Finding the Butterfield

A Journey through Time
in Indian Territory

Susan Dragoo

In memory of my grandfather, Charles Conde Sharp, whose love of history left an indelible mark.

Contents

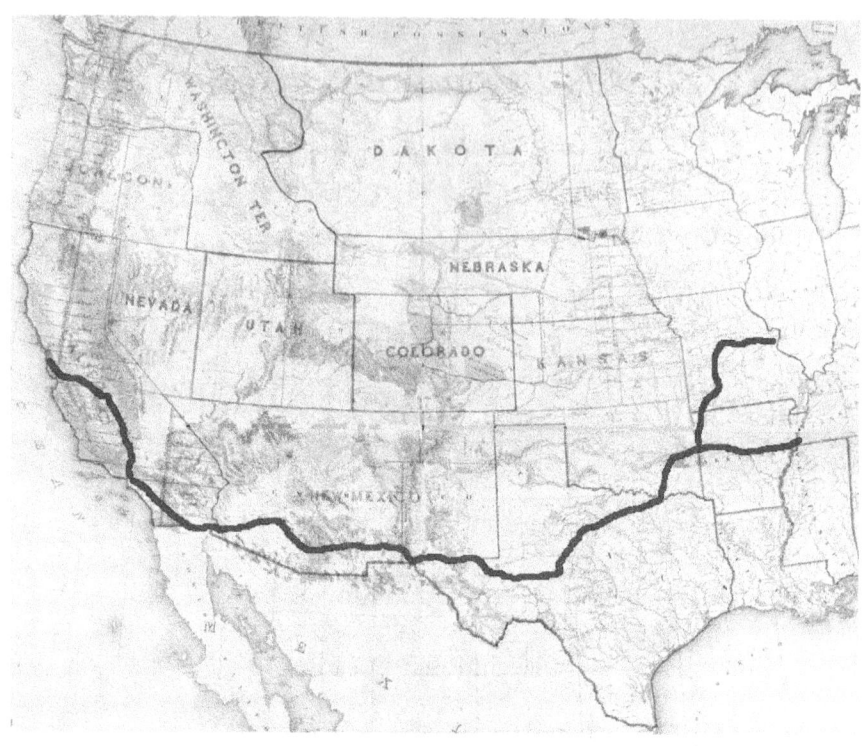

St. Louis and Memphis to San Francisco, September 1858 to March 1861 (Modern depiction, on 1858 War Department map in the collection of the Library of Congress). Retrieved from https://about.usps.com/who/profile/history/overland-mail.htm

Introduction

Brazil Creek near Trahern's Station

In the thick woods of southeastern Oklahoma, on a cold day long after first frost, my footsteps press into layer upon layer of fallen leaves as I walk toward the banks of a stream flowing through the Sans Bois Mountains. Shadowy depths betray only dark trunks of oak and hickory at first, but soon my eyes begin to distinguish scattered blocks of cut stone intermingled with broken bricks, hidden in summer by rank undergrowth but now exposed. A seep, followed to its origin, reveals a walled spring lined with stacked stones, ferns emerging from the joints and moss hiding much of the rock's smooth brown surface. The spring has nestled into the hillside and would be easy to miss, but it once flowed with vigor and supplied clear water to a community here on the edge of what was known as Bayouzil Creek, a name of uncertain origin massaged over the years into "Brazil." A few hundred feet away, an old road runs on a diagonal toward the Red River, its path now largely obscured by the changes of nearly seventeen decades since it saw the passage of the first stage wagon of John Butterfield's Overland Mail Company, rushing to beat a twenty-five-day deadline on its ox-bowed journey from Tipton, Missouri, to San Francisco, California.[1]

For the past eight years, I have gone out into the woods and prairies of eastern Oklahoma exploring the disappearing two-hundred-mile path--sometimes calculated at one hundred ninety-two miles, sometimes two hundred five--of the Butterfield line's Indian Territory segment. My search for historical treasure along that southwesterly diagonal from Fort Smith, Arkansas, to the Red River has borne much fruit and produced unexpected adventures. I wanted to know what had changed since the last significant retracing of Oklahoma's portion of the trail in the late 1950s, and to dig deeper into the stories of both the Butterfield trail in Indian Territory and the people whose lands that trail traversed. This volume is the product of that curiosity.

In the second decade of the twenty-first century, with the instantaneous nature of communications, it is difficult to grasp just how significant it was in the 1850s when, before either a telegraph line or a railroad spanned the North American continent, a stagecoach operation created the first rapid communication and transportation link across the United States, moving mail and passengers over land at record speed and paving the way toward the ultimate goal of a transcontinental railroad. *New York Herald* reporter Waterman Lilly Ormsby, Jr., the only through-passenger on the first westbound Butterfield stage, wrote, "I looked forward in my imagination to the time when, instead of a wagon road to the Pacific, we should have a railroad, and when, instead of having to wait over forty days for an answer from San Francisco, a delay of as many minutes will be looked upon as a gross imposition, and of as many seconds as 'doing from fair to middling.'"[2] His prescient contemplation anticipated not only the coming of the railroad but also our modern expectations for the speed of communication.

The establishment of John Butterfield's stagecoach line, operating from 1858 to 1861 over what was known both as the Southern Route for its geography and the Ox-Bow Route for its shape, fulfilled an imperative driven by the population shift with the acquisition of California and the 1849 Gold Rush. Mail and passengers typically traveled to California by ocean steamship taking, on average, three to four weeks. But the steamship companies were criticized for exorbitant prices and inferior accommodations and seen as a gigantic monopoly. Establishing mail service over land came to be looked upon as the "only escape from the exactions on the ocean route."[3] Perhaps more importantly, completion of the transcontinental railroad was foremost in the country's thinking, an idea promoted since the 1840s to facilitate trade with Asia. New York merchant Asa Whitney, actively involved in trade with China and fixated on construction of a Pacific railroad, unsuccessfully petitioned Congress in 1845 for a charter and land grant for the railroad's construction.[4] In early 1851, the California Senate heard a report stating that a railroad from the Mississippi to San Francisco was, "the best route that can be adopted for the purpose of securing the Commerce of China and India; ... to open a great national highway from California to the Atlantic coast, [and] would be a greater defence and protection than all other military works. It would also be the means of great daily intercourse between the East and West coast of this Republic, ... to prevent those sectional feelings which have ever been the destruction of wide-extended governments."[5]

But that sectionalism —the tension between the slaveholding South and slavery opponents in the North—made progress difficult.[6] One region's concern that the other would win the location for the railroad ultimately made the routing of the cross-country mail service a hot topic, for the stagecoach was a precursor to the locomotive. In

1853-54, the U.S. government conducted surveys for four potential railroad routes: a northern route following the Missouri River along the forty-seventh and forty-ninth parallels from St. Paul to the Puget Sound; a central route along the thirty-eighth and thirty-ninth parallels from St. Louis via present-day Salt Lake City to northern California; a southern route along the thirty-fifth parallel, beginning in Fort Smith, Arkansas, and passing westward through present-day Oklahoma to Los Angeles; and the southernmost route on the thirty-second parallel from Texas along the Gila River to San Diego.

When Congress finally approved funding for overland mail service in March of 1857, the bid from John Butterfield and his associates was the one accepted. A veteran stage operator, Butterfield was born in 1801 in the state of New York, and by 1857 was one of the transportation giants of his day. Butterfield's Overland Mail Company proposed three routes, all incorporating the thirty-fifth parallel: one starting in St. Louis, one in Memphis, and a third, "bifurcated" route with termini at both St. Louis and Memphis, to converge "at the best point to be settled after a full examination" and then to San Francisco. In September 1857 the government awarded Butterfield's company the six-year contract at $600,000 per year and gave him twelve months to put the mail service into operation. The bifurcated route gave the North and South each an eastern terminus, but the nearly 2,800-mile path was far different from the one proposed by Butterfield. Beginning in St. Louis and Memphis, the westbound mails converged in Fort Smith, Arkansas, traversed Indian Territory and Texas on a southwesterly diagonal, then skirted the Mexico border via New Mexico and Arizona into southern California where the path turned north toward San Francisco. Selection of this southernmost route elicited great criticism. Southern interests may have indeed been served by this selection, given Postmaster General Aaron Brown was a southerner, but the path was also extolled as a natural wagon road traversable year-round without the difficulties of snow or high, rugged mountains.

As finally developed, the route combined old and new, following established byways when possible and opening fresh paths when doing so was more efficient. Setting up the stage line in the time allowed was an impressive feat. Butterfield's organization arranged a network of wagons, drivers, horses and mules; estimating about six weeks before the inaugural run that stocking the route required one hundred eighty-eight men, seven hundred seventy-three horses and sixty-four wagons.[7] By the one-year deadline, Butterfield had one hundred forty stations, increasing the number to nearly two hundred the following year. Some stations served meals while others existed only to provide a fresh team of horses or mules. Four-, five- and six-horse teams were used depending on road conditions and the load, but four-horse teams were the norm. Log structures typically housed stations in Missouri, Arkansas and Indian Territory; stone and adobe brick buildings provided shelter farther west.

The first westbound Butterfield Overland Mail stagecoach commenced its journey on September 16, 1858. The mailbags rode by train one hundred sixty miles from St. Louis, moving to the stagecoach at Tipton, then the westernmost point of the railroad, for the long ride west. By the summer of 1859, the railroad had reached Syracuse, Missouri, which became the point for transfer of the mail from the train to the stage and remained so until February, 1861, when the railroad reached Smithton, Missouri, and the transfer point moved there.[8] Butterfield's contract required delivery of the mail in twenty-five days or less and, with the coaches traveling night and day, stopping only to change teams and eat, and carrying only mail and passengers, this goal was often beaten. The inaugural westbound stage arrived in San Francisco October 10, in just twenty-three days, twenty-three and a half hours. The first eastbound coach left San Francisco on September 14, arriving in St. Louis on October 9, with the slightly slower time of twenty-four days, eighteen hours and twenty-six minutes.[9] Brisk times of twenty and one-half days and nineteen days and fifteen hours were also recorded over the life of the stage line, whose timetable did not spare minutes for meals, changing teams, or delays of any sort, which included high water, sand storms, breakdowns, problems with livestock and "Indian trouble," which was infrequent.[10] The Overland Mail Company instead advised drivers to increase their speed sufficiently over the average to make up the time needed.[11]

Average speeds varied considerably, with Ormsby citing five and one-half miles per hour on the Indian Territory segment; only two and one-half miles per hour from Fort Chadbourne to Franklin, Texas; seven and one-quarter miles per hour between Fort Tejon, California and San Francisco; and about five miles per hour overall.[12] Goddard Bailey, a postal employee on the first eastbound stage, reported an overall average of four and one-half miles per hour, and a speed of five miles per hour on the Indian Territory segment.[13] The variation in terrain accounted for most of the difference, although untamed livestock also created delays such as one Ormsby cited at the head of the Concho River in Texas, where catching and harnessing wild mules consumed precious time.[14] William Tallack, an Englishman traveling on an eastbound stage in the summer of 1860, wrote, "Over smooth and level prairie lands we sometimes dashed on at twelve miles an hour, whilst, on rugged or sandy ground, our advance was only two or three miles in the same time, and that often on foot."[15]

On each coach, a conductor guarded the mail, for which the sender paid ten cents a letter. The conductor was responsible for the safety of the mail over the length of his division, which on some segments comprised up to five hundred miles. Drivers changed at shorter intervals, their runs being limited to stages familiar to them. Each conductor had a small brass bugle, blowing a call as the stage approached a station to alert station keepers to prepare meals and teams.[16] Twenty-five days of riding day and night were very tiring for passengers, and some would stay over at an intermediate station to rest. The Overland Mail Company at first set fares at two hundred dollars for the westbound journey and one hundred dollars eastbound. Eventually fares were equalized at one hundred fifty dollars regardless of direction. Passengers riding shorter segments of the road paid ten cents a mile. Forty pounds of luggage were allowed, but no large amounts of money or valuables, to discourage hold-ups. Luggage and passengers shifted into fresh coaches or wagons multiple times over the course of the journey. Tallack reported this occurring about every three hundred miles.[17]

The Overland Mail Company divided the route into two major divisions, East and West, with El Paso, Texas, the dividing point. Nine subdivisions were created, five to the east of El Paso and four to the west. A general superintendent oversaw operations for each of the nine divisions. Hugh Crocker was in charge of the First, Second, and Third Divisions, from St. Louis, Memphis, and Fort Smith to Colbert's Ferry, the Indian Territory segment comprising the Third Division.[18]

On its journey through the Indian Territory, the Butterfield traversed the Choctaw Nation and dipped briefly into the Chickasaw Nation before crossing the Red River into Texas. In the early 1800s, the Indian Territory, though never legally organized as a United States "Territory," was reserved by the federal government for native peoples of the southeastern U.S. who were forced to move from their homes to lands west of the Mississippi. In the early 1830s, at the time of the Choctaw removal, Indian Territory included all of the U.S. west of the Mississippi and not within the states of Missouri or Louisiana, or Arkansas Territory (which would become a state in 1836), or any other organized territory. Mexico still owned Texas and the lands west of the one hundredth meridian. The Choctaws' western lands, owned communally, were bordered on the south by the Red River, on the north and west by the Arkansas and Canadian Rivers, and on the east by a line along the western boundary of Arkansas.

Taking place from 1831 to 1833, the main removals of the Choctaws from Mississippi produced great hardship. The difficulties inherent in the three hundred fifty-mile journey were exacerbated by the government's general ineptitude in organizing the process, a historic blizzard through which the migrating Choctaws suffered during the winter of 1831-32, and a cholera epidemic the following summer, all leading to great loss of life. Before removal, the population of the Choctaw Nation in Mississippi was 17,963 plus 512 slaves.[19] In 1843, the Choctaw population in Indian Territory was reported as 12,690. Small parties of Choctaws continued to migrate west from Mississippi into the 1850s.[20]

In 1837, the leaders of the Choctaw Nation agreed to share their lands with the Chickasaws, granting them a large tract of land in the western part of their domain. Among the Five "Civilized" Tribes, so called because of their adoption of the ways of Euro-American culture, the Chickasaws were the last to sign a removal agreement and accept a home west of the Mississippi.[21] The other three, in addition to the Choctaws, were the Cherokees, Creeks and Seminoles. The Chickasaws were closely akin to the Choctaws linguistically and their eastern lands neighbored each other. While enduring their own travails, most of the Chickasaws, an estimated 4,000, completed removal in 1837-38 without the severe sufferings of the Choctaws, Cherokees and Creeks. The Chickasaw Nation was at first made a political division within the Choctaw Nation, and in 1856 the two separated into independent nations.

The period of Choctaw history after removal and before the Civil War, from 1833 to 1861, presented, in the words of historian Angie Debo, a "record of orderly development unprecedented in the history of any people."[22] Since the last decades of the eighteenth century, white men who had married Choctaw women, known as intermarried whites, along with white traders, had influenced the Choctaws toward adoption of the white man's institutions.[23] The Choctaws had also accepted missionaries who brought Christian teachings and established schools. They began to use livestock as a source of both subsistence and trade and, in 1826, adopted a constitutional form of government. The Choctaws brought these institutions and practices with them from Mississippi to Indian Territory, re-establishing schools, churches, and government in a region of prairie, forest and cane brake. Indian Territory was well timbered with ash, oak, hickory, walnut, gum, hackberry, cottonwood, cedar, bois d'arc and pine, the soil well suited for cultivation of cotton, tobacco, corn, and other crops.[24] In the 1840s and 1850s, the Choctaws lived much like their non-Indian neighbors, mostly dwelling in log cabins on small farms like others in the rural southeast. They hunted wild game and raised corn, potatoes, melons, peas, pumpkins and yams. Along the Red River, planters cultivated cotton on a large scale, using slave labor.[25] Newspapers appeared, the *Choctaw Telegraph* in 1848-1849, and the *Choctaw Intelligencer* in 1850-52, both published in Doaksville, an important Choctaw town and sometime capital, located near the Red River.[26] In 1847, the Choctaws contributed money for the relief of the Irish suffering the Potato Famine. On March 23, a meeting took place at the Choctaw Agency in Skullyville for "the relief of the starving poor of Ireland." One hundred seventy dollars, equivalent to about $6,000 today, was collected, reported the *Arkansas Intelligencer*. "All subscribed, agents, missionaries, traders, and Indians, a considerable portion of which fund was made up by the latter. The 'poor Indian' sending his mite to the Poor Irish!"[27]

With the establishment of the Overland Mail road came increased traffic and new infrastructure through the Choctaw and Chickasaw Nations. Economic benefits for those living on or near the road included exclusive privileges to operate toll gates and bridges, and contracts with the Overland Mail Company to keep relay stations at a rate of somewhere between $125 and $175 per quarter,[28] which converts to between $4,700 and $6,700 in 2024 dollars. Indian Territory's twelve Overland Mail stations, where teams of horses or mules could be maintained and quickly changed at regular intervals, sat an average of sixteen miles apart. Of the station keepers, six were mixed-blood Choctaw or Chickasaw, two were intermarried Choctaws, and the background of the other three is unclear, a matter which I will address later in this book. The Butterfield also brought passengers whose reports made news because of the importance of and controversy surrounding the stage line. Waterman Ormsby's detailed account of the trip presents a particularly vivid picture of the experience. He saw the Butterfield as the first practical step towards the Pacific railroad and forecast that if the overland mail succeeded, the railroad and telegraph would soon follow its course, settlements along the line would build up rapidly, and the United States' western possessions would be opened up.[29] With the disruption of the Civil War, however, Ormsby's predictions for the Southern Route did not come entirely true. In March 1861, Congress voted to move the Overland Mail service north to the Central Route, which ran from St. Joseph, Missouri, to San Francisco. Thus ended the short life of the storied Butterfield Overland Mail on the Southern Route.[30] Both the first transcontinental telegraph line (1861) and the transcontinental railroad (1869) ultimately ran on a course farther north as well. Nevertheless, the Butterfield was the longest stagecoach line of its time, creating significant infrastructure and representing a major step in transportation and communication between the eastern U.S. and the Pacific coast. It has been studied, explored and celebrated. The Butterfield's cultural importance is evident in the many places on or near the route still bearing its name today, and its popularity has inspired fanciful stories involving stagecoaches of the Old West in western novels, motion pictures and television.

In the early twentieth century, historians began to retrace the Butterfield route. Roscoe and Margaret Conkling were the first to explore the full length of the trail, publishing the results in their seminal work of three volumes, *The Butterfield Overland Mail 1857-1869* (1947). Beginning in 1930, the couple tracked down and documented the entire route and its stations, a decade-long process.[31] Since then, other historians and explorers have retraced the mail road numerous times, but the road guards its secrets, even now. The exact locations of some of its stations and segments are still being verified,[32] and with its designation as a National Historic Trail, more exploration and development are on the horizon. For its cultural significance as the first transcontinental stage route and its contribution to the country's transportation system, the route was designated the Butterfield Overland National Historic Trail by the federal government in January, 2023.[33]

In its traverse of Indian Territory, the Butterfield at first followed the Fort Smith-Boggy Depot Road, using wagon trails existing since the 1830s as a result of the Choctaw and Chickasaw removals and U.S. Army movements. Oklahoma historian Muriel H. Wright wrote that if a straight edge were placed on a map of southeastern Oklahoma between Fort Smith and Boggy Depot, the route of the trail would deviate little from that line. With good roadbeds along the valleys, shallow stream crossings and easy passes through the San Bois and Winding Stair Mountains, she extolled it as the best route from Fort Smith across the Choctaw and Chickasaw lands to the Red River, serving as a natural pathway long before the first permanent settlements.[34]

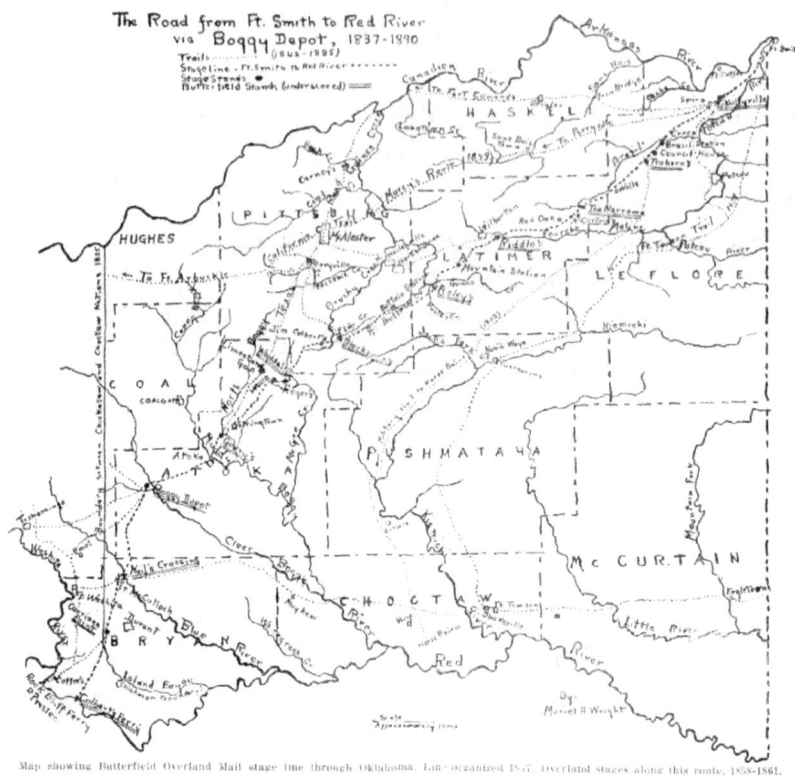

Map showing Butterfield Overland Mail stage line through Oklahoma. Line organized 1857. Overland stages along this route, 1858-1861.

Hand-drawn map of the Butterfield Trail by Muriel Wright, 1933.
Courtesy Oklahoma Historical Society.

Near present-day Atoka, the Fort Smith-Boggy Depot Road converged with the Texas Road, originally a trail leading from St. Louis to trading posts among the Osage people in southwest Missouri and northeastern Oklahoma.[35] First known as the Osage Trace, by the 1820s it was well traveled, continuing into Texas and providing the avenue for thousands of home seekers traveling to Texas before the coming of the railroad in 1871-1872.[36]

U.S. Army Captain Randolph B. Marcy's 1849 wagon road to Santa Fe, New Mexico, on the thirty-fifth parallel, was another important thoroughfare across Indian Territory, following Josiah Gregg's 1839-40 path along the Canadian River. Marcy escorted a company of gold seekers to Santa Fe in the spring of 1849 on this route, which with minor variations was used by Lieutenant A.W. Whipple in his 1853 Pacific railroad survey and Lieutenant Edward F. Beale in his 1857-1859 effort to carry out the government's directive to create a national wagon road. In fact, Beale's survey team left Fort Smith on October 28, 1858, just over a month after the first Butterfield stagecoach passed through. Under Beale's direction, six iron bridges were installed in late 1859 in eastern Indian Territory, including one locally known as "Bridge Edwards" which crossed the Poteau River south of Fort Smith near present-day Pocola, Oklahoma, and was used by the Overland Mail stages. With the establishment of Fort Washita in 1842 as a permanent military post and the extension of the road to that point, it was also sometimes called the Fort Smith-Fort Washita Road.

The Conklings explored the Oklahoma segment of the trail from 1930 to 1932. On their first expedition in 1930 they logged nearly seven thousand miles in three months driving their seven-passenger 1930 model Buick from their home in El Paso, Texas, to St. Louis, then to St. Joseph and over the Central Route to San Francisco and back to El Paso. But before the Conklings' 1947 tome was published, Oklahoma historians Grant Foreman and Muriel Wright wrote of the Butterfield's legacy in Indian Territory and were the first historians to publish state-specific accounts of the trail.[37] Foreman's work in the *Chronicles of Oklahoma*, the journal of the Oklahoma Historical Society, was the earliest. His article, "The California Mail Route through Oklahoma," appeared in September, 1931, and was followed in June, 1933, by Wright's "Historic Places on the Old Stage Line from Fort Smith to Red River," also in the *Chronicles*. While Foreman's 1931 piece was mostly a retelling of Ormsby's account, Wright's work actually retraced the trail and integrated other historical sources specific to Indian Territory. The locations of Butterfield stations in Oklahoma and elsewhere were not by any means a settled matter at the time. Starting with published station names and distances, the Conklings and Wright studied historical maps and government records, talked with local old-timers, found and examined ruins and road traces, and corresponded with people they met, sending hand-drawn maps back and forth for verification and correction. Wright reported personal interviews in 1922-24 with a number of early-day citizens who had traveled over the road both before and after the Civil War.[38]

An August 1930 excursion Muriel Wright made with Mr. and Mrs. John Young Bryce[39] to identify historic sites included placement of some of Oklahoma's first historic markers. The markers were on pine boards and were temporary, "intended only to locate places that had almost been forgotten by this generation." The hope expressed at the time was that, when the Depression had lifted and money was available, "the public-spirited people of our state will see that all of these historic places in Oklahoma are designated by the placing of permanent markers and tablets."[40] Years later, Wright led the effort to see this vision fulfilled, playing a pivotal role in launching Oklahoma's historical marker program in the 1950s.

On November 26, 1930, a little more than two weeks after the Conklings first passed through Oklahoma, Wright wrote that she had just returned from "one of the most interesting field trips" she had ever experienced.

> Beginning with Tuesday, November 18, I traced out every portion of the old Skullyville to McAlester road . . . . I secured the exact location of many of the former homes of old time Choctaws who were prominent in their time, in addition to other persons who lived on the way to Skullyville. I visited old county court house grounds, old graves, school house sites, crossings on the streams,

and talked to a number of persons who were familiar with local history along the way. Returning from Skullyville, traveled clear through to Stringtown on the Boggy Depot Road. Mr. Bryce merely took the highway to a few of the stage stands. But now the Society has complete knowledge of every bit of the Fort Smith-Boggy Depot Road. I visited every historic spot along the way, including Brazil Station, Council Spring, Skullyville County Court grounds and jail, old graves that have been lost, Judge Trahern's home place, etc., taking pictures and noting particularly the traces of the old road.[41]

Contrary to what was written later,[42] it does not appear that Wright accompanied the Conklings on their 1930 journey through Oklahoma, but she must have been well aware of it and perhaps the trip she undertook later that month was prompted by it. She may have felt some pressure to beat them to the punch. In August 1932, Wright did accompany the Conklings along a portion of the Butterfield route through Oklahoma,[43] and corresponded with them for several years following.

Wright's enthusiasm for the subject is fitting. She was born in 1889 in Lehigh, Choctaw Nation, a short distance from the convergence of the Texas Road and the Butterfield. Allen Wright, principal chief of the Choctaw Nation from 1866 to 1870, was her grandfather. In 1866 he famously suggested the name "Oklahoma" for the territory. Muriel Wright authored several Oklahoma history textbooks and wrote for the *Chronicles of Oklahoma* from 1923 to 1971, serving as its editor, unofficially, from 1943 and, officially, beginning in 1955. As she wrote in 1957, Wright believed the Overland Mail Road the most important in Oklahoma's development and settlement. That could be argued, but Wright's work, and her inspiration, is honored here for her deep understanding of and affection for a region that was home to her. "It was the Butterfield Overland Mail," she wrote, "that made the old road from Fort Smith to Colbert's Ferry famous in the history of this country."[44] The intervening years have demonstrated the truth in that statement.

In the 1950s, with the approach of the widely celebrated centennial of the Butterfield, the Oklahoma Historical Society produced a significant body of work about the road's history and its route through Oklahoma. The account of a Historical Society committee's 1958 journey to find remnants of the trail and place markers provides a framework for retracing the trail today. A group of seven—Muriel Wright, Vernon H. Brown, John D. Frizzell, Mildred Frizzell, James D. Morrison, George H. Shirk and Lucyl A. Shirk—undertook this responsibility in connection with the centennial. With Wright as a dedicated guide who believed in the importance of the mission, the Centennial Committee was well equipped to locate Indian Territory's twelve Butterfield stage stands. Mildred Frizzell took notes for the entourage and prepared a first draft of the committee report, which leans heavily toward the sentimental and focuses in particular on the beauty of the landscape during their mid-May journey.

From east to west, the Indian Territory stations and their locations relative to present-day towns or landmarks are Walker's, near Spiro; Trahern's, west of Shady Point; Holloway's, at The Narrows northeast of Red Oak; Riddle's, on the eastern outskirts of Wilburton; Pusley's, southwest of Higgins; Blackburn's, on the edge of the Indian Nation Turnpike; Waddell's, southwest of Wesley; Geary's, now beneath the waters of the Atoka Reservoir; Boggy Depot, west of Tushka; Nail's Crossing, near Kenefic; Fisher's Station, west of Durant; and Colbert's Ferry, on the Red River southeast of Colbert. The Centennial Committee dutifully located the "mute and faded symbols of one of the most important contributions of their age to the growth and progress of America,"[45] and designated spots for historical markers of bronze and concrete, which were in place by 1959. The inscription on each marker reads:

Butterfield Overland Mail
Site Of
_____ Station

Here was located a stage stand of the Butterfield Overland Mail Route, under Act of Congress, March 3, 1857. First mail stage arrived here in September, 1858, enroute to San Francisco. Service continued until the outbreak of the War Between The States.
Oklahoma Historical Society, 1958

As late as the 1950s, explorers could still drive an automobile over much of the old stagecoach road in Oklahoma. Today, however, little of the original roadbed remains accessible for motorized travel, though many county roads are built along or upon the route, which runs mostly through quiet countryside as it traverses LeFlore, Latimer, Pittsburg, Atoka, and Bryan Counties. Many trail fragments are sequestered on private property, but most of the roadside markers are still intact and accessible. The road's path through Indian Territory has, for the most part, long been determined, but for those who enjoy historical exploration, there are discoveries to make along the way. This book, then, is dedicated to the notion that readers of the twenty-first century can appreciate the story of the road and the people and places along its path. It follows the Butterfield, physically and historically, across Oklahoma, building upon the extensive work preceding it while considering new information and perspectives, recording the current state of the trail's remains, and perhaps giving the reader a new appreciation for the state's landscape. Margaret Conkling wrote in 1930, referring to eastern Oklahoma in the 1800s, "There can be no doubt (it) was a real paradise. And we might add that it still is if the traveler is willing to leave the main highway. The Butterfield Trail opened for us one beautiful vista after another."[46]

More than ninety years later it still opens up beautiful vistas far from the main roads.

In 1933, Muriel Wright wrote, "For one who will follow the traces of the old stage line road from Fort Smith to Red River, bearing in mind the part it had in the history of Oklahoma and other sections of the Southwest, there still lingers something of the spirit of Indian Territory days."[47] Although no longer a continuous, discrete pathway, the road abides nonetheless, and something of that same spirit of Indian Territory days does indeed still linger. As I have followed the traces of the old stage line, I have seen the faded scars on the land: a swale through a pasture, a cutdown creek bank, a path worn bare through the forest. In forgotten places, stone-lined wells still stand near the rubble of rock buildings and graveyards of broken tombstones. With each passing year, these few tangible remains of the Butterfield crumble and disappear. Even the concrete and bronze markers are deteriorating. This portal to a different time is closing in a physical sense, disintegrating as earthly things do. But the story of Oklahoma's Butterfield trail offers a journey through time back to Indian Territory's antebellum days, as concrete and steel dissolve into wagon ruts, hewn logs and flowing springs.

Chapter One: The Portal

Fort Smith National Historic Site

Fort Smith, Arkansas

It was the middle of the night when the first westbound Butterfield stage wagon rolled into Fort Smith, Arkansas, welcomed in spite of the late hour by a great celebration: ". . . The news that both the St. Louis and Memphis stages had arrived spread like wildfire," wrote Waterman Ormsby. "Horns were blown, houses were lit up, and many flocked to the hotel to have a look at the wagons and talk over the exciting topic, and have a peep at the first mail bags."[48] By then it was 2:05 a.m. on September 19, 1858, and the St. Louis mail had traveled 468 miles in sixty-six hours. The arrival was twenty-four hours ahead of schedule in spite of the formidable mountain roads in northwest Arkansas. Riding in the wagon with Ormsby and John Butterfield, Sr., were John Butterfield, Jr., driving the stage, and Fort Smith newspaperman John F. Wheeler and his family, as well as division superintendent Hugh Crocker, who had joined the party at Callahan's Station in northwest Arkansas. Leaving St. Louis by train at 8 a.m. on September 16, 1858, they stopped at Tipton, Missouri, the terminus of the railroad one hundred sixty miles distant. There the party, and the two small bags of mail, transferred to a brand-new stagecoach drawn by a four-horse team. A short distance away at Shackelford's Station near Syracuse, Missouri, they dropped off T.R. Corbin, a Washington lobbyist who had traveled with them from St. Louis. The stagecoach then traveled south to Springfield, where the entourage departed the coach and boarded a Celerity wagon.[49] The ornate stagecoaches of the day, with their comfortably padded passenger seats, were used on about thirty per cent of the Butterfield route in settled areas with better roads. But for the rough passage through less developed locales, John Butterfield designed the Celerity wagon to handle steep inclines and rapid passage over rugged trails. The wagon weighed about half a coach's heft and had a lower center of gravity, making it more difficult to tip over. And, with thicker wheels, it was better suited for travel on sandy desert trails in the western reaches of the journey.[50]

From Springfield the road veered southwest through the Ozarks to Fayetteville, Arkansas. Fourteen miles farther, at Park's Station, the team of horses was exchanged for mules, which Ormsby credits with a surprisingly expeditious ride over the steep, rugged roads of the Boston Mountains: "The wiry, light, little animals tugged and pulled as if they would tear themselves to pieces, and our heavy wagon bounded along the crags as if it would be shaken in pieces every minute, and ourselves disembowelled on the spot."[51] The name "Boston" for the mountains may be a corruption of a French phrase for "rough road," although Ormsby wrote that it was slang used in the West for any difficult task.[52] Even as late as 1930, Roscoe and Margaret Conkling found this one of the roughest ten-mile sections of the entire road.[53] Today, automobiles skim across these mountaintops at speeds upward of 80 miles per hour on the modern marvel that is Interstate 49.

Eventually the path wound down to the Arkansas River at Van Buren, where the wagon crossed on a ferry. The river was low, forcing them to traverse a soft bed of quicksand-laden flats before they reached the south shore, a dangerous proposition with their heavy load. But a mounted guide with a lantern helped them pick their way across and they safely ascended the bank on the other side. They entered Fort Smith over Washington Street, now Second, stopping at the John Rogers City Hotel at North Second and A Streets, the site of the Overland Mail agency. The Memphis mail preceded the St. Louis party's arrival by fifteen minutes. Agents joined the two parcels of mail on another wagon, which departed for the Indian Territory at 3:30 a.m. on Sunday, September 19, still a full day ahead of the timetable.[54]

Mother Post for the Southwest

By the time the first Butterfield stage reached Fort Smith, the military installation already had a forty-one-year history. The original fort was established in 1817 on the promontory of Belle Point, at the confluence of the Arkansas and Poteau Rivers. Waterways were then the highways of America, and the fort's position on the Arkansas made it an essential gateway to the frontier. Fort Smith was the westernmost U.S. military installation at the time, placed strategically to quell ongoing violence between the Osages and the Cherokees as pressure grew from Cherokee migration into Osage territory. In 1858, the buildings of the second fort, built 1838-1846, occupied the site and housed an active military post with an adjacent civilian community of 2,500, incorporated as the town of Fort Smith in 1842. Since its inception, Fort Smith played a prominent role in the western expansion of the U.S., militarily and through the creation of infrastructure, including the building of roads eventually used as part of the Overland Mail route. Characterized in Bearss and Gibson's *Fort Smith, Little Gibralter on the Arkansas,* as the "mother post for the Southwest," Fort Smith's history is inextricably linked with that of Indian Territory.[55]

Only five years after its start, however, Fort Smith seemed to have already served its purpose. In August of 1822, the Osages and Cherokees signed a peace treaty and post commander Colonel Matthew Arbuckle, for whom Fort Arbuckle and the Arbuckle Mountains in central Oklahoma would later be named, recommended relocating the Fort Smith garrison to a more strategic spot farther west. The frontier town growing at Belle Point was troublesome, with opportunities for gambling, whiskey and women among the motivations to move the troops. Other forces were also at work. In 1820, Choctaw leaders in Mississippi signed the Treaty of Doak's Stand, exchanging their lands east of the Mississippi River for about thirteen million acres in Arkansas Territory south and west of Fort Smith. Some Choctaw families then migrated west, but by 1825 they were few. A significant portion of the lands granted to the Choctaws encompassed established settlements of Arkansas Territory, triggering strong protest from territorial leaders who hoped to expand their domain in anticipation of statehood, rather than see it shrink. Their delegate to Congress proposed that Arkansas Territory annex land west of Fort Smith on a line from the mouth of the Grand River south to Red River, expecting the troops at Fort Smith to move west as well. Added to that, a resumption of violence among the Cherokees and Osages deeper in Indian Territory strengthened the case for relocating the garrison to a new location on the east bank of the Grand River. In April of 1824, Arbuckle received orders to abandon Belle Point, and the troops traveled overland along an existing trail on the north bank of the Arkansas River to their new post at Cantonment Gibson, cantonment being a term for temporary troop quarters.[56]

In the garrison's absence, the structures at Fort Smith deteriorated, but the government still found official uses for the post. In 1825-26 the Choctaw Boundary Commission headquartered there for, instead of approving Arkansas Territory's request to expand westward, the 1825 Choctaw Boundary Treaty did the opposite, setting the Choctaws' eastern boundary and Arkansas' western boundary on a line beginning on the Arkansas River one hundred paces *east* of the fort and running south to Red River. The federal government promised to remove whites who had settled west of the boundary, and Choctaw leaders agreed to relocate their people who had settled on the eastern side. In November, 1825, the boundary commission began survey work at Fort Smith and by January, 1826, established the new boundary. Also in 1825, the government's western Choctaw Agency set up headquarters at Fort Smith to manage relocation of Choctaws who were living on the east side of the new boundary and to provide a supply depot during the move.

Whiskey and Malaria

On March 18, 1825, Major William L. McClellan was appointed agent for the Choctaws west of the Mississippi. The role of Indian agent evolved from that of the "factor," who carried out treaty provisions as a representative of the United States, usually in connection with a trading post or "factory." When responsibilities increased and required a more supervisory role, especially in the removal process, the title changed to "agent." McClellan was the second agent to the Choctaws west of the Mississippi, succeeding George Gray (or Grey) who was appointed in March of 1821 following the 1820 Treaty of Doak's Stand.

McClellan was directed to prepare the Indians in the southern part of Arkansas Territory to move west across the new boundary and to establish his agency at the western limits of Arkansas. At first, McClellan headquartered at Fort Smith, but soon he moved the agency across the river into Indian Territory to put some distance between his constituents and the Belle Point townspeople, for whom the illegal selling of whiskey to the Indians was a lucrative activity.[57] Ultimately, McClellan had very few Choctaws in his charge. In September, 1828, he reported eight who had presented themselves at the agency and forty to sixty settled on the Red River, attributing the small numbers to the fact that white settlers had occupied the land for a long time, and the Choctaws' fear that the settlers would commit "outrages" on them and their property. The whites would soon be removed east of the Choctaw line, McClellan noted. Upwards of one thousand Choctaws were then located west of the Mississippi, he wrote, settled on the Red River and scattered in small villages in the state of Louisiana.[58] McClellan was later made a sub-agent to the Cherokee Agency and died in 1829. In 1830 McClellan's brother David became sub-agent to the Choctaws.

Attempts to prevent importation and sale of intoxicating liquor into Indian communities were nothing new. Before the arrival of Europeans, few Native Americans used any kind of fermented beverage. Alcohol use was, however, pervasive among early European colonists, who substituted alcohol for often-contaminated drinking water and used it for medicinal purposes. The availability of hard liquor grew over time with local brewing and distilling, and alcohol consumption increased. Between 1800 and 1830, the annual per capita alcohol consumption in the U.S. was somewhere between 5 and 9.5 gallons, compared with 2.45 in 2020. Frontiersmen and soldiers drank heavily, modeling high consumption of alcohol. And, liquor was used in trade and as a diplomatic tool in spite of legal restrictions. Combined with Native Americans' lack of experience with alcohol, the effects were destructive and demoralizing. Both U.S. and tribal governments enacted laws to forbid alcohol sales among the Indians but enforcement was a constant challenge.[59] See William Unrau's *White Man's Wicked Water: The Alcohol Trade and Prohibition in Indian Country, 1802 to 1892,* for a more in-depth study of the subject.

William McClellan had other concerns motivating his departure from Fort Smith as well. In a letter to Colonel Matthew Arbuckle on February 2, 1827, the agent wrote from Fort Smith, "I am erecting buildings for the Chocktaw Agency, 18 miles above this, at a fine spring, it wou'd be call'd good water in the States. I am in great hope that it will prove to be a healthy place as we have all suffered here." At the place he called Pebble Spring, McClellan's hope for better health addressed the common problem of malarial illness.[60] Six years later, Captain John Stuart, recommending the establishment of Fort Coffee up the Arkansas River in a more healthful spot, wrote that Fort Smith would always be "extremely sickly" in summer, given its nearness to the river and the surrounding swampy land with "pools of stagnated waters, which are very unhealthy."[61] Miasmas, or poisonous atmospheres rising from low-lying areas, were then believed to cause malaria. It was 1880 before Alphonse Laveran, a French Army surgeon, discovered a parasite to be the cause of the disease, and 1897 when Ronald Ross, a British officer, demonstrated its transmission by mosquitoes.[62]

Road Builders

Military survey and building crews also operated out of Fort Smith when, between 1825 and 1827, Congress authorized construction of military roads on the Arkansas frontier. Intended to improve defenses and communication and to facilitate the anticipated relocation of Native American tribes from the southeast, two of these military corridors extended west from Fort Smith.[63] One went to Cantonment

Gibson and another to Cantonment Towson, established in 1824 near the confluence of the Kiamichi and Red Rivers to strengthen the international boundary with Mexico, which was then the Red River, and later to provide a buffer between the Choctaws and the Plains tribes.

In the summer of 1827, road construction began between Cantonment Gibson and Fort Smith as well as east from Fort Smith to Little Rock, Arkansas. Civilian contractors built the road from Fort Smith to Little Rock, but fifty-five soldiers from Gibson used basic hand tools on the road between Gibson and Fort Smith, creating a roadbed sixteen feet wide, reducing stumps in the roadway to less than a foot, and building causeways over wetlands.[64] In March of 1827 Congress authorized a road between Fort Smith and Cantonment Towson on the Red River, but it took nearly six months to survey the route and in November of that year Major Alexander Cummings, the Towson commander, complained that he lacked the manpower to complete the project. Work stopped in October, 1828 after ongoing delays.[65]

Meanwhile in Mississippi, pressure grew for the Choctaws to vacate. In 1830, President Andrew Jackson gained Congressional approval for the Indian Removal Act and Choctaw leaders signed the Treaty of Dancing Rabbit Creek, ceding the rest of their eastern territory and agreeing to move west. Soon, in preparation for the impending removal, new western Choctaw agent Francis W. Armstrong, appointed in 1831, renewed the attempt to complete a passable road between Fort Smith and the re-designated Fort Towson. Armstrong intended to move the Choctaws up river on boats to the Choctaw Agency on the south bank of the Arkansas River, then send them over land toward Towson, where supplies would be distributed. With the poor condition of the old road, Captain John Stuart, an infantry officer then stationed at the re-designated Fort Gibson, was assigned to build a new one and, with twenty enlisted men, two officers and a medical doctor, he commenced the project on March 28, 1832 in spite of his concerns that both transport and food supplies were insufficient. Work began with cutting down the west bank of the Poteau River for a boat landing. Clearing a path through thirteen miles of dense canebrake and undergrowth required more than two weeks, and it was April 15 when Stuart finally reached the Choctaw Agency. Heavy rain, rocky, steep terrain, a dwindling food supply and fear of Indian raids plagued his efforts as he continued south, but Stuart kept moving over the mountains and across countless streams. Having no blasting powder, his crew used sledge hammers, pry bars, and blocks and tackles to remove large rocks. On June 16 his team completed the road to Horse Prairie on the Kiamichi River, about twenty miles west of Towson.[66]

Captain Stuart was a pivotal figure in another aspect of the removal. As the Choctaws were re-settling in the Indian Territory in 1834, the ongoing problem of illegal alcohol sales to the Indians prompted the Army to establish Fort Coffee under Stuart's command, just nine miles west of Fort Smith at Swallow Rock, a bluff on the south bank of the Arkansas River. With a wide view up and down the river, the fort's directive was to stop boats carrying liquor into Indian Territory. The Army maintained Fort Coffee as a military establishment for only four years, but during the removal it also served as a receiving point for Indians arriving from the east. By the end of 1837, more than 3,500 Chickasaws waited there for a road to be opened to the western lands allocated for them by the Choctaw Nation. The opening of that road began on December 21, 1837, when scouts set out to mark it. Following the Fort Towson Road for about twenty-five miles, they turned west and traveled another twenty-five miles to the Fourche Maline River, then southwest for another sixty-nine miles to Gaines, Brushy, and Little Boggy Creeks and, finally, Clear Boggy Creek. "Boggy" is a translation of "Vazzures," the French name given the stream by early traders, from the word "vaseux," meaning silty or muddy. There, they found good water, excellent pasture for livestock, and enough cane to subsist horses all winter. Its location was central enough to serve as a depot for provisions for the Chickasaws. William Armstrong, who succeeded his brother Francis as Choctaw agent after the elder Armstrong's death in 1835, sent out men to open the road shortly after. On February 18, 1838, five hundred Chickasaws with twenty-eight wagons and teams left Fort Coffee to move to the depot on the Boggy, which became known as "Boggy Depot." [67] The road would soon be known as the Fort Smith-Boggy Depot Road and would later carry the stage wagons of the Butterfield Overland Mail. [68]

The lack of a standing military force eventually became a source of dissatisfaction for Fort Smith citizens and politicians. They campaigned for the post to return from Fort Gibson to Belle Point, claiming they feared Indian attacks. The campaign bore fruit, and construction began in 1838 on a new fort, completed in 1846. These were busy years at Fort Smith, where troops based for exploration across the Southwest and armed and equipped for the Mexican War. [69]

With the discovery of gold in California in 1848, Fort Smith found yet another opportunity for distinction. Local newspaperman John F. Wheeler, who was the printer for the first book printed in Indian Territory in 1835[70] and rode in the first Butterfield stage with Ormsby in 1858, saw potential in Fort Smith as a launching point for the overland journey to the California gold fields. He led an effort to petition the Arkansas legislature and, ultimately, Congress to survey a road up the Arkansas and Canadian River valleys to Santa Fe, New Mexico. Wheeler contended this would be the most efficient route, with terrain over which wagons would roll relatively free of mountains and good range for livestock most of the year. [71] Wheeler's work paid off, and the Army authorized a military escort to Santa Fe for California-bound emigrants gathering at Fort Smith in the spring of 1849. Troops would protect the gold seekers from Indian attack, smooth the roads on steep grades, and mark fords along the route, which followed the south bank of the Canadian River and the watershed between the Canadian and the Washita Rivers. A detail led by Lieutenant Frederick T. Dent of the Fifth Infantry went ahead to reconnoiter the route, crossing the Poteau on March 27, 1849 to open the California Road.

U.S. Army Captain Randolph B. Marcy arrived at the end of March to command the military escort. On April 4 he struck out along the road and, during that month, four hundred wagons moved through Fort Smith, with more gold seekers departing through the spring and summer. Marcy reached Santa Fe on June 30 and wrote that caravans using the more northern Santa Fe Trail lagged about two weeks behind his own company, validating the pronouncements of folks back in Fort Smith about the efficiency of the Southern Route. The Gold Rush lasted about ten years, and thousands of emigrants passed through Fort Smith annually until 1861 and the outbreak of the Civil War. On his return, Marcy escorted a wagon train bound for El Paso, Texas. Sixty miles north of El Paso at Doña Ana, New Mexico, he turned east toward Fort Smith, and found the return route shorter than his westbound path along the Canadian. This became known as the Doña Ana Road and gold seekers used it heavily. Between Boggy Depot and Fort Smith, this route primarily followed the road established for the Chickasaw immigration from 1837 to 1839, later used by the Overland Mail. Thus the road through Indian Territory that would soon be used by Butterfield's stages became a well-established thoroughfare as a result of the removals, the Gold Rush, and the military's need to improve supply and communication routes to its posts south and west of Fort Smith.[72]

In the year of heavy activity preceding the start of the Overland Mail, Fort Smith and neighboring Van Buren newspapers reported on Butterfield's men and equipment passing through. In April 1858 the Van Buren *Arkansas Intelligencer* announced that an Overland Mail exploring party including John Butterfield, Jr. had traveled the route from San Francisco to Van Buren in fifty-two days' time, calling the path "practicable and free from Indians," having seen none but the friendly sort.[73]

That same month, the news that Fort Smith would be the connecting point for the mails from Memphis and St. Louis was welcomed with great enthusiasm: "The forming of the junction on our frontier will be of great advantage to Western Arkansas. It will serve to draw attention to the many advantages possessed by us, and will undoubtedly, draw a large emigration to settle upon our cheap and fertile lands."[74] In early August 1858 a large number of Butterfield's horses, mules and stages passed through Fort Smith on the way to take their places along the route.[75] During the life of the Butterfield, the Overland Mail stages made twice-weekly stops in Fort Smith, at 3:30 a.m. each Friday and Monday, then taking forty-five hours to travel the 205 miles to Sherman, Texas, if westbound, or seventeen and one-half hours to cover the sixty-five-mile distance to the next major eastbound stop at Fayetteville, Arkansas.

Belle Point Today

Today, the Fort Smith National Historic Site occupies the riverside portion of the town's historic district and graces the elevation of Belle Point. A city of 90,000 fans north, east and south from the fortress and original town site. Structures of the second fort are still prominent, including the commissary building and the barracks, now serving as the visitor center but used from 1875 to 1896 as courthouse and jail for "Hanging Judge" Isaac C. Parker's court. The foundations of the second fort walls have also been excavated and enclose the campus. Closer to shore, overlooking the river, the stone foundations of the 1817 fort lay exposed. Standing there, I consider the view, trying to summon a sense of the past. At the confluence of the Arkansas and

Poteau Rivers, where once seasonal variation and sand bars impeded navigation, the water is now maintained at a minimum depth of nine feet for cargo-carrying barges. In 1971, the locks and dams of the McClellan-Kerr Arkansas River Navigation System tamed the Arkansas, and the junction of the two rivers has since been engulfed by the marine highway.[76]

Hand forged mooring ring on the shore at Belle Point

Down at the water line, I perch on a ledge of black rock at the river's edge, waves lapping at my feet. Hand-forged mooring rings protrude from the stone, testifying to the busy landing this once was, with steamboats and ferries coming and going. Quiet now and cleared of structures, the pristine condition of the historic site harkens back more, perhaps, to pre-settlement days than to the time when the Butterfield stage passed through. By 1858, docks and shacks would have lined the riverbank, stairs and other structures placed here and there to facilitate loading and unloading of people and cargo.

Walking down to the shore of the Poteau, I look upstream into the river's mouth, puzzling over the actual location of the ford used by the first Overland Mail. From the agency at North Second and A Streets, the wagon would have made its way southwest past the present visitor parking lot for the Fort Smith National Historic Site to the ferry landing near the southwest extensions of North Third and Fourth Streets.[77] Ormsby's stage forded rather than ferried across the Poteau for some unknown reason. Ferries operated at Fort Smith for many years before that, but river conditions may have made fording practical and expeditious given that the Arkansas River was quite low when Ormsby crossed at Van Buren. J.M. Farwell, correspondent for San Francisco's *Daily Alta California* newspaper, crossed the Poteau on a ferry on his eastbound journey a few weeks behind Ormsby.[78] And in August 1859, westbound traveler Albert Richardson crossed the Poteau into Indian Territory on a "shaky" ferry.[79] By 1860, the Overland Mail was using Bridge Edwards. That year the Choctaw General Council granted Tandy Walker and Joseph R. Hall the privilege to establish a toll gate at the western end of the bridge, on a turnpike road to be covered with stone or plank, extending west to the John Ring plantation. Federal troops destroyed Bridge Edwards the following April as they evacuated just ahead of Arkansas volunteers aligned with the Confederacy, who then took possession of the fort.[80]

From the top of the Belle Point bluff, I look across the Arkansas River into Oklahoma. Among historic views, this one ranks highly. It is everything English botanist Thomas Nuttall described during his 1819 visit to Fort Smith: ". . . more commanding and picturesque, than any other spot of equal elevation on the banks of the Arkansa."[81] It is still commanding and picturesque, but the forested banks beyond the water reveal nothing about what lies ahead. For the stagecoach traveler from the east in 1858, looking across the river was to contemplate jumping from the familiar into the mystery of Indian Territory and many miles of wilderness beyond. The intrigue of discovering what remains of the old road and what it reveals about the people whose land it crossed draws me in the same direction.

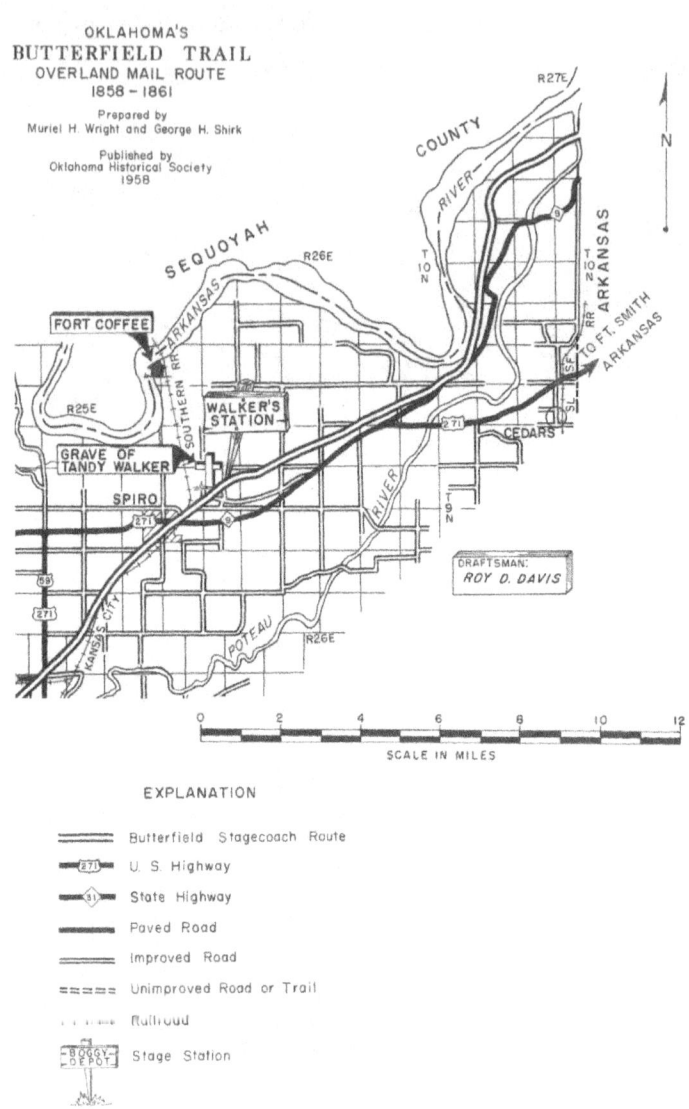

OKLAHOMA'S
BUTTERFIELD TRAIL
OVERLAND MAIL ROUTE
1858 – 1861

Prepared by
Muriel H. Wright and George H. Shirk

Published by
Oklahoma Historical Society
1958

EXPLANATION

======= Butterfield Stagecoach Route
U. S. Highway
State Highway
Paved Road
Improved Road
===== Unimproved Road or Trail
Railroad
Stage Station

Butterfield Trail – Eastern LeFlore County, from the Arkansas border to Spiro. Adapted from original map courtesy of Oklahoma Historical Society.

Chapter Two: The Source

Drinking from Agency Spring

The water is clear and cold coming from the pipe at the side of the road, overflowing my cup in a second. I quaff it and fill it again, only later wondering whether it is a good idea to guzzle water from an unfamiliar source. But the folks living here use it every day for their drinking water and it is piped to the road for the community's use. More than that, for nearly two hundred years it has been the source of life for dwellers and travelers at Walker's Station, Indian Territory's easternmost Butterfield stage stand. And, centuries before, it may have slaked the thirst of the people who built the Spiro Mounds just a few miles away on the south bank of the Arkansas. Drinking from the same spring, still flowing with vigor, is a nearly mystical connection to the past.

I reach this place from Fort Smith by a route slightly different from Waterman Ormsby's and am certainly much more aware of my surroundings. No doubt numb from lack of sleep after sixty-eight hours of wakeful travel, and finally accustomed to the rough ride of the stage wagon, Ormsby fell into what must have been blissful oblivion on the road between the Poteau River and Walker's Station. In the Butterfield stage wagon behind the driver were three wooden bench seats which converted to one bed when the backs were lowered. It was intended to accommodate four to ten passengers, according to their size and how they positioned themselves. Ormsby found it "a very agreeable bed for one" after the other passengers disembarked at Fort Smith, suggesting it did not work at all well for a group of any size.[82] As the only through passenger on the journey, Ormsby was spared the crowded experience reported by others. Raphael Pumpelly, an American geologist, traveled in 1860 on a Butterfield stage from St. Louis to Tucson, Arizona, with eight other passengers. He wrote that since the occupants of the front and middle seats faced each other, it required six passengers to interlock their knees and "there being room inside for only ten of the twelve legs, each side of the coach was graced by a foot, now dangling near the wheel, now trying in vain to find a place of support." Pumpelly had to take a seat in the front and an unusually heavy mail weighed down the rear, keeping the passengers in the front seat always bending forward without any support for their backs, a position in which rest was impossible.[83]

From the ford and ferry landing on the Indian Territory side of the Poteau River, the mail road ran south for about ten miles down the finger of land between the Arkansas and Poteau Rivers, then turned southwest toward Walker's. When Captain Stuart opened this portion of the road in 1832 the first miles were "very tedious and extremely unpleasant," struggling through a cane brake so thick, heavy and entangled with briers and vines as to render it "almost impenetrable."[84] H.C. Benson, a minister teaching at a boys' school at Fort Coffee from 1843 to 1845, agreed with Stuart's assessment of the land between Fort Smith and Skullyville, claiming there was hardly language to describe the density of the cane in the bottomland, "so thick there seemed to be little room for other timber," although he did admit to the presence of "a few cottonwoods, elms, and pecans."[85] Ten years later, artist Heinrich Balduin Möllhausen, traveling with the Whipple expedition, described "roots of trees and decaying trunks" so close that they "arrested the procession." The canopy so shaded the ground that it would not dry, and so "the last of the wagons had to be literally drawn out of the mud as from a morass."[86] It continued to be a difficult section, described by another passerby as "one quagmire for ten miles,"[87] but later travelers could avoid it using Bridge Edwards to get across the Poteau. The iron bridge is long gone, its location near Pocola obscured beneath the elevated waters of the McClellan-Kerr Arkansas River Navigation System.

Ormsby awoke as the sun rose, catching only about three hours' slumber. The Butterfield mail wagon's first stopping place in Indian Territory was a large farm "owned by an Indian but worked by a white man from the East."[88] This may have been the plantation of John G. Ring, located in the Braden vicinity about ten miles southwest of Fort Smith. The Ring home and store faced the mail road and sold supplies to travelers.[89] The house was built in what Benson called "Texas style," with "wide piazza in front and rear, united by a broad, open passageway through the center of the building," a form of architecture typical of the southeastern U.S. and Indian Territory known as a "dogtrot," since the family dogs could find a spot of shade and cool air in the breezeway. Ring also operated a stage station there during the 1840s.[90] He was, observed Benson, a white man with an excellent farm and a Choctaw wife. Mrs. Ring made quite an impression, for Benson wrote that "although an Indian," she was "sensible, tolerably well educated, energetic in business, and altogether a superior woman," indicating he considered such qualities unusual in a woman of her race.[91] By marrying a Choctaw woman, Ring, who died in 1854 at the age of fifty-five, possessed a valuable estate on his wife's behalf.[92] White men could not on their own acquire title to land or reside in the Choctaw Nation without government permission, but the tribe adopted them as citizens and bestowed attendant privileges if they married Choctaw women.[93]

Governor Walker

Ormsby's Celerity wagon continued to Walker's Station, a meal and change station located at Skullyville, northeast of present-day Spiro, at the home of Choctaw Governor Tandy Walker. A mixed-blood Choctaw born in Mississippi, Walker was serving as Governor under a new constitution adopted by the Choctaws at Skullyville in 1857. The constitution generated great controversy, a subject about which Ormsby would learn more down the road in Boggy Depot. Like other influential Choctaws and Chickasaws, Walker viewed the Butterfield company favorably.[94] He was among the citizens who maintained relay stations at their homes and obtained government permits to build bridges and toll gates, charging usage fees to non-citizens.[95] "Toll bridges," wrote John Young Bryce, "were the order of the day, provided a stream large enough could be found across which to build one. If not, sometimes they would ditch around in such a way as to make it impossible for a wagon to pass other than on the bridge."[96] Otherwise, most roads in the Choctaw and Chickasaw Nations were primitive trails. The Choctaw government did not appropriate money for road improvements, but required all male citizens between the ages of eighteen and fifty to work the roads for six days a year.[97] The Chickasaw government required the same of all males from sixteen to fifty. It fell to county judges to administer these laws, appointing men to mark new roads when petitioned by the community, assigning overseers, and notifying people when to bring their axes, hoes and spades and show up for work.[98]

In October, 1858, the Choctaw General Council approved multiple six-year permits for building and operating infrastructure along the Overland Mail route. Authorized tollgate keepers on the Butterfield route charged fifty cents for a four-wheeled wagon with a four-horse, mule, or oxen team; twenty-five cents for a four-wheeled wagon pulled by one or two livestock; ten cents per man and horse; and one cent each for livestock being driven through. The legislature granted these privileges to A.W. Geary on the Little Boggy; the heirs of William R. Guy on the Clear Boggy; James D. Davis on the Middle Boggy; John Riddle on the Fourche Maline; and Washington McDaniel and Charles M. James for erecting a bridge on Bayouzil Creek (also spelled Brazil, Brazeale and Brazile at various times) and establishing a toll gate near their place of residence. William Holloway received permission to construct a turnpike road and toll gate at the Narrows, "grading the earth and leveling with stone."[99] And in October 1859, the Council granted Silas Pusley a permit to erect a toll bridge across Gaines Creek.[100] Some of the work legitimized in October 1858 had likely been completed the summer before. On July 7 that year, the *Fort Smith Times* reported an Overland Mail crew leaving there soon to work on the road in the Choctaw Nation.[101]

The structure housing Walker's Station predates the Overland Mail by at least twenty-five years. Tradition has it that the dwelling was built around 1832-1833 to house the western Choctaw agency. The building may, however, be the same one erected in 1827 when agent William McClellan moved his headquarters from Fort Smith to Pebble Spring. In 1830, after William McClellan's death in 1829, his brother David reported the property was still in the hands of McClellan's widow and she wished to turn it over to the U.S.[102] On September 7, 1831, Major Francis W. Armstrong was appointed agent for the Choctaws west of the Mississippi as the Choctaw migration was commencing.[103] Two years later, Armstrong brought his family to Indian Territory and a year after that, on September 25, 1834, he wrote to Elbert Herring, Commissioner of Indian Affairs, requesting $362 to complete the agency building. He stated that when he arrived, presumably referring to the year before, there was nothing but the body of a double log house. He found the roof and porches rotten and the agency dilapidated, with only one chimney. With the requested money, Armstrong planned to put on a new roof and provide the house with a good stone foundation, new floors, and chimneys. "The agency," he wrote, "will then be comfortable, plain and substantial and nothing more will be required as long as the roof lasts." In urging the granting of his request he added, "The comfort of my family makes it necessary that the work should be done before the winter sets in."[104] It is possible that William McClellan's widow lived in the original agency building for some time after his death and by the time Armstrong took possession of the building the structure was dilapidated. He and his family may have lived in the old dogtrot cabin for a year before he took steps to make it sound. Had the building been constructed in 1832 or 1833, or even in 1831, as one secondary source states, the onset of its dilapidation seems premature, but Armstrong's language can also be interpreted to suggest the structure had never quite been completed.[105]

Reconciling the distance to the agency is another matter. William McClellan reported Pebble Spring was eighteen miles above Fort Smith, a distance incorporating the meanders of the Arkansas River. With Captain John Stuart's 1832 road work, the distance was shortened to thirteen miles.[106] But Francis Armstrong called it fifteen miles[107] and Captain Randolph B. Marcy fourteen.[108] Whatever the precise origin of the building and its exact distance from Fort Smith, the United States established a post office at Choctaw Agency in June 1833 with Armstrong as postmaster. This was the third post office established in the Indian Territory, preceded by one at Miller Courthouse in 1824 (then Arkansas Territory) and Fort Towson in 1832.[109] Postmasters in such far-flung outposts of the federal government usually operated out of their homes or businesses, sorting mail delivered by another contractor via stage or horseback, and distributing it to local citizens for a small commission.[110]

Skullyville

At the Agency, the Choctaws received annuity payments from the U.S. in exchange for land cessions, and those settled in the area called the locality "Iskuliville" or "Moneytown," "Iskuli-fehna," meaning "money" in Choctaw. The name became anglicized to Skullyville and the post office was renamed the same in 1860.[111]

Skullyville became a center of trade, social and political activities, and education. Möllhausen described the community in 1853:

> You come . . . upon fields of Maize and wheat, the log-houses, surrounded by flourishing young fruit trees, which announces the commencement of the rising Indian town. The town consists of a kind of broad street, formed of log-houses and gardens, and does not differ much in appearance from many other thriving villages; Indians, Negroes, and Europeans are seen moving about –

domestic animals of all sorts enliven the farmyards, gardens, and streets; the sound of the threshing machine is heard, and the regular falling of the smith's hammer upon the anvil, and in general there is an appearance of lively industry about the place."[112]

In 1844, Fort Coffee Academy opened for Choctaw boys north of Skullyville in the buildings of the abandoned military fort.[113] The boarding school was part of the Choctaws' robust educational system. Its development was strongly influenced by descendants of intermarried whites, who saw education and adoption of "civilized" institutions as the best hope for their people. Beginning in 1818, the Choctaws invited missionaries to establish stations and open schools in their country. Three years later, Presbyterian Cyrus Kingsbury opened the first mission school, with the tribe bearing the bulk of the school's expenses. A Choctaw boys' academy, where many future Choctaw leaders were educated, opened in Kentucky in the fall of 1825. By 1830 there were eleven schools in the Choctaw Nation.

Once re-established in the west after removal, the Choctaws began to rebuild their school system. By 1836 eleven schools boasted two hundred twenty-eight students. In 1842, the Choctaw government took steps to establish a comprehensive school system, leading to the 1844 opening of both Spencer Academy, ten miles north of Doaksville, and Fort Coffee. Two years later New Hope opened, as well as Armstrong Academy, in the Pushmataha district. The Choctaw Council also appropriated money for schools at Pine Ridge, Stockbridge, Goodwater, and Wheelock.[114] In 1848 the Choctaws had nine boarding schools supported by tribal funds, usually operated under a contract with a mission organization, which furnished teachers. Besides the boarding schools, neighborhood schools emerged in a number of communities and eventually they received public monies for support. In 1860 five hundred children attended these neighborhood schools, which with the boarding school attendance brought the total school enrollment up to nine hundred.[115]

Skullyville was also capital of the Choctaws' Moshulatubbe District, named for a full-blood leader who was one of the signers of the Treaty of Dancing Rabbit Creek.[116] An influential district chief, Moshulatubbe was born in 1770, his early exploits as a warrior giving him the name "Determined to Kill." He served in the Creek War of 1813-14 with General Andrew Jackson and was present at the Battle of New Orleans in 1815. At the time he signed the Treaty of Dancing Rabbit Creek, he had in Mississippi two homes, eleven slaves, thirty acres under cultivation and large herds of cattle and horses. Remembered as a great orator, Moshulatubbe was an important representative for Choctaw interests both before and during the removal. He strongly opposed missionaries and their teachings and complained that the government was wasting money by giving it to missionaries for the education of their children. Moshulatubbe served as district chief until 1836 and died from smallpox August 30, 1838.[117] The location of his burial is uncertain.[118] W.B. Morrison wrote that Moshulatubbe was buried in an unmarked grave, probably in the Skullyville cemetery. Farther along the Butterfield trail, other possibilities emerge.[119]

Located between the Arkansas and Canadian Rivers, Moshulatubbe District was northernmost of the Choctaw Nation's three original political sectors in the Indian Territory. The others were Red River or Okla Falaya, later renamed Apukshunnubbee, east of the Kiamichi River; and Pushmataha, west of the Kiamichi River and south of the Canadian. Each district was an autonomous entity with representation in the national legislature, or General Council, composed of twenty-seven elected members. District chiefs were ex-officio members of the council, and any two of them could veto legislation unless over-ruled by a two-thirds majority. In 1837 the

Treaty of Doaksville gave the Chickasaws the right to form a fourth political district in the western region of the Choctaw Nation.

Western Choctaw Agent Francis Armstrong died in August 1835 at the Agency and was succeeded by his brother, William Armstrong, who occupied the building until his death in 1847. Tandy Walker purchased the agency building after it was abandoned.[120] In 1859, Butterfield passenger Albert Richardson described the structure as long, low and hospitable, surrounded by stately oaks and graceful locusts, with outbuildings serving as kitchen, executive office and slave quarters.[121] To reporter Waterman Ormsby, Governor Walker looked like a "full-blooded white man." The governor came out in his shirt sleeves and helped hitch the horses, an act which was notable because slaves took care of the horses at Walker's and usually hitched them to the stage.[122] Walker had a large farm and several hundred head of cattle and would have used slave labor in managing those operations as well as supporting the Butterfield station. In 1860, the federal census recorded sixteen people whom he enslaved. The bottomlands along the Arkansas and Poteau Rivers near Skullyville, and the Red River to the south, supported large-scale agriculture and the labor of enslaved people was commonly used by Choctaw planters for cultivation.

Slavery in the Indian Territory

The Choctaws and other southeastern tribes adopted chattel slavery as early as the late eighteenth century, a byproduct of the influence of and intermarriage with whites.[123] Benson's impression was that even poorer Choctaw full-bloods managed to enslave one or two black people to "perform their heavy work,"[124] although the 1860 census reports that only 2.5% of Choctaws and 2.6% of Chickasaws owned slaves. Most slaveowners, according to census data, held fewer than five slaves and fewer than thirty people in all of Indian Territory owned thirty slaves or more. But some owned hundreds.[125] By 1860, enslaved people made up fourteen per cent of the Choctaw Nation's population, with more than half living along the Red River where mixed-blood planters settled, taking advantage of both fertile soil and the availability of steamboat transportation to get cotton to market.[126]

Indian slaveowners were often, but not universally, characterized as more lenient than others. Ormsby wrote that the Choctaws appeared to let their slaves do "pretty much as they please."[127] William Tallack's impression from an 1860 journey on the Butterfield echoed Ormsby's. He observed a large amount of "comfort and moderation in . . . the condition and treatment" of slaves.[128] Möllhausen thought slaves received from their Indian masters more Christian treatment than among the Christian whites. "The negro is regarded as companion and helper, to whom thanks and kindness are due when he exerts himself for the welfare of the household."[129]

Major Ethan Allen Hitchcock offered a broader perspective after spending five months in Indian Territory during 1841-42 on behalf of the federal government investigating fraudulent practices among agents and contractors. Distinguishing between slaveholding full-bloods and mixed-bloods, he wrote that the full-blood "rarely works himself and but few of them make their slaves work. A slave among wild Indians is almost as free as his owner . . . ." But the mixed-bloods, whom Hitchcock called the "true civilizers," required more service from the slave until "they become slaves indeed in all manner of work."[130] And, in contrast, W.B. Parker's observations in 1854 convinced him that "the general government would subserve the cause of humanity by prohibiting any Indians from holding (slaves); they look upon them as mere beasts of burden, and treat them accordingly."[131]

In general, the living conditions of slaves in the Indian Territory were similar to that of slaves in the United States. Men worked as field hands and women attended to household duties.[132] Some slaveholders among the Choctaws allowed slaves to farm and raise their own livestock, live with a spouse owned by another, or serve as translators between Indians and whites.[133] At New Hope Academy, Aunt Hetty, an enslaved woman of about forty, managed the dining room and kitchen and acted as an interpreter. "She was about the most important character on the place," wrote Reverend William Graham, a Methodist missionary.[134] Traveling in the Choctaw Nation in 1844, N. Sayre Harris, secretary and general agent for the Protestant Episcopal Church, visited a Choctaw widow whose family had a "number of people of colour among them, who seem to be very happy: fare as well as the Indians, and are of great service to them in many ways."[135]

During his time at the Fort Coffee boys' school, Benson, anti-slavery in sentiment, lived as a missionary within the slaveholding society until such time as his denomination could no longer reconcile the ethical dilemma of the situation. His accounts of daily life illustrate the contradictions inherent in the institution of slavery. In one instance, Hannah, an ancient female slave too disabled to work, was discarded by the man who enslaved her. Benson wrote, "As Hannah was too old and frail to labor, Jones concluded not to furnish her any more provisions. As she was not useful to any one, (Jones) thought it would be strictly proper, and in good taste, for her to die as soon as convenient." The starving woman, withered and weak, crawled to the mission seeking help, taking three hours to travel less than a mile. This same Jones also "had the reputation of a good *master*, which was not contradicted by the appearance of his slaves; they were fat and sleek, cheerful, welldressed, and apparently quite happy." Hannah was taken in by Mrs. Hall, a mixed-blood woman who also enslaved a number of people. This slave owner "kindly consented" to house Hannah in a vacant cabin and take care of her as long as she lived, doing this "cheerfully, from a conviction of duty, and without any compensation whatever." Benson wrote that Hannah was still living and "quite comfortable" when he left Indian Territory."[136]

In the 1930s, former slaves talked with Works Progress Administration interviewers about their lives. Polly Colbert, enslaved by Holmes Colbert, a mixed-blood Choctaw, was interviewed at the age of 83.[137] She thought "Indian masters was just naturally kinder any way, leastways mine was." Polly was a small child when her parents died, and Colbert and his wife provided well for her and her siblings. She remarked that other slaveowners who lived on nearby plantations were also "good" to their slaves.[138] Kiziah Love, aged 93 at the time of her interview, was enslaved by Chickasaw Benjamin Franklin (B.F.) Colbert, who ran Colbert's Ferry. She and other slaves on the Colbert plantation "loved Master Frank" and were "about as well off as the best of 'em." On the other side of the coin, Colbert's half-brother, Buck, "the meanest man the sun ever shined on," habitually whipped slaves and generally behaved badly until one day he killed one of his own brothers and was then killed by a surviving brother. "Everybody was glad that Buck was dead," said Love.[139] Mary Grayson, who was enslaved by a Creek Indian, recalled at age 83 that "we slaves didn't have a hard time at all before the War" but that the Chickasaws didn't treat their slaves like the Creeks did, instead they were more strict, like the people in Texas and other places.[140]

Illustrating the danger of generalization, Matilda Poe, 80, enslaved by Chickasaw Isaac Love, said he "was sure good to his slaves. . . . I never did know I was a slave, 'cause I couldn't tell I wasn't free. I always had a good time, didn't have to work much, and allus had something to eat and wear and that was better than it is with me now.[141] These detailed reports do provide insights about the experiences of these individuals, although they were quite elderly at the time of the interviews and the events they recounted occurred more than seventy years earlier.[142] And, looking back so many years from the depths of the Great Depression to their childhoods, those times may have indeed seemed better.

Farwell's additional observations are telling. At a stop in Indian Territory he saw an aged black woman smoking comfortably at the door of an outbuilding, watching several small black children play, "some of whose seniors might, however, have been less at ease . . . for in front of the verandah, there was a notice offering 'two hundred and fifty dollars reward for the apprehension of my slave Frank,' who had run off in search of a happier allotment."[143] Newspapers from the antebellum period in Indian Territory and Arkansas contained regular posting of rewards for runaway slaves. Some listed by slaveholders from Arkansas or Texas indicated they suspected the runaway of going to the Indian Territory. An 1851 notice in the *Choctaw Intelligencer* of Doaksville, Choctaw Nation, placed by a man from Fulton, Arkansas stated that if the slave, named Bob, was not stolen, "he is likely gone to some of the neighboring Indian nations, and may have obtained forged papers and attempted to pass himself off as free." Another notice, from an 1844 Van Buren, Arkansas, newspaper, reports, "It is expected he (Henry) will endeavour to make his way to the Cherokee nation and pass for a free boy." One runaway, Pun, escaped from the Fort Towson, Choctaw Nation, area in 1844 and it was supposed he "went among the Creeks or Seminoles." Some enslaved people apparently saw the potential for greater freedom in the Indian Territory or in parts of it other than their own. An 1851 notice in the Doaksville newspaper by a Choctaw Nation slaveholder offering $200 for a runaway slave named Aleck is chilling: "If the boy cannot be taken alive, I will pay a reward of $25 for his scalp."

Suspected destinations for runaways changed with the times. An 1849 notice in the Fort Smith newspaper about an escaped slave indicated he may have fled for California during the Gold Rush. Postings in 1859-61 sometimes mentioned the slaves going to Kansas, which was admitted to the Union as a free state in January, 1861. Clearly, enslaved people in Indian Territory ran away, so whether or not their owners were "lenient," they knew there was a better life outside of slavery and some chose to pursue it. Some enslaved people in Indian Territory may indeed have experienced relatively mild conditions, but generalizing these experiences to that of Indian Territory's enslaved population as a whole is probably best avoided. For more on this subject see *Black Slaves, Indian Masters: Slavery, Emancipation and Citizenship in the Native American South* by Barbara Krauthamer.

Slaves also worked cattle on Choctaw ranches, a significant source of the tribe's wealth.[144] Although Ormsby observed little farming along the road between Skullyville and present-day Atoka,[145] he met many bands of Choctaws driving large herds of cattle and reported they were quite wealthy in cattle and slaves, owning large herds of cattle and "liv(ing) well on the increase."[146] In 1837, a government agent reported, "The country is so well adapted to raising stock, and so prolific has been the increase, that (the Choctaws) have furnished large quantities to the Creek contractors, without apparently diminishing the main stock, and they assure me that they have an abundance to stock the Chickasaws upon their arrival at their new homes."[147] By the late 1840s, Indian Territory's cattle industry had become a major player in the southern U.S. market.[148]

Ormsby described Choctaw dwellings along the road as squalid and miserable.[149] They certainly stood in stark contrast to what he was accustomed to seeing in New York City and the settled areas of Missouri and Arkansas. Parker's 1854 account echoes Ormsby's and goes deeper into what he saw as lacking: "These buildings are stuck (almost invariably) upon the road; no neat door yard, with a substantial fence and neat gate, enclose them; no flower or vegetable garden is seen, but the ornamental figure of a half-starved hog, grunts lazily on one side, and a pack of miserable curs lounge on the other, the whole presenting an untidy picture of squalid discomfort."[150] These statements from easterners on the frontier are harsh but instructive. We would like to think they saw these differences in a positive light somehow but this was a time when it was still common to think of Native Americans (even, apparently, the Five "Civilized" Tribes) as "savages." Like Benson's backhanded compliment to Ring's wife, these criticisms may not set well with us in 2024, but they illustrate an attitude that did exist in the 1850s.

Ormsby also described a lack of farming and many deserted houses along the road, a condition which may be connected with a severe drought. In October, 1858, Elias Rector, government agent for the Southern Superintendency, attributed a preponderance of deserted houses to the practice of communal landholding, stating all five tribes cultivated the soil to a small extent but, lacking individual ownership, they moved from place to place, "and one sees, in traveling through their country, more deserted than inhabited houses."[151] But since 1854 the Indian Territory had been suffering from sparse rainfall and crop failures and, rather than being culturally itinerant as Rector suggested, many Choctaws may have moved to survive. Drought and starvation continued as the onset of the Civil War approached and would influence the Choctaw Nation's decision to align with the Confederacy.[152]

The Road Today

Neither fording the Poteau nor crossing on Bridge Edwards is possible these days, so the next best way to reach Oklahoma from Fort Smith is via the Tom Traw bridge over the Poteau on Oklahoma Highway 9A, winding through the community of Arkoma and across the state line. West of the river, the bottomland on the peninsula separating the Arkansas and the Poteau is now mostly clear of timber, replaced by sod farms and corn fields. I glimpse a few tall cane brakes there, faint vestiges what was once nearly impenetrable. Highway 9A approximates the path of the old trail, passing through the site of Ring's Plantation and the Braden community. Traveling west, Cavanal and Sugar Loaf Mountains in Oklahoma's LeFlore County appear in the distance. Portending the landscape ahead, Möllhausen wrote that these and the Sans Bois Mountains "bound really paradisaical valleys, over which Nature has poured out every kind of loveliness with inexhaustible profusion."[153] He and other travelers described the forests, meadows and mountains of Indian Territory in romantic terms, right up to the mid-twentieth century. In 1930, the Conklings found segments of the abandoned mail road navigable here, but much of it was very rough and sometimes submerged by backup from the Arkansas River.[154]

Side Trip: New Hope

On the potholed pavement of New Hope Road, the Butterfield trail passes New Hope Cemetery and the site of New Hope Academy, a boarding school for Choctaw girls opened in 1846. Today on the eastern edge of Skullyville, the old cemetery spreads out, shaded and mysterious, containing about 5,000 burials. Many of them are long-forgotten, including students of the Academy, which once stood a short distance east of the graveyard. Health concerns were common in the days when infectious diseases took many lives, and being congregated in the common space of a boarding school encouraged the spread of illness. In fact, the school closed early in 1849, ending the term in April after ten months because of a cholera epidemic among Choctaws then arriving in the country. New Hope experienced a pneumonia epidemic in 1852 but all the victims survived. During the 1852-53 school year, however, nearly half the boarding school's fifty students contracted pneumonia and whooping cough, and four died. A teacher, Mary Talbott, also died, the school suffering "more (that) year than at any other time since it commenced operations."[155] Local tradition has it that three of these students were the first to be buried in New Hope Cemetery. I visited the graves with caretaker Dale Stout, located on the south end of the twenty-seven-acre tract. A large plot surrounded by stones contains the resting places of two of the girls and the other one, a single grave nearby, is surrounded by a rock wall and covered with a slab bearing an ornate carving. The names of these unfortunate girls are unknown. In 1937, this cemetery was in "deplorable condition," with numerous graves overgrown and more unmarked than marked, prompting WPA writer Gomer Gower to consider that the graveyard might hold "the remains of those whose memory we would revere in an appropriate manner did we but know who they were."[156] It is now tidy, exuding a hallowed aura thanks to the massive oaks and hickories sheltering the old graves.

Less than one-half mile east of the cemetery, New Hope's school buildings burned in December, 1896, and the academy did not reopen.[157] Vestiges of the structure's rubble remain – stones, bricks, pieces of metal and shards of pottery— west of a historical marker placed by the Oklahoma Historical Society in 1969. The school's water supply, New Hope spring, is down the hill to the north of the site, its vigorous flow supplying water to nearby homes and flowing into a nearby branch. During the 1920s, J.W. Hood, whose descendants still own the spring property, delivered water from the spring to customers in Fort Smith for thirty-five cents a five-gallon bottle.[158]

Walker's Station

Less than a mile west of New Hope, a turn to the north on aptly named Spring Road brings Walker's Station into sight. The spot would be easy to miss but for a green sign indicating the turn for Roselawn Cemetery, where a dirt path provides a parking spot. The marker of concrete and bronze placed by the Oklahoma Historical Society in 1958 remains intact on the west side of the road just inside the fence and in the center of the easily visible trace of the stagecoach road.

When the Conklings passed through in 1930, the original structure housing the Choctaw Agency and stage station was still standing "in a fine state of preservation."[159] The property was then owned by the Ainsworth family, Thomas D. Ainsworth having purchased the structure in 1881. Fire destroyed it on September 12, 1947; at the time it was the oldest structure in Oklahoma and one of only four extant log house Butterfield Mail stations of the original forty-seven.[160] Another of those was also in Indian Territory at Nail's Crossing; none of them still stand in the twenty-first century.

Northeast of the house is a "never-failing spring of water famed for its purity." In 1853, Möllhausen commented that this spring gushed out from the rock near the agency.[161] A few years later, Tandy Walker was said to have diverted the spring water into wooden troughs in a nearby milkhouse where milk, cream and butter could be kept cool in the fresh running water.[162]

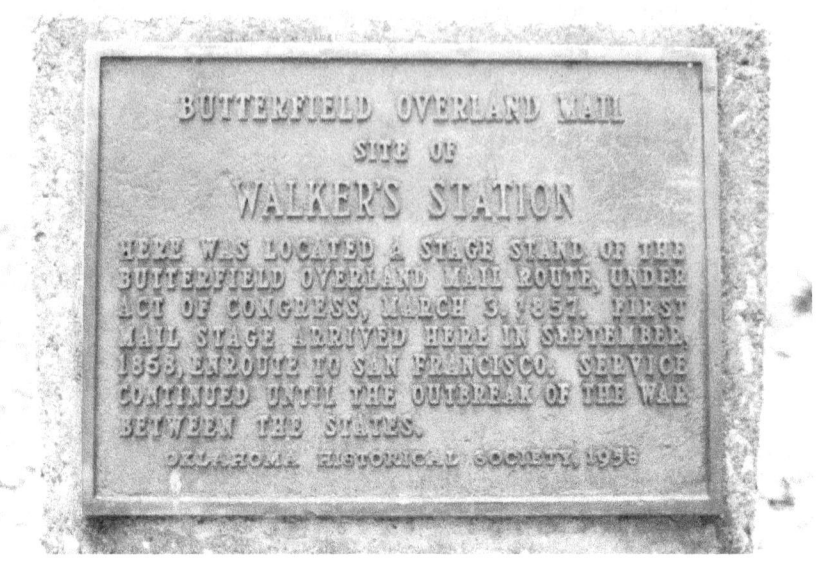

1958 Historical Marker at Walker's Station

In 1958, the Centennial Committee parked their automobiles and drank from the spring "at the same spot so much enjoyed by the countless passengers riding across the Choctaw Nation via Overland Mail stages a century ago." Scattered foundation and chimney stones up the hill from the spring were all that remained of the station then, except for overgrown iris and spirea in bloom, demarcating paths, gardens, and the front of the house. The committee considered Walker's Station one of Oklahoma's most beautiful Butterfield sites with its lush blue grass and the "aura of dignity and importance" its "tall and stately" hickory, walnut, oak, and elm trees provided.[163] In 2022 the trees of 1958 had gone, the lawn dominated instead by a massive, living bois d'arc, impressive in its own right. On one of my visits, I find the property owner, Joy Terry, out working in the yard. She has just acquired the site and is unfamiliar with its history, so I have the pleasure of educating her. I am delighted when she calls my attention to the spring, still flowing with cold, sweet water. Like the committee members sixty-four years earlier, I relish the experience of drinking the water from that historic spring as a tangible link to yesterday.

Tandy Walker's grave marker in the Skullyville Cemetery

The Skullyville cemetery is southwest of Walker's Station, housing the resting places of many Choctaw leaders, including Tandy Walker, who died on February 2, 1877. The cemetery was in mediocre condition in 1937[164] and evidently had deteriorated further by 1958, since the Centennial Committee found the graveyard "almost completely grown rank with dense blackberry bushes, wild honeysuckle and weeds."[165] They called it a disgrace to the state of Oklahoma.[166] Now it is managed by the Choctaw Nation and well groomed. Tandy Walker's ornate marble gravestone, fractured but still intact, is easily located near a wrought-iron fence. Like New Hope, the Skullyville cemetery is a quiet place of antiquity.

Side Trip: Fort Coffee

A few miles north of Walker's Station on the south bank of the Arkansas River is the site of Fort Coffee.[167] There at a landing at the foot of a tall bluff, people of the Five Tribes disembarked from steamboats in their new homeland and goods arrived from other ports for distribution. Atop the bluff were the buildings of the 1834 fort, later used for the Choctaw boys' school and as a Confederate encampment. The buildings burned during the Civil War but I am curious to see what remains at the site. Dennis Peterson, curator of the Spiro Mounds Archeological Center, now retired, is kind enough to take my husband Bill and I there one late November day.[168] Located just east of Fort Coffee, Spiro Mounds is Oklahoma's only Native American archaeological site both accessible to the public and predating European contact. Excavated in the 1930s, the site contains twelve mounds and has yielded one of the country's most significant collections of artifacts from the Mississippian culture. Dubbed the "King Tut of the Arkansas Valley" in 1935, Spiro Mounds was inhabited from about A.D. 800 and A.D. 1450 by people who spoke a Caddoan language and functioned within an extensive trade network.[169] Today it is owned and operated by the Oklahoma Historical Society.

We walk a mile or so to the remains of Swallow Rock, upon which Fort Coffee was situated. In 1819, Thomas Nuttall described this landmark as "a projecting cliff, about 150 feet high, adorned with bushes of cedar, in the centre of which there appears to be an entrance into a cavern, and several other fretted excavations scattered over with clusters of martin nests."[170] Benson wrote in 1843 the Fort Coffee site was surrounded by an impenetrable thicket of heavy timber and brush. He continued, "At the point of the promontory the river bank was a bluff or wall of solid rock, rising, almost perpendicularly, sixty-four feet above low-water mark. The edge of this bold precipice was bordered with a growth of old cedars, the roots of which had penetrated the fissures and crevices of the rocks. Their gnarled trunks and scraggy branches were weatherbeaten and hoary with years."[171] The south slope led down to the water on a flat rock, where the steamboat landing was located.[172] In 1853, Möllhausen found Fort Coffee on a hill rising abruptly from the Arkansas with a gentle downward slope on the landside and a white building gleaming out pleasantly from the dark cedars.[173]

On this cool, sunny day in 2018, our hike takes us through fields and woods to the edge of the river. There, we find that Swallow Rock is gone, obliterated when limestone was quarried during construction of the McClellan-Kerr Arkansas River Navigation System. With dredging beginning in 1963, the once-shallow Arkansas River became a 250-foot-wide channel to facilitate commercial navigation between the Mississippi River and Tulsa's Port of Catoosa.

Neither is there anything to see of Fort Coffee except the disrupted cemetery and broken stones where Choctaw Agent Francis Armstrong was laid to rest.[174] In 1936 the vandalism of Armstrong's neglected grave was reported in the *Chronicles of Oklahoma*: "An iron gate to a lot of one of the three cemeteries at Fort Coffee bears his name . . . This gate was recently broken by vandals. Part of the rock wall around the lot remains on the two stone posts between which the gate was swung."[175] What became of Armstrong's remains is unknown.

Skullyville declined rapidly after the Civil War. The railroads passed it by, and trade moved to nearby Spiro. But reminders of the past abound. With recorded history dating back to the 1820s, its significance as Walker's Station, the Choctaw Agency, and the Spiro Mounds, Skullyville and its surrounds offer a high concentration of sites important to the early history of Indian Territory and life in the Choctaw Nation after removal. Continuing southwest, the stagecoach road probes deeper into the heart of Choctaw country.

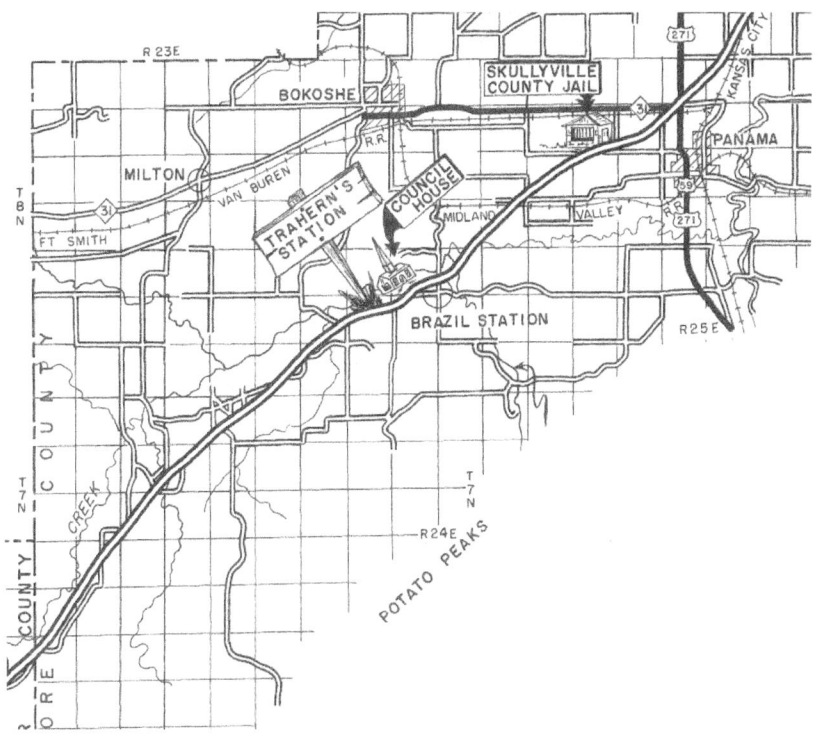

Butterfield Trail - Western LeFlore County, including Brazil Station and Trahern's Station. Adapted from original courtesy of Oklahoma Historical Society. See Eastern LeFlore County map, page 40, for map legend.

Chapter Three: Lies and Legends

Crossing Brazil Creek on the old steel truss bridge, now out of service

Gravel flies as a Jeep skids to a halt in front of us. "What are you doing here?" the driver shouts as he jumps out. Joseph Wolf and I are both startled, and I am definitely puzzled. I had secured permission from the property owner to visit the site of Brazil Station, or so I thought.

Located about fourteen miles from Walker's Station, Brazil was not an official Butterfield stand, but the Choctaw legislature awarded Washington McDaniel and Charles M. James the concession for a toll bridge across Brazil Creek near the site in October 1858, concurrent with the initiation of the Overland Mail. After the Civil War, David Robert Welch, an Irishman who came to Indian Territory via Alabama, founded a trading post here, and the location served as a local mail stop.[176] Both the Conklings and Muriel Wright stopped here on their explorations. Following suit, Joe and I have been examining the ruins, a cemetery and a road trace. Oblivious to the possibility that we could be trespassing, we showed up on a game camera and the land owner alerted a friend, who is accosting us now. I explain that we have the property owner's permission to be here, making sure he knows that Joe is with the Choctaw Nation's Office of Historic Preservation in hopes that it will lend us some credibility.

"Who's the property owner?" he demands, maintaining his sternness but becoming somewhat less threatening. I tell him her name and he informs me she sold the property to his friend some time ago. At first I am shocked and then feel utterly betrayed. I was in contact with her that very morning, even at the moment Joe and I parked at the gate. I knew she was eccentric, but never dreamed she would intentionally deceive and endanger me. At our first meeting, she arrived in a pickup studded with auxiliary lights for catching poachers, making threats about what she would do to trespassers and stating not so subtly how suitable old wells are for hiding bodies. From that moment on I knew not to cross her and scrupulously obtained her permission for each subsequent visit, but now I see that my ginger handling of the relationship was for naught. Thankfully, the Jeep driver softens up and gives me the name and phone number of the current owner for future use. And, on the bright side, I have now made four visits to Brazil Station without getting shot. Certainly, Waterman Ormsby and other travelers did not feel entirely safe during their traverse of Indian Territory so I suppose it could be considered a meaningful moment of empathy.

My experience with property owners has been consistently positive other than this, and even this one seemed friendly at first. Trespassing on private property is taken seriously here, and with few exceptions (which will become apparent later), I have been scrupulous about contacting the owner and asking permission before visiting a site on private property.

Brazil Station

Before arriving at Brazil Station, the stagecoach road passed the present town of Spiro to the south, running southwest toward the Coal Creek crossing. U.S. Highway 271 is close to the line of the old road over part of this distance. About two miles west of Spiro, the road branched into three: the left fork the Overland Mail route, the right fork the road to Edwards Trading Post on Little River in the Creek Nation, and the middle fork Marcy's California wagon road.[177] Near the Coal Creek crossing, the mail road curved sharply west and then southwest again, passing to the south of the Skullyville County Jail, which sits along Rock Jail Road west of Panama, Oklahoma. On private property but easily viewed from the road, the jail is a one-story sandstone building with walls two feet thick and an iron-barred door and window. Although it did not exist contemporaneously with the Overland Mail's use of the route, the structure is important as the only surviving building connected with the Skullyville County government of the Choctaw Nation.

Counties emerged as political divisions within the nation with constitutional changes made in 1850 which reorganized the judiciary, vesting power in a national supreme court, district circuit courts, and county courts. District court had original jurisdiction over all criminal cases as well as civil cases involving property worth more than fifty dollars. At the county level, court convened monthly and recorded marriage licenses, discovery of minerals, and sale of improvements on land. The county court also addressed probate matters and could examine criminal cases and commit them to a higher court.

In order to organize the courts at the county level, the Council divided the nation into nineteen counties. Each county was required to provide its own courthouse and jail. Some courthouses were shacks sitting unused between court sessions, and jails were inadequate, although in the early days were rarely needed because Choctaw criminals could be trusted to present themselves on the day of execution and those convicted of lesser crimes were usually punished by immediate whipping.

Legislation enacted in 1860 required Choctaw district judges to hold court in each county but the population in some counties was so small that a panel of competent jurors could not be assembled. An 1883 law removed the 1860 requirement and provided that court would be held at only one place in each district. After this the Choctaw government built more substantial facilities, such as Skullyville's stone jail.[178] Originally a courthouse and execution tree also comprised the government complex, built between 1888 and 1895.[179] The Skullyville County courthouse, once located north of the jail, burned sometime before 1937.[180]

From the jail, the mail road continued southwest across Buck Creek, where a mail station was located on a later stage route. It then crossed Brazil Creek, a tributary of the Poteau, and what is known today as Mack Watson Creek. About a quarter of a mile southwest of this last crossing is the site of Brazil Station.

Fences through which county roads do not extend now obstruct the path of the old road between the jail and Brazil, but a detour over Buck Creek Mountain on Blue Goose Road affords a scenic crossing of Brazil Creek, until recently on a picturesque 1941 Pony Truss bridge, now out of service but still visible off the main road.[181] It was replaced with a bridge of concrete and greater safety but certainly less charm. South of the bridge, an obscure lane running east accesses the Brazil Cemetery and ruins of Brazil School. The cemetery is still in use, with recent graves near the road and countless old resting places spreading into the woods, their uninscribed stones scattered among the brambles. North of the graveyard, a pile of rubble that once was Brazil School hides in the trees, its clearly defined foundation enveloping the stones of the collapsed walls. In November 1930, the Conklings visited the remnants of the Brazil settlement. "After driving all morning without meeting anyone on the road," wrote Margaret Conkling, "we felt that we were in a deserted countryside. But when we arrived at Brazil School, there were perhaps thirty children out for recess with the teacher directing their play. All looked modern enough and quite happy even though their school yard was a continuation of the cemetery. Not even a fence line to protect the early graves."[182] By 1958 the school was abandoned.

North of the cemetery, a locked gate now blocks access to Brazil Station. This was not the case in 1930, and the Conklings drove past the cemetery and school right up to the D.R. Welch house, near the site of the stage station. They were told the house was built in 1868. Welch also owned land in the Arkansas River bottom at Geary Lane, later renamed Braden. "The only way through this bottom land was by Geary Lane and as father had control of the land, he made this a toll lane," said Robert Anderson (R.A.) Welch, D.R.'s son. "However, this toll fare was only charged for the passage of people who were not citizens of the Territory and all the Choctaw Indians were allowed to go through free of charge." The younger Welch, born in 1877 to D.R. and his third wife, Phoebe, dated the Brazil settlement's origins to 1876, contradicting the 1868 date reported to the Conklings.[183] In an 1885 newspaper article, however, a current resident of Brazil Station wrote that Welch established his trading post in 1872, effectively beginning the Brazil settlement then.[184] The correct date may be one of these, but is difficult to determine.

A post office named Brazil Station was established on April 11, 1879, with Phoebe Welch as its first postmaster. She was the fifth female postmaster in the Indian Territory, at a time after the Civil War when across the United States more women were being appointed to the role.[185] When the post office name was changed to Brazil in 1895, the postmaster was Phoebe Reagan, who, we may surmise, remarried after D.R.'s death in 1892. The Brazil post office was discontinued in 1913.[186]

The Conklings and the Centennial Committee found the ruins of the Brazil stage station northwest of the Welch house, near the creek. The station ruins are no longer evident, but the Welch family grave plot near the house, an old well and a row of bois d'arc trees mark the site, changed little since 1958.[187] A lane east of the house leads to the locked gate blocking entry from the south. This would have been the access point for both the Conklings and the Centennial Committee. Black locust trees also observed in 1958 still flourish, their long thorns creating a hazard for the distracted walker, especially near the small cemetery. An ornate wrought-iron fence topped with the fleur de lis surrounds the picturesque graveyard. D.R. Welch's tombstone is in the southeast corner, broken off at the base but otherwise in good condition. The small plot contains several other markers including that of D.R. Welch's second wife, Lucinda.

On another day I walk the mail road's path from Brazil Station northeast to the Brazil Creek crossing. From the Brazil settlement, the trail quickly enters a deep rut flanked by large trees, the width of a narrow road. It is difficult to walk in the depression, where small trees and briers grow thickly. I cross Mack Watson Creek, the water shallow and the rocks slippery. Continuing through a pasture, I see an old house on a slight rise. Its roof has collapsed but a stone-lined well remains intact, sheltering a snake in its cool interior. On a well-defined and recently used two-track, I soon arrive at Brazil Creek. A likely crossing site is evident where the creek bank is cut down on the east and a path gradually ascends from the creek on the west. The location is consistent with the crossing on a historic map, and a modern aerial view shows a road trace continuing northeast on the east side of the creek. Returning from the crossing, the change in perspective makes the deep swale of the old road more distinct. With increased resolve to push through the undergrowth, I walk most of the way back to Brazil Station in the trace, about a mile, detouring occasionally for incessant tangles of briers.[188]

Later, as I explore the area with Joe Wolf before our encounter with the Jeep driver, a cow path beckons us around a pond southwest of the house and well. Soon we enter a depression lined with massive bois d'arcs. The swale ends at the fence bordering the county road, where the stagecoach road continues toward Trahern's Station, the second official stop on Butterfield's Indian Territory itinerary.

Trahern's Station

Trahern's offers two mysteries related to district chief Moshulatubbe: the possible site of his grave and the location of his Council House.[189] Sometimes dated to 1834 but probably built in 1837, the log structure served as Chief Moshulatubbe's residence.[190] The house of station keeper James N. Trahern and Moshulatubbe's Council House flanked the stagecoach road, and later mail routes sometimes gave "Council House" as the name for the station.

In June of 1836, specifications for three chiefs' houses, one for each district chief, and a national council house were published by Choctaw Agent William Armstrong, seeking bids for their construction under the terms of the Treaty of Dancing Rabbit Creek. Completion of the houses in the "most workmanlike manner" was expected by September 1, 1837. Each log house was to be fifty-two by twenty feet, with a twelve-foot passage between the two rooms. A ten-foot porch the length of the house both front and rear was required, along with eight windows and shutters. The houses would have two chimneys built of stone and lime mortar and four-foot fireplaces with good mantel-pieces. The interiors were to be painted white, and the doors and windows green.[191] William Lowry was awarded the bid of $8,400 for the chiefs' houses and council house, $2,100 each, and in October, 1836, construction of the chiefs' houses had begun. In late September 1837, Armstrong reported that Lowry would be unable to complete all three chiefs' houses by the contracted time because of difficulty obtaining workmen, but the third chief's house was then underway. He did not specify the locations of the houses nor the order of their construction.[192]

Muriel Wright cited tradition in writing that one or more sessions of the Choctaw General Council may have occurred at the Moshulatubbe Council House before the 1838 completion of the national council house at Nunih Waya, named for a sacred site in Mississippi and located a mile and a half west of present Tuskahoma.[193] An 1854 account by W.B. Parker, traveling with Marcy to Texas, describes the Moshulatubbe Council House as a long and rambling log building, similar, except for its larger size, to the typical houses he observed among the Choctaws. The Council House no longer served official purposes when Parker passed through, sixteen years after Moshulatubbe's death; he wrote that the nation had moved its place of assembly to Doaksville, but an Indian family occupied the building. Parker placed the structure west of the Fourche Maline crossing but this location is erroneous.[194] Trying to reconcile his statement, there were other Choctaw governmental structures in the vicinity which Parker theoretically could have mistaken for the Council House: Gaines County and Sugar Loaf County Courthouses. These, however, were smaller buildings and were also located east of the Fourche Maline. And, at least in the case of Gaines County, the courthouse was still in use in the 1850s and served official purposes until 1907.[195]

Twentieth-century visitors attempted to pinpoint the location of the Moshulatubbe Council House, and their physical descriptions often differed widely from one another.[196] That is not surprising, since by 1932 the structure had "long since" disappeared, although in 1958 the Centennial Committee reported seeing chimney stones and a few scattered foundation stones.[197] The presence of the nearby spring at least provides a consistent indicator of the general proximity of the Council House. In 1930 Council House spring was a "fine flowing spring of permanent water"[198] and nearly thirty years later it still flowed copiously, its walls covered with ferns.[199] It endures to this day although it is now only a trickle of clear water seeping through the fallen leaves of countless autumns in a shallow recess still partially lined with cut stone. Just down the bank in Brazil Creek, the spring water mingles with run-off from other mountain springs and ethereal streams on a twisting journey northeast to the Poteau River.

Bill Dragoo at Council House Spring

Our brief stint as unwitting trespassers at Brazil Station behind us, Joe Wolf and I drive over to Trahern's and walk to Council House spring, having double-checked with not only the land owner but also our new Jeep-driving friend, who confirms that the Trahern's property has not changed hands unbeknownst to us. Above the spring sits a cluster of large cut stones. I have noticed them on previous visits but their meaning escaped me. This time, the recent fall of a large tree has disrupted one side of the spring's rock enclosure. I notice fragments of cut stone and broken brick embedded in the massive root ball. About the same time, Joe remarks on the pile of cut stones; through his eyes their appearance signifies remnants of a structure. And among them is brick, indicating the presence of a collapsed chimney. He stands where the chimney would have been and says we have found it. The old Council House, then, may have been right here, not twenty-five feet south of the spring. Or so I thought at the time. And so the Centennial Committee apparently thought, citing the chimney stones and scattered foundation stones. A later visit with historical archeologists from the Choctaw Nation and the Oklahoma State Historic Preservation Office casts doubt on this conclusion,[200] so the exact location remains a mystery.

Moshulatubbe's legend also lives on south of the Council House and across the county road, one of several sites believed to be his burial place. W.B. Morrison stated Moshulatubbe was probably buried in the Skullyville cemetery, and others have proposed two different burial sites. In a November 26, 1930 letter to Judge Robert L. Williams of Muskogee, governor of the State of Oklahoma from 1915-1919 and president of the Oklahoma Historical Society at the time,[201] Muriel Wright wrote that it had "almost been established historically" that Chief Moshulatubbe was buried at Emachaya graveyard on the creek of the same name west of Whitefield in Haskell County.[202] But since Wright was a party to the 1958 report placing the Moshulatubbe grave at Trahern's, she may have dismissed the Emachaya location by that time.

In 1965, the Oklahoma Historical Society installed a granite memorial to Moshulatubbe in Hall Cemetery near Poteau. This marker indicates Moshulatubbe made his home in the prairie off the Fort Towson Road north of Sugar Loaf Mountain, near which he died and was buried, his grave covered with unmarked stones. Those associated with the Choctaw Nation remain mum about the location of Moshulatubbe's grave, preferring not to tempt vandals, so another mystery remains.

Whether or not his grave is located here at Trahern's, legend has it that Moshulatubbe was buried with his horse in keeping with the Choctaw tradition of burying the deceased with their belongings. This custom represented several iterations of change from the burial practices observed among the Choctaws in the 1700s, in which they placed their dead upon scaffolds, accompanied by favorite belongings, food and drink, and dogs or horses to provide companionship or transportation for the spirit.[203] Once the corpse decayed sufficiently, an individual appointed as bone-picker stripped the flesh from the bones The skeletal remains were then gathered into a box and placed in a community house set apart for that purpose. Once a bone-house was filled, the contents were taken to another location, deposited in the form of a pyramid and covered with earth, forming a conical mound. Many of the mounds observed in Mississippi and Alabama were cemeteries of the ancient Choctaws.

By the early years of the nineteenth century a pole-pulling ceremony largely replaced the bone-picking custom. In this practice, when a Choctaw died, friends set up poles around the grave on which they hung hoops and wreaths. The survivors gathered around the poles daily at sunrise, noon and sunset, mourning for the loved one.

This continued for several weeks, then the neighbors assembled and pulled up the poles, ending the mourning period with "feasting, drinking, and great disorder." This tradition retained the killing of favorite horses or dogs and their burial with the deceased's gun and hatchet.[204]

These practices waned over the years, but between 1843 and 1845 Benson observed the continuing occurrence of both the pole-pulling tradition and the practice of placing the gun, bow and arrow, hatchet and knife in the grave.[205]

In 1958 a row of stones still marked the site believed to be Moshulatubbe's large grave. These were remnants of a rock wall but are no longer visible. North of the Moshulatubbe grave, the 1958 historical marker was in fair condition during my early visits to Trahern's Station, its bronze plaque intact but the concrete base damaged at the upper corners. Sometime before February, 2022, however, LeFlore County's road equipment unearthed the monument. It stood askew as of March, 2023, its concrete base pulled from the ground. It had fallen over on the roadside by November of that year.

Station keeper James N. Trahern, having served on the Choctaw Supreme Court and as county judge of Skullyville County, died in 1883 at the age of 65. His gravestone was still in place in 1930, when the Conklings found only a cultivated field where the Trahern home and station had stood. The Trahern burial ground was, however, still intact beneath some small trees on the eastern edge of the tract.

By 1933, Muriel Wright reported that the entire field on the south side of the county road had once been a cemetery but had been cleared of gravestones.[206] Trahern's marker lay under a grove of large trees near the station in 1958, but is now in safekeeping elsewhere, along with that of his wife Sarah.

Another house occupied by the Traherns at some point is referenced several times in the literature. In 1931, the Conklings photographed this log structure, located one and one-quarter miles southwest of Council House. In August, 1932, traveling in the company of Muriel Wright, they referenced the house again in their notes but ultimately concluded the Butterfield station was co-located with the Trahern graves and Council House.[207]

The Trahern family lived in the area until the 1880s and operated a store. From June 1881 to February 1882, a post office called Opposum (sic) operated there, named for nearby Opossum Creek, although misspelled. In 1901, another post office at the site was named Latham, for U.S. Commissioner Thomas B. Latham, and operated until 1918.[208]

With the remnants of the Brazil settlement; the spring, Council House and graves at Trahern's; and the Skullyville County Jail, the segment between Walker's and Trahern's Stations makes for a rich historical journey. Just ahead, a better sense of the old road begins to emerge on the way to Holloway's Station.

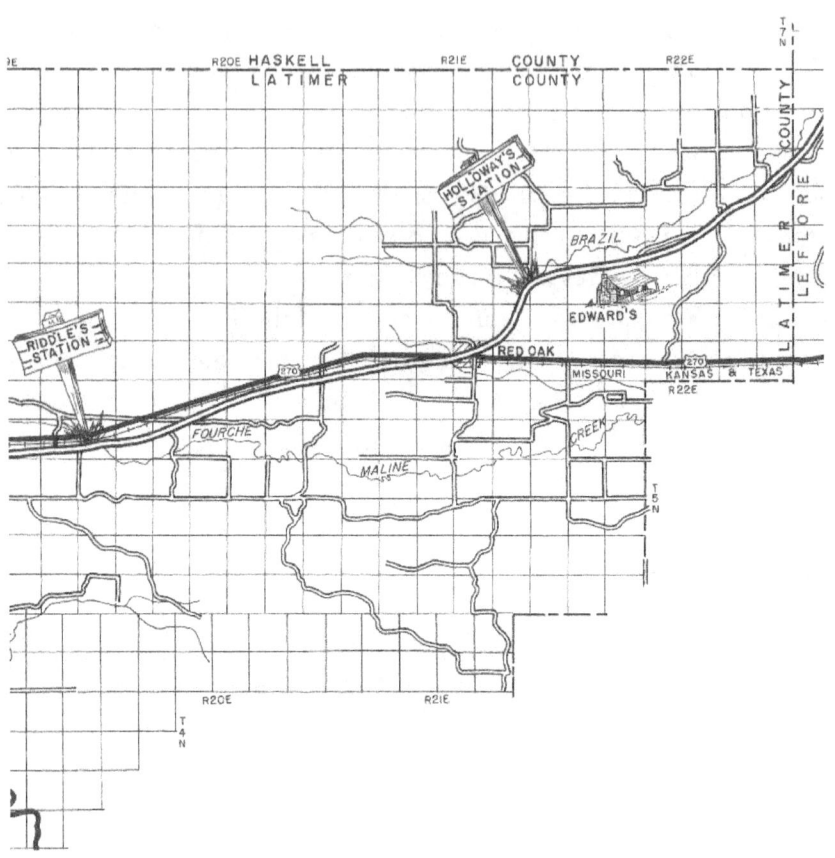

Butterfield Trail - Eastern Latimer County, including Edwards Store, Holloway's and Riddle's Stations. Adapted from original map courtesy of Oklahoma Historical Society. See Eastern LeFlore County map, page 40, for map legend.

Chapter Four: The Store and the Narrows

The Edwards cabin

From Trahern's Station the stagecoach road continues through the valley south of Brazil Creek. Dirt roads follow the route, sometimes zigzagging on section lines at ninety-degree angles and in other places curving with the contours of the old trail as it winds between mountain ridges toward the southwest. The segment between Trahern's and Holloway's crosses Wild Horse and Dog Creeks, now bridged where they were once forded. Other than fences and power lines, little of human existence appears along some stretches of the road, even today. After a heavy rain the slick mud can be a handful for a modern automobile, and must have been equally challenging for a wagon pulled by a four-horse team. Other challenges of travel in the 1850s are illustrated by Parker's description of immense numbers of insects as he passed through in the summer of 1854, reporting "a large, greenish brown horse fly, the most inveterate blood sucker of the genus. So ravenous are they, that after settling down to their bloody work, they will allow themselves to be picked up in the fingers, making no effort to escape. At every stroke of their bills, the blood flows as if from a lancet, and they come in such myriads that I have seen a horse bathed in his own blood."[209]

Dog Creek Settlement

The road passes through Dog Creek Settlement, once an active community of descendants of Choctaw freedmen, black people formerly enslaved by the Choctaws. After the Civil War, the process of emancipating and assimilating enslaved people in the Choctaw and Chickasaw Nations was slow and difficult.[210] Slavery in the United States was abolished through the Emancipation Proclamation in 1863 and the 13th Amendment in 1865, but these provisions applied to the states, not the Indian nations, although Creek loyalists acknowledged the Proclamation's authority in 1863. On October 14, 1865, before the negotiation of reconstruction treaties with the United States, the Choctaw General Council enacted regulations which technically abolished slavery but continued the subjugation of black people. The law required former slaves to negotiate a contract with their former enslaver or another employer, the employer becoming a guardian to the laborer and providing clothing, housing and medical care. Wages were deducted in the case of illness or absence without leave, and rations withheld if the person refused to work. Working hours were prescribed but an exception made when "forced labor was necessary to save the crop." Freedmen who left the Choctaw Nation were not permitted to return, and black people discovered without an employer were considered vagrants and would be arrested and their services sold to the highest bidder.[211]

By the spring and summer of 1866, the United States and the Indian nations negotiated reconstruction treaties confirming the abolition of slavery and laying out the terms of black people's citizenship in each nation. Each treaty provided a different route to citizenship for former slaves. The Seminoles granted them all the rights of native citizens. The Cherokees and Creeks did the same but required that refugee freedmen return to the nation within six months and one year, respectively, to secure citizenship. The treaty made jointly with the Choctaws and Chickasaws was more convoluted. If the two nations extended full citizenship to former slaves by June of 1868 they would receive monies owed them for the Leased District, lands west of the ninety-eighth meridian ceded to the United States under the Treaty of 1855 for occupation by other tribes. If the nations failed to comply, they forfeited the funds, to be used for the benefit of their former slaves, who would then be removed from the nations if the former slaves were willing. Neither the tribes nor the federal government adhered to the treaty's provisions, leaving an estimated 3,500-5,000 freedmen and their descendants in limbo regarding their citizenship status and rights.[212] The Choctaw government eventually fulfilled the citizenship requirement with the Choctaw Freedmen Bill of 1883, granting former slaves the right to vote, equal educational opportunities, and equal process in civil and criminal matters in the Choctaw courts. Freedmen were also granted forty acres of land to be held in the manner of other Choctaws, who held property communally and could improve as much of it as they wished.[213]

Former slaves in the Choctaw Nation lived largely in segregated settlements. Around 1885, the first neighborhood schools for children of Choctaw freedmen were established in several settlements in Skullyville County, and one of these was at Dog Creek.[214] Susan Lewis, born in 1870 to former slaves, reported that Dog Creek was a "good size little settlement of about thirty families" with a country store run by an Indian named Jim Darnell. She went to school at a "little log house" on Dog Creek and went to church with the Choctaws there, meeting most of the time under a brush arbor.[215]

Nothing remains of the original Dog Creek neighborhood school, but a one-room rock schoolhouse built for the Dog Creek community by the WPA in 1936 still stands in good condition on the roadside along the Butterfield trail as a reminder of the community's existence.[216] And, hidden at the end of a dirt road running west of the school house, Dog Creek cemetery abides in isolation and beauty.

Passing through Dog Creek in 1958, the Centennial Committee stopped at a "rustic and dilapidated" log cabin occupied by B.H. Thompson, a black man who welcomed the visitors. When committee member John Frizzell admired some large gourds Thompson had hanging up to dry, the two, "in a matter of minutes . . . realized they were gourd 'soul mates.'" The account continues,

> After inviting him into his cabin to expound further on the greatness of the lowly gourd he gave (Frizzell) a hand full of seeds for our 'red earth.' Mr. Thompson 'lowed there was nothing better than a drink of spring water out of a cedar bucket from a gourd. A shaft of sunlight coming down the open stone fireplace chimney revealed a pan of delicious looking fried rabbit cooking on a small log fire. He proudly showed Captain Brown and John (Frizzell) his method of storing sausage in dried, neatly wrapped corn husks, hanging from the rafter of his home.[217]

During this stop the committee saw a slice of life in a primitive log cabin, and rhapsodized about it perhaps a bit too condescendingly. We do not know whether they sampled the fried rabbit and sausage, but such fare might have sounded appetizing to Waterman Ormsby one hundred years earlier. About this stretch of road he wrote little except to wax poetic about the two meals he took between Walker's and Holloway's Stations from a provision basket provided by John

Butterfield, who had remembered to include "the needful with which to wash it down":

> Though it consisted of but a few cold cuts, my memory still clings to it as the last civilized meal between Fort Smith and the barren plains where I now write. . . . Ever since I left that last meal of cold ham, cakes, crackers and cheese, fond recollection recalls it to view. Though I am no epicurean, I could not forbear writing its obituary.[218]

At the time, Ormsby was writing from Fort Belknap, Texas, about sixty miles beyond present-day Wichita Falls, planning to post the update upon arrival at Fort Chadbourne, at which point he would have traveled 945 miles from St. Louis. The farther west he traveled, the more the food declined in quality. Indeed, the cold cuts he enjoyed would have been a luxury on the frontier when the fare available at stops at a price of forty cents to one dollar consisted of bread, tea, and fried steaks of bacon, venison, antelope, or mule — "the latter tough enough," according to Tallack, who at least acknowledged that the food was "better than could be expected so far from civilized districts."

In Indian Territory, eastbound *Daily Alta* correspondent Farwell enjoyed sweet green corn and the first potatoes since he left San Francisco, noting he found milk, butter and vegetables only toward the two ends of the routes, in California and at stations in the settled parts of the western Mississippi valley.[219] At Colbert's Ferry, his last stop in Indian Territory, Ormsby had sugar, butter and pastry, "the first two of which have been exceedingly rare articles since I left Fort Smith, and the last of which I have not seen anywhere else since I left Fort Smith."

Other than Farwell's reference to sweet green corn, Overland Mail passengers failed to mention partaking of any traditional Choctaw fare. The Choctaw diet was primarily corn-based, their principal dish,

Tafula, anglicized to "Tom Fuller." To make this dish, beaten corn was boiled with lye, then kept warm until it had thoroughly soured, when it was considered ready to eat. This was such a staple that the corn patches tended by Indian women were called Tom Fuller patches. Meat, boiled so thoroughly that it fell off the bone, put into a mortar and beaten, then combined with Tafula, was called Pashofa. Cornmeal was also used in bread, one form of which was called Banaha, or Shuck Bread. Sweet potatoes and beans augmented these ingredients, and acorns and hickory nuts were also part of the Choctaw diet.

Famine

After 1854, however, abundant harvests of the previous twenty years succumbed to a period of scarce rainfall, poor crop yields and severe famine. The winter of 1860-61 was particularly hard, with the corn crop failing and some Choctaw families struggling along with only acorn mush and acorn bread supplemented with wild potatoes found in the swamps.[220] Sue McBeth, a missionary to the Choctaws in 1860-61, wrote that those Choctaws who had money were sending to Texas for flour, although the Texans were nearly as bad off as the Choctaws. "I hear they have good crops in the states, but the difficulty is in getting it here," she wrote. The idea of reassigning school appropriations for famine relief was discussed. " . . . Life is the first thing to be taken care of in such times as these, although there will still be a great deficiency even of the cheapest food." But she notes the appropriations would be only a drop in the bucket to feed 20,000 Choctaws, and the Choctaw government had "no possible means . . . to feed them."[221]

Of this period, Lycurgus Pitchlynn wrote from Eagletown, Choctaw Nation, on February 10, 1860 to his father, Peter Pitchlynn, the Choctaw statesman and later chief, who was in Washington, D.C. at the time, "It is hard times – many of the Indians are starving. Corn can't be had for love or money. Hogs, horses and cattle have died and are dying by the wholesale or retail. I have lost all my hogs. Lavinia and in fact all of us are in pretty straightened circumstances." In July of the same year Lycurgus wrote again, describing a "hot, burning, deadly wind," such weather as he had never seen in that country before. The corn crops in the adjoining countries of Arkansas and Texas were completely burnt up. "Starvation stares us in the face." [222]

In September, 1860, Peter Pitchlynn urged immediate relief, describing the suffering from the drought and writing that what made it more distressing was that it followed "a hard year for something to eat; . . . now another year of scarcity, unparalleled is before (the Choctaws) and makes it truly deplorable."[223]

In his 1860 annual report to the Commissioner of Indian Affairs, Elias Rector urged federal funding to relieve this hunger, describing the loss of crops and the suffering of the tribes. " . . . as we aided in sending food to starving Ireland, so we should preserve from destruction and misery these faithful allies . . . ." [224]

Appealing to the federal government for funding owed them, the Choctaw General Council on January 9, 1861 wrote,

> In consequence of the unprecedented drought of the past summer . . . there has been almost an entire failure of the corn crop, and a large portion of our people are now entirely destitute of the means of subsistence. Almost daily the homes of those of our citizens who have been somewhat more favored, and enabled to raise a small surplus of corn, are besieged by families of poor starving women and children who are without bread.[225]

The Overland Mail did not escape the effects of the drought. In a letter to his wife on August 9, 1860, Butterfield agent Hiram Rumsfeld wrote of the scarcity of grain to feed the stock between Fort Smith, Arkansas, and Fort Chadbourne, Texas, stating there was not one bushel to be had along the entire distance. "The drought has absolutely destroyed everything," he wrote. "The grasshoppers have even perished from want of sustenance."[226]

Southern Alliance

The federal government's failure to help in these dire circumstances undermined the Choctaws' faith in the U.S. government and made them more open to the Confederacy's promises at the onset of the Civil War. Although the Union promised to provide funding in accordance with treaty obligations, no drought relief was forthcoming and in 1860 the federal government further eroded trust by unsuccessfully proposing to the Creeks, Choctaws and Chickasaws the allotment of their lands in severalty. Ultimately, although Congress appropriated most of the requested funds in early 1861, little of the money made it to Indian Territory and by then the Choctaws felt they had little choice. Seven years of drought had created a desperate situation and the people were in dire need of relief. The Choctaws could stay loyal to the U.S. and starve, or trust the Confederacy to alleviate the suffering. There were other factors at play as well. Most of the money held in trust for the Choctaws by the federal government was invested in southern stocks, which Confederates warned would be forfeited by the war. The southerners also promised to assume the United States' obligations for the annuities owed and guaranteed protection for slavery; retention of land titles for the Indian nations; and Indian representation in the Confederate congress.

Peter Pitchlynn assured the Commissioner of Indian Affairs that his people would remain neutral if war broke out, and once back in Indian Territory tried to convince them to do so. But withdrawal of federal forces from Indian Territory at the onset of the war left the Indian nations vulnerable, and they felt intense pressure from the Confederate government and from Arkansas and Texas, pro-Confederate states bordering Indian Territory. Threats from Texas secessionists silenced Pitchlynn's voice and that of others who advocated neutrality. One Choctaw wrote, "If the north was here so we could be protected we would stand up for the north but now if we do not go in for the south the Texans will come over here and kill us."[227] Many full-bloods favored loyalty to the Union but even their government agents were southern, and pressure to align with the South arose from within as well. Principal Chief George Hudson advocated neutrality but was overruled by Robert M. Jones, a Choctaw planter with numerous plantations and hundreds of slaves, who gave a fiery address threatening anyone who opposed secession.

The situation is summarized by a missionary teacher who left the Choctaw Nation in September, 1862:

> The Choctaws received quite a bundle of promises from the rebel government . . . . and when I think of these, of the belief of their oldest missionaries in the final success of the rebels, of the fact that all of the old officers of the U.S. government were in the service of the rebels, of the occupation of the forts there by the rebels, of the activity of a knot of bitter disunionists led by Capt. Jones who has long been a very influential man, of the Texas mob law which considered it a crime for a young man to refuse to volunteer, of the fact that there was no way for them to hear the truth as to the designs of the U.S. government concerning them, except through Col. Pitchlyn (sic) who was soon silenced & of the falsehoods told them as to the designs of the Government, I do not wonder that they have joined the rebels." [228]

Foreshadowing the ultimate outcome, a discouraged pro-Union Choctaw said of the alignment with the Confederacy, "We expect the Choctaws will be buried. That is what we think will be the end of this."[229]

On July 12, 1861, Choctaw leaders signed a pact with the secessionist government, citing common "natural affections, the educations, institutions and interests of our property."[230]All five nations in Indian Territory aligned with the Confederacy that year and fought for the South during the war. The Choctaws and Chickasaws raised one regiment of soldiers, the 1st Regiment of Choctaw and Chickasaw Mounted Rifles, with Lt. Col. Tandy Walker as commander. The Creeks and Seminoles also raised a regiment, as did the Cherokees. See *Choctaw Confederates: The American Civil War in Indian Country* by Fay Yarbrough for more on this subject.

The Edwards Store

In the later years of the Civil War a store keeper along this segment of the Butterfield played an unexpected leadership role among the Choctaws. Sixteen miles southwest of Trahern's Station is the Edwards Store, the only structure contemporaneous with the operation of the Overland Mail still standing along the Choctaw Nation segment of the stagecoach road.[231] The Conklings, who had possession of records from the Edwards Store for a number of years, wrote, "That Edwards's store was a mail station on this route is confirmed by reference to meals to stage passengers at forty-five cents each." Although the ledger has been lost and no other confirmation exists that stage passengers were served meals at Edwards Store, Conkling's statement provides strong evidence.[232] See "Side Trip: Lost Historical Treasure" below for more on this subject.

Storekeeper Thomas Edwards[233] was an Englishman who married into a Choctaw family when he wed Nancy Hardaway. In 1850 they built a home from hand-hewn logs raised on a stacked sandstone foundation. The same stone was used to build the chimney on the east side of the cabin. In 1870 they built a second log room and stone chimney west of the original structure, connecting the two rooms by a covered breezeway and creating the dogtrot design common to the era. Separate from the residence on a knoll about thirty feet in front of the house, a single log room fifteen feet square housed the Edwards mercantile operation.[234]

In 1864 Edwards was made governor of a provisional Choctaw government organized to attempt a reconciliation with the U.S. at a time when the Choctaws were still almost universally aligned with the Confederacy. Official documents record only a few hundred Choctaws who remained loyal to the Union. Some of them escaped Confederate-occupied Indian Territory, seeking refuge in Kansas along with several thousands from other tribes. The Creeks following prominent leader Opothle Yahola comprised the largest group. Confederate forces followed Yahola's contingent in late 1861, attacking them three times. In the last battle, on December 26 in the Osage hills north of present-day Tulsa, the Creeks were completely routed and abandoned their possessions and fled to Kansas.[235] Among the loyal Indians taking refuge at the Sac and Fox reservation in Osage County, Kansas, were about three hundred Choctaws.

By June of 1864 the Union reoccupied Fort Gibson and proceeded to move about 5,000 refugees, including the handful of loyal Choctaws and Chickasaws, from Kansas back to their homes. The refugees were temporarily located at and around Fort Gibson because their homes were still "overrun and infested by the enemy."[236] That fall Isaac Colman, U.S. Choctaw and Chickasaw agent, reported he left the refugees in his care temporarily at Fort Gibson until he could provide for them in the vicinity of Fort Smith, which the Union had re-occupied in September, 1863. At Fort Smith, Colman also found about three hundred loyal Choctaws in need of provisions and clothing, and he issued rations of flour, beef, salt, and tobacco. It is possible that Thomas Edwards and his family were among these. In all, Colman indicated he was trying to restore to their homes some four hundred Choctaws and Chickasaws.[237] At the end of the war, U.S. Indian Agent

George Reynolds reported only two hundred and twelve Choctaws who remained "true allies" of the U.S. government, praising twelve loyal Choctaws who volunteered in the Union army.[238]

By late 1863 the Choctaw and Chickasaw Nations, having avoided the worst upheaval and devastation of the war, were being flooded with refugees from other parts of Indian Territory. Rumors circulated that the federal government planned to confiscate Choctaw property, including land and livestock, to be given to freed slaves and Indian tribes from other states who would be settled in Indian Territory. In February 1864, President Abraham Lincoln's proclamation of pardon and amnesty was circulated to the Confederates in Indian Territory. For the Creeks, Seminoles and Chickasaws the war was all but over by this time. And, having lost confidence in the Confederacy, a small faction of Choctaws attempted to organize an opposition government, meeting near Skullyville at New Hope Academy on March 14. They approved a resolution of allegiance to the United States and established a provisional government, perhaps hoping for leniency and to avoid the seizure of their property.[239] Thomas Edwards was nominated and confirmed governor, and ten days later he issued a proclamation to the citizens of the Choctaw Nation, exhorting them to return to allegiance to the Union.[240] But a much larger element of Choctaws meeting near Fort Towson had not yet made up their minds to accept peace and the response to Edwards' proclamation from Union leadership was less than enthusiastic. Colonel William S. Phillips, commander of the Union's Indian Brigade, wrote to William P. Dole, Commissioner of Indian Affairs, from Fort Gibson that the Choctaw Nation was still *de facto* rebel, and "about the only Indian nation that can be said to be so at the present day." [241]

"That a handful of men about Scullyville would like to be the 'Choctaw Nation' is, I think, probable, and that a portion who have not fled from the northern section might be willing to accept an assurance of Choctaw nationality, and pay for acting as militia to expel all invaders is, I think, also probable," he wrote, expressing his skepticism.[242] Fearing reprisals from those loyal to the Confederacy, many among the opposition faction sought protection at Fort Smith until the end of the war.[243] A record book kept by Thomas Edwards lists the names of two hundred forty-one Choctaws who took refuge at Fort Smith, his family among them.[244]

Ultimately, the federal government gave no recognition to either the provisional Choctaw government or Edwards' office as governor.[245] After the war, Edwards was not involved in Choctaw governance but continued to operate the store. In 1868, an official U.S. post office was established there and designated "Red Oak," with Edwards as postmaster. He died October 16, 1883. His wife's nephew, Jesse Hardaway, ran the store until around 1890, when a town sprang up along the railroad about eight miles to the southwest at the site of present-day Red Oak, and the post office was moved there.

The Edwards homeplace still sits on a hill overlooking the county road. In 1956, during the planning of the 1958 centennial, Muriel Wright wrote that John Frizzell would be restoring an old stagecoach for use during the centennial and that Frizzell wanted to "take his horses and the coach over to some place along the old Butterfield road for a real ride!" Wright suggested that a good place for such an excursion would be Red Oak, near the Narrows. "I told him about the Edwards' place, the old log cabin, the people who are relatives of Edwards of the Butterfield stage days, and then the idea of having those people serve us a dinner on the day of our visit! So, the plan has been thought over, and we might do this by September!"[246] Sadly, this wonderful idea did not materialize, but the Centennial Committee's stop at the Edwards Store was clearly one of the highlights of their 1958 journey. As they arrived, an old bois d'arc hitching post caught the group's attention. "It was probably near this old hitching post that the Overland Mail coaches would stop, while the passengers would walk up to the Edwards' home where they were served good food. This would also give the horses a chance to blow for the pull up over The Narrows, as from here on the gradient is much steeper."[247]

The account of this stop is effusive:

> The minute one steps on the well packed yard from long years of use, and the steps leading to the porch (which are giant cut slabs of sandstone), it is sensed that this is a very old and important building. Upon seeing the great, hand hewn logs of the original home on the Butterfield Mail, at once one knows this is the real thing. Perhaps the most convincing features of all are the great stone chimneys at either end of the home. The stones are so perfectly fitted on the earliest chimney that they laid without mortar.
>
> The original appearance of the home will have to be imagined because of the later additions, but the vista from the house, of the wooded Brazil Creek valley and hills beyond, to the north is one of majesty. It has not been appreciably altered. It is an everlasting joy to the visitor of Edwards' store, and looked to us much as it looked to Ormsby, assuming he wasn't too tired to look![248]

Jesse Hardaway's youngest son, Edgar, and his wife, Lula, were living in the cabin in 1958 and occupied it until 1981. In 1972, the site was added to the National Register of Historic Places and is still owned by Hardaway descendants. The Centennial Committee expressed the hope that the structure would be preserved, a wish now in the process of being fulfilled. In 2016, I found the structure intact but abandoned, its chimneys still in surprisingly good condition. The structure was listed on Preservation Oklahoma's Most Endangered Places in 2013, 2018 and 2019, a recognition which raises awareness of the need for protection of historic sites at risk of demolition or deterioration. The efforts of supporters culminated in a restoration project begun in February 2020 with funds from an Oklahoma Historical Society grant used to stabilize the structure's chimneys, a process conducted by log-cabin preservationist William Bailey, who encased the chimneys in industrial shrink-wrap embedded with wooden lathe to prevent their collapse.[249] By early 2022 the roof was protected and windows closed up, with more restoration efforts underway. Archeological examination of the site began in 2023, and work was expected to continue into 2028.

West of the log cabin is the cemetery where Thomas and Nancy Hardaway Edwards are buried, their graves marked only with rough-hewn unmarked stones.[250] Their two children, who died in infancy, are interred nearby. Looking north from the homestead and cemetery, the view across the Brazil Creek valley toward the Sans Bois mountains extolled as "one of majesty" is still impressive. A marker placed by the Oklahoma Historical Society in the same style as other Butterfield station markers sits at the bottom of the drive.

In early 2022, I travel this segment of the mail road with Latimer County historians Earl and Cindy Shero and June Chubbuck, Board member and champion for the Edwards Store. We spend the day touring the county's segment of the mail road, which includes more Butterfield sites than any other in Oklahoma. At lunchtime, we pick up chicken salad sandwiches in Wilburton and drive to the Edwards Store, where we sit in the sunshine and enjoy our picnic on the front porch of the cabin, near the spot where stagecoach passengers took nourishment so long ago.

As of mid-2024, when active reconstruction work is not underway, the Edwards Store site is open to the public.

Side Trip: Lost Historical Treasure

"That Edwards's store was a mail station on this route is confirmed by reference to meals to stage passengers at forty-five cents each."[251]

- Roscoe and Margaret Conkling

On August 23, 1932, Roscoe and Margaret Conkling and Muriel Wright visited the Edwards Store, where they met with Riley Hardaway.[252] Hardaway was the oldest son of Jesse Hardaway, who took over the store from Thomas and Nancy Edwards. Roscoe sketched the construction of the Edwards cabin, producing a detailed pencil drawing of dressed oak and walnut logs on a corner of the structure. His notes locate the house atop a hill on the north side of the road, and report the presence of an old post in front of the house containing lead bullets.[253] The Hardaways showed the Conklings and Wright a daybook dating to the 1850s containing records from the operation of the Edwards mercantile. The Conklings, finding that the book contained valuable historical data, borrowed it.

Margaret Conkling's diary from that date records Riley Hardaway's address, below which she documented sending a letter to Hardaway November 9, 1932 and the statement, "(We have record book to be returned to above.)" beneath Hardaway's name and address. An undated comment which appears to have been written later states, "The book was returned."[254]

A copy of that November 9 letter resides in the Conkling archives at the Seaver Center for Western History Research in Los Angeles. In it, Roscoe Conkling reassured Hardaway that the "old store book you so kindly loaned" was safe and sound and would be returned in perfect order. Conkling also blamed the delay in returning the book on the time it had taken to copy its contents, and other things which had kept him busy. Clearly, he saw it as an important artifact, writing that he would like to have the book to preserve with other relics of the mail road. He asked Hardaway to let him know if he ever decided to part with it.[255]

Nearly forty years later, on August 12, 1970, I.C. Gunning wrote to Roscoe Conkling at his home in Inglewood, California. Gunning was president of the Eastern Oklahoma Historical Society; he was writing a story on the Edwards Store and needed the daybook. "Mrs. Hardaway still lives in the old home," wrote Gunning, "and she tells me that you borrowed the account book, it really was a notebook, for a few days on the promise to return it, but that she never got it back." Gunning had been trying to track down the book, contacting museums and other agencies in Oklahoma on the strength that the Conklings had left it with some of them. Finally, it was Muriel Wright who advised Gunning that she had accompanied the Conklings for a few days and that the couple had borrowed the book. The book had never gotten back to the Hardaways, and Mrs. Hardaway wanted it returned, wrote Gunning, adding, "I promised her I would search for it."[256]

On August 24, 1970, Margaret Conkling responded. First, she pointed out that Roscoe had just returned from the hospital after a serious operation and thus she was responding on his behalf. She went on to state that Gunning had been wrongly informed that the book was in the nature of a loan.

"We recall the incident although it was about forty years ago, when Mr. Riley Hardaway made the book a gift to us," she wrote. "He said that he had no use for the book and that the children were scribbling in it. Had it been otherwise, it goes without saying that the book would have been duly returned to Mr. Hardaway. We sent the book to the Oklahoma Historical Society for safe-keeping." Because they had recently moved and did not have access to their files, they could not provide the date the book had been returned.

Unbeknownst to Gunning, fifteen years before he reached out to the Conklings the book had indeed been returned to Oklahoma. On May 28, 1955, the *Daily Oklahoman* reported that a ledger kept by Thomas Edwards had been added to the Phillips Collection, now part of the Western History Collections, at the University of Oklahoma. Dr. Eugene Hollon received it for the University, according to the newspaper, as a gift from the Conklings.[257]

The daybook the Conklings borrowed appears to have been quite the historical treasure. Among its contents was a register of Choctaw citizens living in the region in the 1850s-1860s, and those who were refugees at Fort Smith during the Civil War, including Thomas Edwards, his wife and a child. The account book also listed prices of commodities, livestock, building materials, labor, and medicine. It recorded the number of letters passing through the post office, and the selection of newspapers and periodicals to which the citizens of the area subscribed. But perhaps most pertinent to this discussion is reference made to meals sold to stage passengers for forty-five cents each, suggesting that the Butterfield Overland Mail stage wagons stopped at the Edwards Store for meals.[258]

In some respects, the suggestion seems unlikely. The Edwards Store was not an official Butterfield station, where passengers usually obtained a repast. In Indian Territory, Walker's, Blackburn's and Colbert's Stations have been documented as stands where food was served during the rushed twenty-minute stops. Speed was of the essence for the Overland Mail line and, in an early version of the drive-through restaurant, food was sometimes brought out to the stage for the passengers. The rationale for stopping between stations seems unclear.

But neither was Mountain Station an official Butterfield stop and it is well documented that the Butterfield stage stopped there, and meals were served. (See Chapter Five).[259] Mrs. Flack's in Atoka was a widely known meal stop along the road and may have served Butterfield customers between official stops. Given the timing of the Overland Mail stage's passing of the Edwards Store, which would usually have been just past mid-day, a stop for food may have been welcomed if the stage were ahead of schedule. And the terrain was about to become steeper as the incline increased with the approach to the Narrows, so a stop at Edwards would have given the horses a chance to breathe before the ascent.[260]

Although she does not mention it in writing until after the Conklings' 1947 book was published, Muriel Wright clearly believed the store had been a meal stop on the Overland Mail route. Her source for that knowledge may also have been the daybook. In her account of a tour of the Butterfield trail in 1955, Wright described Edwards Store as an important stop where meals were served to travelers on the Butterfield stages, starting soon after the first mail passed there on its way west. She also stated the following: "The old log building that housed Edwards Store is still owned by an elderly nephew of Thomas Edwards, Mr. Edgar Hardaway, who can show an early account book in his uncle's handwriting."[261]

While this suggests that the 1850s account book was back in the hands of the Hardaway family, Gunning's 1970 inquiry and the source material cited for the booklet he published on the Edwards Store circa 1972 do not support that line of thinking. Gunning's publication lists record books dating back to 1869 but not before. It may have been one of these later ledgers to which Muriel Wright referred in 1955.

As of this writing, the 1850s Edwards Store daybook is still missing. There is no trace of it in OU's Western History Collection, where its presence was last recorded, nor in the Oklahoma Historical Society's archives or the Conkling papers at the Seaver Center in Los Angeles.

In the end, absent the primary evidence for Butterfield stage passengers stopping at Edwards Store for meals, one must ask, was the idea wishful thinking on someone's part? Did the Conklings manufacture the story? Such a notion is far-fetched. They had no incentive to do so. Roscoe Conkling did, on the other hand, find in that daybook a historical gold mine, and one of its gleaming nuggets was evidence that Overland Mail stage passengers stopped at Edwards Store for meals. Muriel Wright seems to have had good reason to believe it as well. Perhaps someday the book will materialize. Until then, it is plausible that the Edwards Store, the only standing structure along the Choctaw Nation segment of the Overland Mail Road, served meals to hungry stagecoach passengers.

Holloway's Station

Beyond the Edwards Store, the valley contracts for the next five miles to a gap in the mountains permitting passage to a prairie and an easy road for the next twenty miles. In 1958, the stagecoach trail was still visible lacing back and forth along the county road. The pass, described in 1854 as a "rugged mountain gorge, very difficult for wagons,"[262] is known as the Narrows, and Holloway's Station was located at its northern entrance, in a clearing near Brazil Creek.[263] Between 1840 and 1850, the Brazil Gap stage stand, established by Edmund McCurtain, preceded Holloway's Station at the Narrows, according to a writer for the WPA Federal Writer's Project, although I have found no other evidence for this.[264] Butterfield station keeper William Holloway was granted the privilege to establish a toll gate near his home some distance west of the Narrows in October 1858, but little is known about him.[265] He is listed on the 1860 federal census as a 57-year-old farmer from Tennessee, with two stage drivers from Connecticut and Illinois also dwelling at his address. He may have been a Butterfield employee who moved away when the Southern Route was discontinued in 1861.[266] Muriel Wright speculated that, though not a Choctaw citizen, Holloway may have obtained the toll gate concession through a partnership or employment relationship with the Edwards family since, according to Wright, the Edwards family lived at "the old station or in its vicinity," presumably meaning Holloway's, after the Civil War.[267]

Jackson McCurtain, brother of Edmund McCurtain, obtained the toll gate concession at the Narrows after the Civil War.[268] The gate itself may have been positioned at the bottom of a spur of the mountain over which the mail road rose and fell. Its design probably involved a large log spanning the road with each end supported on a stone pier, built to allow the barrier to swing open. Another toll gate design incorporated a crotched post supporting the toll bar, which was attached on one end to a stone providing a counterweight.

From Edwards' to Holloway's, the modern road closely follows the Butterfield route. In 1930, the Conklings saw a well-preserved section of the trail north of the station site. In 2024, I visit the site and find a section of the trail in that same spot, still quite evident. Across the road on the hillside the Conklings found an old cemetery.

In 1854, Parker reported nearby, and perhaps at this same location, the grave of an emigrant, covered with a house of logs and marked with the tail board of a wagon nailed to a stake. The board bore the following inscription in tar with crude lettering: "George Bemshaus, born in Prussia, October 13th, 1812; died March 2d, 1854."

"Poor fellow!" wrote Parker. "All his hopes of home and fortune in the land of freedom, lay here on a barren hill-side in this wild Indian country,--such is life, a vision, a struggle, a grave."[269] If Bemshaus was buried there, his grave may have been the victim of road construction, as by 1958 the Centennial Committee found only a few markers remaining in the cemetery high above the modern county highway. Today the Holloway's Station marker sits in good condition inside a fence on the north side of the county road amid large boulders. Climbing up the embankment to the south, I easily find the cemetery. The principal marker remaining is that of Dolphus C. Jackson, born September 23, 1874 and died October 18, 1875.

Over its twenty-one-mile length, the sparsely populated and mostly unpaved segment of the stagecoach road from Trahern's to Holloway's offers a feeling of remoteness. The presence of the Edwards Store gives it an important distinction and a quiet spot where the modern traveler, like those long before, can stop for a rest.

Chapter Five: Choctaw Justice and Moving Pictures

The Jack McCurtain Place

Passing through the Narrows, the mail road crossed the land holdings of the McCurtain family. Patriarch Cornelius McCurtain was chief of the Moshulatubbe District from 1849 to 1854 and three of his sons, Jackson, Edmund, and Green, later served as principal chiefs of the Choctaw Nation.[270] Jackson was born in 1830 in Mississippi and moved with his parents to Indian Territory in 1833. He was living at the Narrows at the time he became principal chief in 1880, when he moved to the Antlers area.[271] He later moved to Tuskahoma, where he died in 1885. The McCurtain estate at the Narrows included a knoll east of present-day Red Oak where "Jack" McCurtain built an impressive home and operated a stagecoach station. The presence of a Choctaw courthouse was also reported on the site. Apparently, there was a lot going on at the Jack McCurtain place.[272]

William D. Fields, interviewed for the Indian-Pioneer Papers, helped to haul lumber from a saw mill in Arkansas to build the McCurtain house, which he called the "Governor's home." The outside walls were made of hewn logs and sealed with rough-sawn lumber. The house's six chimneys required McCurtain to employ a number of "younger Indian men to come and live there with him and to get all the wood for all those fire places in the winter time." R.A. Welch, a son of D.R. Welch of Brazil Station, bought the property and kept it intact for many years but eventually sold it and by 1930 the house was gone. Seven years later, J.A. Blalack owned the place and only the "fine well" remained, still in use, with curb stones and walls of native stone.[273] In 1930 the Conklings photographed the well, finding it adjacent to a chicken house. Margaret Conkling recorded near the well the presence of a sandstone trough "made by Indians," cut from an oblong stone. A solid slab of limestone four and one-half feet square with an opening twenty-two inches in diameter comprised the well coping.[274]

One winter day I find myself at the McCurtain place, again with Latimer County's Earl Shero and June Chubbuck of the Edwards Store, looking for that same well. Such stonework should have endured at least the ninety-odd years since the Conklings' visit and would be hard to hide. But Earl and June and I come up empty-handed. Those historic rocks may be buried under the large pile of debris we find behind the barn.

We are not prepared to give up easily, however, and we wander off to the east. There in the forest an avenue appears, leading north, back toward the Narrows. We turn and follow it, and I am reminded of the Conklings' fortunate timing on November 3, 1930 when they saw "one of the best preserved abandoned sections of the road on this portion of the route, traversing a dense oak wood on the McCurtain place." It still appeared like a "straight narrow aisle" through the woods, and the bark on the trunks of some of the larger trees displayed "old scars, long healed, . . . scored by the hubs of many passing vehicles." The Conklings traced the road distinctly up the hill, past the McCurtain station site, and on still farther toward the Narrows. The next day, the trees were scheduled to be cut down, erasing "this relic of the old thoroughfare that has been a trail followed by man as long as he has inhabited the region."[275]

Are we walking the same trail? The foot travel is easy except for some ups and downs through small streambeds. Our path exactly matches a road on an early map running north and south from the Narrows to a point just east of the Jack McCurtain place. We continue north, reaching a fence running east and west. There we look out upon a meadow and, beyond it, the Narrows. The road we are traveling is certainly an old one, and it may have been the north-south connector between the Narrows and McCurtain's later stage stand. But before McCurtain established his station around 1864, the original mail road likely curved in a diagonal around the southeastern flank of Red Oak Mountain along the same course as the present highway before veering west. The "straight narrow aisle" the Conklings observed may indeed be the one we walked, but is perhaps the ghost of that later branch of the road.

Near the McCurtain station, the Conklings reported that until shortly before their visit an old log building used by Choctaw chiefs and citizens as a kind of "lodge room" stood in a fair state of preservation.[276] Founded between 1850 and 1860 and abandoned in 1866, this structure was the Moshulatubbe District Courthouse and "Shuka Lof" or Sugar Loaf County Courthouse. In 1937, a WPA writer stated there was nothing left of it but the "old whipping tree."[277] In the Choctaw Nation's system of justice, whipping was a common form of punishment for stealing and many other crimes, including arson, perjury, forgery, selling intoxicating liquor, gambling, adultery, polygamy, bribery, carrying pistols, skinning dead animals on the range, disturbing the peace, defacing public buildings, and disturbing religious services.[278] When an individual was sentenced to whipping, the sheriff and his deputies stripped the accused to the waist. Two men then grasped his hands and held him with his chest against a tree while others took turns laying on the number of lashes ordered. Sometimes this occurred with a "good sized green hickory switch."[279] The whipping tree in the yard of this courthouse was a large red oak, to which J.A. Blalack attributed the name of the town of Red Oak. That belief is, however, inconsistent with the fact that the post office at the Edwards Store was named "Red Oak" before the town was moved to its present site. By 1884 the courthouse for Sugar Loaf County was relocated near Summerfield, about halfway between Red Oak and Heavener.[280]

In the old days, murder and accidental killing among the Choctaws were avenged by the victim's relatives by killing the murderer or a member of his family. The murderer seldom tried to escape, it being a matter of honor to submit to his just punishment. This law of retaliation began to change in the early nineteenth century. Under Choctaw law post-removal, the death penalty was prescribed for murder, a second offense of rape, armed robbery, and treason. In carrying out a death sentence, the sheriff and his deputies exposed the chest of the accused and drew a mark over the heart. The condemned man sat on a blanket facing his executioner while a man on each side drew his arms apart and held them extended. Then the fatal shot was fired.[281]

In 1894, on a plain southwest of Red Oak known as Brown's Prairie, what some consider the last legal execution administered under the jurisdiction of the Choctaw Nation occurred.[282] Silan Lewis, the condemned man, was punished for a killing associated with political conflict between the Nationalist and Progressive factions of the Choctaws.[283] In 1892, the election for principal chief became a showdown between the two factions. Results were hotly contested and when the Progressive candidate, Wilson Jones, was declared the winner by a narrow margin over Nationalist Jacob Jackson, a faction of Nationalists decided to take matters into their own hands. On September 11, 1892, a group of them, including Silan Lewis, met and plotted the murders of a number of Progressives, then split into two groups and killed five Progressives, including former Gaines County Sheriff Joe Hokulatubbee and two boys who got in the way. By the end of September, Lewis and the other Nationalists surrendered. All of them were subsequently convicted of the crimes, but a series of delays and reprieves left Lewis the only man condemned to die. After his sentencing on April 20, 1894, Lewis was released to go home and get his affairs in order. True to Choctaw tradition, he did not flee although he had ample opportunity. "To be regarded as a coward was a doom more fearful, a thousand-fold, than death itself; he is altogether too brave to shun a judicial investigation; he is not afraid to die, but ready to face death with boldness,"[284] wrote Benson of this Choctaw characteristic. Lewis refused to take advantage of the freedom he was given, walking in from the woods in time for his execution.[285]

On November 5, 1894, the execution took place at the Gaines County Courthouse on the western edge of Brown's Prairie. Photographer Frank Raymond witnessed the event. He had taken a portrait of Silan Lewis and his wife in Hartshorne a few months before, then traveled from Hartshorne to Red Oak by train and rode fourteen miles on horseback to the courthouse to photograph the execution. Raymond described the courthouse building as fairly small, about twenty-four by thirty-six feet. It had been painted white but on execution day was a dingy gray. Lewis had camped nearby with his wife and family and was brought to the south side of the courthouse, about thirty feet away from the building. He took off his coat and vest and sat on a blanket facing north toward the courthouse. Lyman Pusley was the executioner, delivering one rifle shot to the chest. Lewis did not die right away and after about fifteen minutes one of the men smothered him with a bandana.[286] Raymond took the only known photo of the event. It shows Lewis lying on the ground surrounded by men, with a handkerchief over his face. The site of Gaines County Courthouse is at Courthouse Gap, about three miles south of present-day Panola and about two and one-half miles south of the Butterfield Trail.

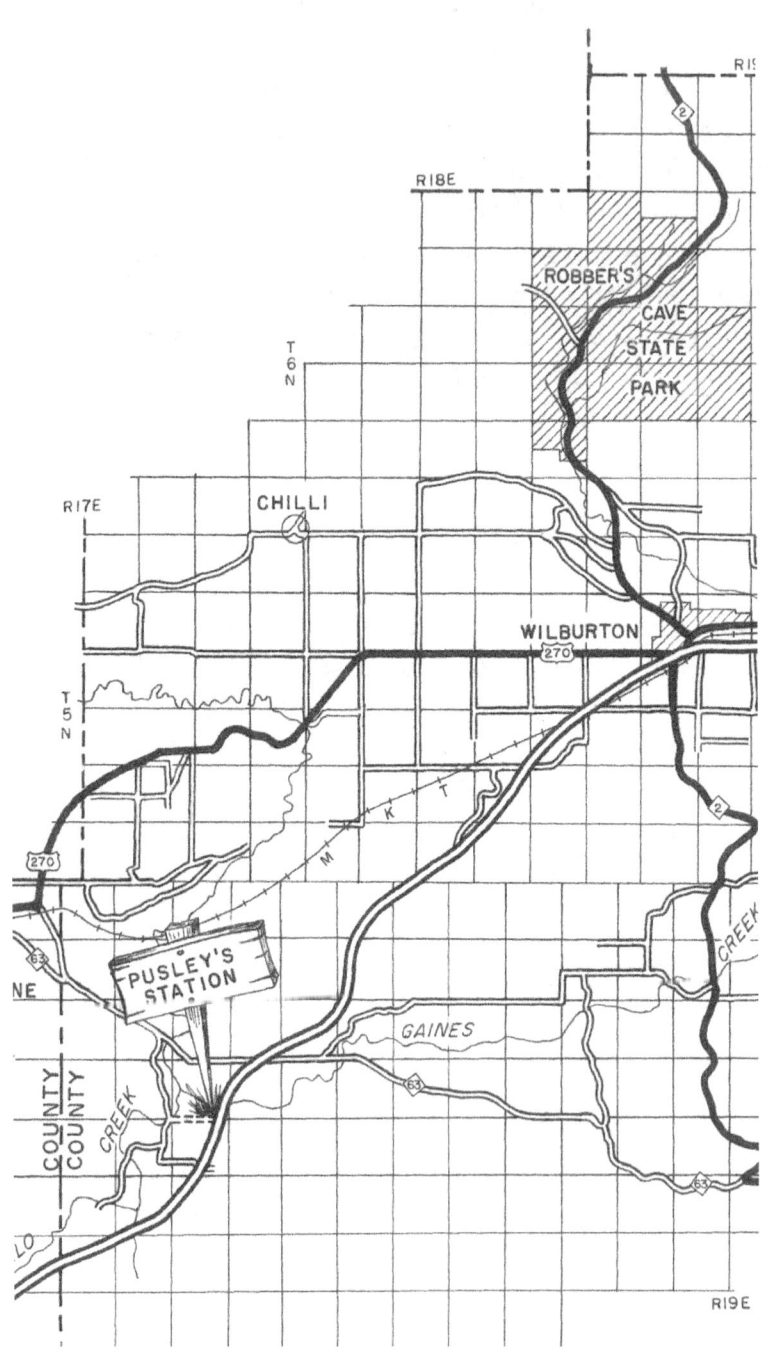

Previous Page: Butterfield Trail - Western Latimer County, including Mountain Station (unmarked but about 2/3 the distance from Wilburton to Pusley's) and Pusley's Station. Adapted from original map courtesy of Oklahoma Historical Society. See Eastern LeFlore County map, page 40, for map legend.

Riddle's Station

Beyond the Narrows, the mail road emerged into the first prairie of consequence in Indian Territory, then ran due west, veering slightly toward the southwest again as it approached the Fourche Maline.[287] The Butterfield wagons stayed on the higher ground along the edge of the valley, south of present-day Red Oak and U.S. Highway 270. In the 1930s, some of the stagecoach trail could still be traveled on this fourteen-mile segment, where the old byway had been improved for automobile use. Today, less than a mile south of Highway 270, a road named Butterfield, or County Road E1430, runs through the foothills, following the approximate trace of the old road. It dead-ends and requires a brief detour on the highway about a mile east of Panola, but reconnects at Northeast 104th Road and soon crosses a tributary of the Poteau River, the Fourche Maline, meaning "treacherous fork" in French.[288] The crossing was first facilitated for the Overland Mail by a toll bridge built by station keeper John Riddle. Just beyond the Fourche Maline bridge and east of Lutie Cemetery is Riddle's Station.

Born in Mississippi about 1809, Riddle was the son of an Irishman and a Choctaw woman, and moved to Indian Territory as a young man. He attended the Choctaw Academy in Kentucky and served as a member of the Choctaw Council.[289] At Riddle's the stable for Butterfield stock was located in a grassy area south of the house. John Riddle's two sons cared for the horses, harnessing them and bringing them out to hitch to the stage as the wagon approached the station. In December 1866, one of Riddle's sons, George, who served with the

Choctaws in the Civil War and was later county judge, obtained a renewal of his father's toll bridge concession, which he continued to operate along with the mail station. Riddle's retained its identity until 1873, when it was renamed Big Fourche Maline post office, with George Riddle as postmaster.[290] During the 1930s and 1950s, only chimney stones and a caved-in well remained of the Riddle home, although the Centennial Committee made sure to note that the station site was almost knee deep in blue grass.[291] Today a modern home is located at the station site. Just to the west on the hillside is the stone-rimmed Riddle family cemetery plot, abiding near a towering oak. The grave of John Riddle is not evident, although many Riddles, including John's son George, are buried there. A trace of the trail is still visible as a slight depression running east to west across the cemetery through the turf. South of the cemetery, on the north side of the county road, sits the 1958 historical marker in fine condition.

Side Trip: (Station) Keeping It In The Family

John Riddle was at the center of a family network of station keepers. Tandy Walker was his nephew, and Sarah Hall Trahern, wife of Judge James Trahern, was his niece. Another niece, Mary Walker (Tandy Walker's sister), was married to Casper Blackburn, keeper of Blackburn's Station farther west near Brushy Creek. Riddle's daughter Martha operated a stand at Mountain Station with her husband, William Chapen.

Connecting the line farther southwest, James Trahern's half-sister Lucy Juzan was married to A.W. Geary, who operated Geary's Station on North Boggy Creek. Another half-sister, Eliza Juzan Flack, was "Mrs. Flack" of Atoka fame. (See "Side Trip: Mrs. Flack's" in Chapter Seven).

James, Lucy and Eliza were from the same mother, Margaret, the Choctaw daughter of Nahomtima. The Juzans were sisters of Pierre Juzan, chief of the Choctaw Nation's Pushmataha District from 1838 to 1841.[292]

Coal Country

About four hundred yards south of Riddle's Station, a vein of coal outcropped in the ridge, described by Ormsby as "a curious ledge of black sandstone rocks, which had very much the appearance of the ruins of a large building, so regularly were they laid."[293] The presence of coal was frequently mentioned in early descriptions of the country, such as Parker's reference to a vein of bituminous coal seventeen inches thick.[294] Coal was used for the blacksmithing needed to support the Overland Mail, and by Choctaw farmers and ranchers. Less than twenty years after the Butterfield stage wagons passed through, mining became a major industry in the Choctaw Nation. From 1873, when bituminous coal was first mined commercially, through the 1980s, more than 200 million tons of coal were extracted from Oklahoma mines.[295] The town of Wilburton, to the west of Riddle's Station, was one of many communities which sprang up around coal mines in southeastern Oklahoma.[296]

From Lutie west to Wilburton, the Centennial Committee saw the tracks of the Rock Island Railroad superimposed on the trace of the stagecoach trail, lacing back and forth, often only a few feet away from the tracks.[297] Traveling that way today, such traces are no longer apparent, but the road's now invisible path leads the traveler to more discoveries on the Butterfield in Latimer County.

Mountain Station

At the crest of a hill between Riddle's Station and the next Butterfield stand, a tale with far-reaching consequences and an air of mystery awaits. The mail road continued west from Riddle's, curving around the east face of a gap in the ridge now in the center of Wilburton, and, turning southwest, emerged onto the prairie. Here the country opened up to smoother roads, well trafficked with Choctaws herding cattle up the road and emigrants coming from Texas toting all their worldly goods in covered wagons when Ormsby was passing through. Since this was a period of great migration *to* Texas, the trajectory of these travelers going the other direction is noteworthy. Some were likely traveling to Colorado seeking their fortunes in the Gold Rush of 1858-59.[298] Ever the jester, Ormsby took the opportunity to lampoon the emigrating families who, when camping at night, were "luxuriating" on the obviously spartan fare of "dried beef, coffee, and perhaps corn from the nearest cornfield."[299]

The mail wagon skirted the edge of the hills before ascending a "steep, stony hill"[300] to the site of Mountain Station at the crest of Blue Mountain, at an elevation of 920 feet above sea level. Though not an official Butterfield establishment, this was a small relay station[301] and after the Civil War a stop on a later stage line. Olasechubi, a full-blood Choctaw, was granted the concession for a toll gate at the summit in 1867. The stop was well known as a place for watering both passengers and horses, it being "hard driving over the rough road" on Blue Mountain.[302] Old-timer James W. Baird said his father, William G. Baird, operated a trading post there for three years, and there was ample water of good quality in a large spring.[303] Another pioneer said a stone house was built over the spring and in 1937 some of the rocks were still there and the spring was still running.[304] Mountain Station was considered one of the county's "principal stage coach stops," had a trading post, and was the site of an early Indian burial ground where, in 1937, numerous graves were visible in the three-acre plot. There were no markers and the ground over most of the graves was level with the growth of vegetation, but rotting remains of small houses once covering the graves were still evident.[305] The custom of erecting houses over graves has an uncertain origin. W.B. Morrison attributed it to a tradition that rain must not fall upon the grave.[306]

Tobacco, food, clothing, and treasured belongings were placed either in the grave with the deceased or in the grave house.[307] The custom continues to this day in some communities, and one may still see new structures covering graves. They are often made of wood, about two feet high with a gabled roof, or concrete with a flat top. Some families put tomb stones at the head and foot of the grave house and place a picture of the deceased on the headstone.[308]

Driving a (possible) trace of the stagecoach road near Mountain Station

For several miles on either side of Mountain Station, the county road runs very near the trail; in fact, the Centennial Committee saw the depressions of the old road within a few feet of the roadway.[309] When

Bill and I explore this segment, we spy what may be the same traces, on the west side of the county road. They are easily visible only feet from the pavement and the opportunity to drive the path is sorely tempting. There is no gate, nor a No Trespassing sign, and we give it a try, rolling several hundred yards along the rugged rut before reaching a swollen creek. With its large wheels, a Celerity wagon could have forded the stream. But we are not prepared to try, so we turn back. Whether or not this is the old road, it is easy to imagine we are riding in its traces and thrilling to have the experience.

In 1860, an eastbound stage of the Overland Mail carried Eadweard J. Muybridge, traveling as a through passenger from San Francisco, from whence he departed July 2. Best known for his use of photography to capture animals in motion for the first time in 1878, Muybridge laid the groundwork for modern motion pictures, developing a shutter system to stop motion and one of the earliest motion picture projectors, the zoopraxiscope. But in 1860, the Englishman was living in San Francisco and selling books. Traveling to the east coast on his way back to England, on Friday, July 20, Muybridge's stage wrecked when the horses ran away on the descent of a hill. The wagon left the road, collided with a tree and was broken to pieces. Muybridge sustained a serious head injury and a passenger by the name of Mackey was killed. Every person on board the vehicle was injured. Newspaper reports of the day placed this accident at Mountain Station. Some have identified the location of the accident as Mountain Pass Station, located on the Overland Mail route near Merkel, Texas, seventeen miles west of Abilene, about two hundred fifty miles southwest of Sherman, Texas, and nearly twice that distance from Fort Smith.

Muybridge's testimony in a murder trial fifteen years after the accident is the basis for the statements that the accident occurred in Texas. In 1875, standing trial for the killing of his wife's lover, Muybridge recollected that on his eastbound stagecoach journey he dined at a stage house, then boarded the stage, drawn by six wild mustang horses. "That is the last I recollect of that nine days," he said. "After that, I found myself at Fort Smith, 150 miles distant, lying in bed."[310] He was treated for his head injury in Fort Smith before traveling on to New York, where he continued under the care of a physician. Muybridge sued the Butterfield company for $10,000 in damages but settled for $2,500. Although Muybridge claimed no firsthand memory of the accident, he relayed that a fellow passenger told him the stage had traveled probably half an hour and they were just then entering the Texas Cross Timbers. "Just as we were getting to the Timbers I remarked that the best plan would be for us to get out of the back of the stage, because I saw that an accident would take place. He told me that I took out my knife to cut the canvas back of the stage, and was preparing to leave when the stage ran against either a rock or a stump and threw me out against my head."[311]

Muybridge's mention of the Cross Timbers region of Texas is noteworthy. These post oak-dominated woodlands, once covering 28,000 square miles from central Texas across Oklahoma into southeastern Kansas, separate the more arid southern Great Plains from the eastern deciduous forests. The region was known to early travelers as a "cast iron forest" because the dense, tangled growth made for a very difficult passage.[312] The western edge of Texas' western or "upper" Cross Timbers (because they are higher in elevation than the eastern Cross Timbers) lies just east of the Mountain Pass Station area in Texas. At Mountain Station in Indian Territory, Muybridge was actually near the eastern border of the Cross Timbers when the accident occurred, passing out of the thickly wooded region.

Muybridge's retelling of the incident took place in support of an insanity defense in his murder trial. He was found not guilty, although insanity was not the basis of the verdict. Rather, the jury believed the killing justified. Still, some believe the long-term effects of the head injury led to significant abnormalities in his personality. "Prior to his accident," testified a close friend, "Muybridge was a good businessman, genial and pleasant in nature; but after the accident he was irritable, eccentric, a risk-taker and subject to emotional outbursts."[313] Following his acquittal, Muybridge went on to achieve renown in the world of photography. The head injury did not appear to inhibit his intellectual or creative achievements; rather, it may have actually enhanced his creative abilities because he became more willing to take risks, and pursued his art obsessively.[314]

Contemporary news reports make it clear, however, that the accident occurred in Indian Territory, not Texas. On July 23, 1860, the New York Times reported that a dispatch from Van Buren, Arkansas announced an accident to the Overland Mail coach, delaying its arrival about thirty hours. The horses, it said, ran away in the mountain pass of the Choctaw Nation.[315] Another newspaper report directly quotes a passenger on the stage, S.P. Nott, of Sherman, Texas, also referring to its location in "the Choctaw country."[316] Nott's is the most detailed contemporary account of the accident identified by this author. The item, originating in a Fort Smith newspaper, states the following:

> . . . Fifty miles from this place, in the Choctaw country, on Friday night last, the stage arrived at the station a little before sundown, and after getting supper it was about eight o'clock when the stage started, with eight passengers, Mr. Stout, road agent, and the driver. The brake was out of order, and one of the horses was refractory, and the team started in a run, but was soon checked, and Mr. Stout got upon the seat with the driver, and the latter gave his whip a crack, and away went the team down the hill full tilt, and as the brake was useless, there was no way to stop them. While the stage was at the top of its speed, the curtains being down, Dr. Denton took out his knife and cut them, and jumped out, and in cutting the curtains, cut Mr. Nott severely in the back. Dr. Denton was badly bruised in the fall.

The stage soon after struck a tree and smashed to pieces, and the fore wheels became disengaged, and the horses ran some distance, dragging the driver and bruising him severely. Mr. Nott says he braced himself, and when the stage struck the tree he landed some distance from the place where it struck, and the top of the stage with him. In recovering he heard the groans of the wounded, and on going to one he found the blood gurgling in this throat, and it being dark, he raised him up, and receiving no answer from him, he put his hand to his head and found the forepart of the skull broke in. The man proved to be Mr. Mackey, of Cass County, Missouri. He was killed immediately. Mr. Nott returned to the station and there he soon fainted from the loss of blood. Mrs. Chapin, the lady of the house, had all the wounded bodies taken to the station, and went to work and dressed their wounds with her own hands. Mr. Nott speaks in the highest terms of the kindness of Mrs. Chapin.

Mr. Stout, the road agent, was seriously injured, his face badly bruised, and his upper lip cut through, and the lower lip is not in much better condition, besides his bruises in the chest are very serious. Most of the passengers were injured more or less, and only two of them, young men from Ohio, were able to walk about. The names of the passengers are Messrs. Nott, McCarty, Halsey, Denton, of New York, and two young men from Ohio, and Mr. Mackey, of Missouri, who was killed.[317]

On Saturday, about eleven o'clock, an express arrived here with the news of the accident, and a coach was dispatched immediately, taking Doctors Bomford and Dunlap, to attend to the wounded.

This is the first serious accident to the stage in the region of this place, since the Overland Line went into operation.[318]

The Mrs. Chapin to whom Nott refers would have been Martha Riddle Chapen, daughter of John Riddle, keeper of Riddle's Station.

She and her husband, William Chapen, operated Mountain Station "a few years after its establishment." Martha provided meals and sleeping quarters for passengers and William provided a change of fresh horses for the stagecoaches, although it is unknown to what extent this occurred during the life of the Overland Mail.[319] A post office was established there in 1873, with Martha J. Edwards as postmaster, likely the same person as Martha Chapen.[320] Muybridge refers to a "Dr. Bowie" caring for him in Fort Smith, who could have been Dr. Bomford.

An interview with Latimer County resident James A. Blalack in 1937 provides another clue. Blalack's grandfather was Andrew Mackey.

> He had been to California to the Gold rush in about the year of 1848 and he . . . was almost home when the stage coach team ran away. This happened at the top of a large mountain called Mountain station. This stage station was located about ten or eleven miles southwest of where Wilburton is now located where all stages that ran on the through road from Fort Smith to the Texas border had to stop for food and water. As they started down this mountain, the team ran away and my grandfather was killed in the smash. He was buried in the Mountain Station burying place.[321]

At the time of the interview, Mr. Blalack was sixty-nine years of age, and his mother, who would have been Andrew Mackey's daughter, Sallie Mackey Blalack, was living with him, in her early eighties. She would have been ten years old at the time of the accident, probably old enough to remember the event, and perhaps in 1937 still had a clear memory of it. Historical records place Andrew Mackey in Cassville, Missouri in the 1840s and in Athens, Missouri in 1850 when his daughter Sarah (Sallie) was born.[322]

Earl Shero took me to the spot where the accident may have occurred, pointing out the steep descent where the stagecoach would have careened out of control, crashing into the trees on the rocky hillside. A grave marker for Andrew Mackey is easily found in the Mountain Station cemetery, obvious because it is so new in this old cemetery. Mackey's true burial place is unknown, but a Mackey descendant had the plaque made and placed it in the family plot. The marker reads:

In Memory
Andrew J. Mackey
1821-1859
Returning from Calif. Gold Field
Killed in Stage Coach Wreck at
Mt. Station

The year of death on Mackey's grave marker may be incorrect, but in the end the clock tells the story. The accident occurred on the evening of Friday, July 20, 1860. Late the following day, July 21, news of the accident reached Fort Smith. The only way this could have occurred would have been via a person on horseback or by stagecoach, as the telegraph line did not yet extend to northwest Texas or Indian Territory. A stagecoach traveling at the average speed of 5.5 miles per hour expected over Indian Territory roads could have traveled the nearly 100 miles from Mountain Station to Fort Smith in about seventeen hours, a man on horseback even faster.

Mountain Pass Station in Texas was 487 miles from Fort Smith, requiring nearly five days' travel in a stagecoach and at least two days by horseback under the best possible circumstances.[323] When the report of the accident was received in Fort Smith, a coach was dispatched immediately to attend to the wounded and by July 23, 1860, thanks to extension of the Missouri and Western Telegraph line to Fort

Smith, word of the accident was disseminated all over the eastern United States. By the time the injured passengers arrived in Fort Smith on Sunday, July 22, a wagon carrying passengers from Mountain Pass, Texas would have still been about three days away. The timeline stands on its own in clarifying that it would have been a physical impossibility for the passengers to arrive from Mountain Pass Station, Texas, to Fort Smith, Arkansas, by July 22, 1860. Thus it is reasonable to conclude that Mountain Station in the Choctaw Nation of Indian Territory, not Mountain Pass Station in Texas, was where Mackey met his maker, Muybridge's life was changed, and the invention of moving pictures was, perhaps, set in motion.

A settlement grew up around Mountain Station into a community large enough to be designated a post office by 1873.[324] But like so many other communities along the old mail road, the population dwindled with the coming of the railroad. Today a cemetery and a historic marker indicate the site of Mountain Station. When the Centennial Committee stopped here in the spring of 1958 the iris were in bloom and the cemetery in excellent condition and "an inspiration of rustic beauty." They found the view to the south from Mountain Station one of grandeur and designated a site on the west side of the county road, opposite the cemetery, for a historical marker stating the following:

Old Ft. Smith-Boggy Depot Road.
A stage stand for changing horses and a toll road over this mountain pass were established here in 1866 under Choctaw law.
This road was the Butterfield Overland Mail route in 1858–61.

Toll-gate keeper Olasechubi's house sat about fifty yards west of the old cemetery. In 1933, traces of the old road could still be seen passing within the shadow of a large oak that stood within a few feet of the house, both ends of which were indicated by a heap of chimney stones.[325] Today, stones remain in the field west of the county road, although there is no evidence of the oak. Beyond the house site, traces of the old trail are still evident through the woods, diverging from the county road in a southwesterly direction. Mountain Station Spring, which furnished water for the stage stand, is located about one hundred yards south of the cemetery.[326] In 2016 a sign at the roadside advertised the spring as a stop along the Butterfield, but has since been replaced with one warning off trespassers. Just off the road, enshrouded no longer in rock but in protective concrete, the spring still flows. Beyond the iron-stained streambed going up the hill is a rocky trail which may have served as a path from the station to the spring.

Pusley's Station

Descending from the Blue Mountain summit, the mail road traversed a sloped prairie extending toward Gaines Creek.[327] It crossed present State Highway 1 about a mile west of Higgins School.[328] At the community of Higgins, the Conklings traced the road for a short distance south of a country store, now long gone, and saw a deep depression leading away through the fields. About a mile and a half southwest, the road crossed Gaines Creek and soon arrived at the next Butterfield station at the home of Silas Pusley.[329] Station keeper Pusley was the grandson of George Pusley who, until 1850, maintained the Moshulatubbe District's blacksmith shop at his place near Mountain Station.

An abandoned segment of the stagecoach road near Mountain Station

Pusley's Station, sixteen miles from Riddle's, occupied a plot of land between Gaines Creek and its tributary, Pusley Creek. Silas Pusley was granted the privilege of erecting a bridge and establishing a toll gate on Gaines Creek on October 22, 1859. The date of this permit suggests that the Overland Mail wagons forded the creek for some time before a bridge was built. The mail road traversed Pusley's land between the two creeks. In 1933, Muriel Wright wrote that worn ruts of the road, a well, a portion of an old log structure, and the Pusley family graveyard remained at the site. Some of the older graves in the cemetery were unmarked, and other marble tombstones bore the names of Pusley and Seeley. The graves of Narras Pusley and Eastman Pusley (a son of George Pusley[330]), who died in 1887 and 1899 respectively, were then still covered with ruins of gravehouses.[331] At Pusley's, the fenced graveyard is now grown up with trees and brush and many of the stones are broken or fallen. Tall marble markers for M.A. Seeley, who died in 1907, and Betsey Pusley, who died in 1909, dominate the plot.

The Conklings found the stone foundations of the Pusley's Station chimneys about a quarter-mile southwest of the Gaines Creek crossing and about one hundred feet west of an old log house which still stood on the east side of the trail. This was the former home of Eastman Pusley, and was then occupied by J.W. Green. By 1958, Green was living in Higgins and agreed to accompany the Centennial Committee to the station, where they examined the Eastman Pusley home, "an excellent example of the Butterfield Station home" although it was built after the Civil War. The committee urged that it be preserved, citing a beautiful old tree to the north of the house, and the adjoining well, as indications of the structure's importance. "The well was built waist high out of carefully cut and fitted slabs of sandstone and adjoined the house at the south corner of the west or front porch." As usual, they could not resist mentioning that the wire fence outlining the yard was covered with early spring roses and fragrant honeysuckle in full bloom.[332]

Old well at Pusley's Station

For the Pusley's historical marker, the committee chose a spot on the south side of the section line road, in the center of the depression made by the stage road. It was this information and a photograph of the remnants of the marker on civilwaralbum.com which helped me find the site. The memorial's bronze plaque has been removed and the base is mostly destroyed, but enough is visible to indicate its location. The stump sits directly in the trace of the mail road, which runs southwest toward Pusley Creek. The well adjacent to the Eastman Pusley house is still present. The home, however, was not preserved, despite the committee's wishes.

At Pusley's, Ormsby met an "old Indian" with seven hundred head of cattle and a pretty daughter, "willing to give the half of the one to the white man who will marry the other." The reporter seemed to be enjoying himself at this point, at least in retrospect, as he had the opportunity to clean up and change to attire more apropos of the setting than whatever city duds he was wearing when he left St. Louis.

"Here I gave an Indian boy a paper of tobacco to give me water enough to wash my face, put on a blue flannel shirt, and considered myself pretty well on my way out West."[333]

In 1972, historian Kent Ruth wrote that while one could drive long stretches of the old Butterfield stage route in a car, mostly on pleasantly meandering county roads, few places offered more of the feel of the route than along the two or three hundred yards of rutted trace that leads northeast from the ruins of Pusley's Station to the property line fence, an abandoned section line road, and the crossing of Gaines Creek just beyond.

Here parallel ruts, formed first by iron tired wagons and then by rubber tired motor vehicles, indicate the flow of a century's traffic across the unbroken prairie. Now seemingly deserted (the nearest house, that of owner R. W. Watts, is more than a half-mile to the southwest, and out of sight), the site must appear much as it did in 1858. One need only to reconstruct the log station house, if only in one's eye, to recreate the scene that greeted Ormsby when he arrived, fresh from the east. When this writer was there even the cattle were present, crowding curiously around his car. So strong was the mood evoked that he was almost tempted to inquire about the pretty Indian girl, just to see if her hand, and half the cattle, were still available.[334]

Butterfield Trail - Pittsburg County, including Blackburn's Station. Adapted from original map courtesy of Oklahoma Historical Society. See Eastern LeFlore County map, page 40, for map legend.

Chapter Six: Rough Play and Bad Dreams

Driving a segment of the trail west of Pusley's Station

Today a locked gate on the Watts Ranch blocks the trail beyond Pusley's Station, but on our first trip down the Butterfield road, Bill and I found the gate open and drove through. We wandered most of the way across, fording several creeks in our four-wheel drive truck. Close to the western boundary of the ranch, locked gates blocked the way and we turned around, retracing our path. It was a rare opportunity to travel the route of the old trail in the isolation of Buffalo Creek valley, seeing cattle and deer but no human inhabitants. The view has changed very little since the 1950s, when the landscape was devoid of houses, cars and telephone lines for perhaps the longest distance of any section of the mail route through Oklahoma.[335] Beyond the Watts Ranch, the road traverses Ti Valley along Pittsburg County roads bounded by private ranch land and, in particular, the large Ti Valley Ranch owned by the Choctaw Nation of Oklahoma.

Choctaw Ball Games

Along its seventeen-mile course to the next Butterfield station at Blackburn's, the mail road passed through "little plains" along Buffalo Creek. There Waterman Ormsby saw tall posts the Choctaws used in playing ball. "The players divide themselves into two parties, one standing at each post," he wrote. "The throwers aim to hit the posts, and the catchers must capture the ball in little bowls, with which each is provided, a penalty being inflicted for catching the ball with the hands. They become very much excited at this game, and gamble with it very often."[336] The game he mentions is stickball, or *ishtaboli,* played long before the removal by the southeastern tribes .[337] *Ishtaboli* in Choctaw is roughly translated "little brother of war," and tribal communities sometimes played the game to settle disputes.

Travelers through Indian Territory often commented on the sport, impressed with its spectacle. One wrote, "The grotesque appearance of the players, the excitement, yells and shouts of the crowd, old and young, and the gaudy finery displayed, all combined to make an indelible impression upon our memories."[338]

The men who played were elaborately painted, naked except for a belt and breech-clout. In the course of play they ran and "literally leaped over each other's heads, and tripped and dodged and foiled their opponents in every possible combination of agility and grace."[339]

Möllhausen offers a vivid description from his 1853 journey through Indian Territory:

The players instantly rush madly forward and become mingled together in one wild struggling mass of human bodies and limbs in which no individual or group can any longer be distinguished. The turf is trampled into dust,—the crowd sways this way and that,—now one has the ball, but it is immediately torn from his grasp,—the next moment another has snatched it, and it is seen flying through the air towards the goal; but it does not reach it, for it has been arrested in its progress by a watchful eye and a sure hand; the struggle begins again, and at last it is really pushed through one of the gates.[340]

The game was so rough that casualties were frequent, and betting on the games was common. Into the 1880s, stickball remained the game into which the Choctaws "entered with the zest of primitive days,"[341] but its popularity waned in later years. Between 1890 and 1910, newspapers advertised "Indian ball games" as exhibitions and amusements, although reports of competitive games between local teams still appeared.[342] The *McAlester Daily News* reported as something out of the ordinary a "genuine, old fashioned Indian ball game" occurring in Krebs in 1905.[343] Revitalization efforts by the Choctaw Nation of Oklahoma began in the mid-1970s and the game continues to prosper, with a few modern trappings, such as clothing.[344]

The Conklings noted a "last great ball game" played about 1910 near the "old Pulcher place," with Judge John Pulcher as one of the referees.[345] This event probably occurred among the same plains Ormsby passed, a few miles southwest of Pusley's Station on the present-day Watts Ranch. Pulcher, a mixed-blood Choctaw born about 1860, served as county judge and clerk for Gaines County. His mother, Phoebe, was George Pusley's daughter. His father, Albert, was born in Germany in 1824 and died in 1860. Both Phoebe and Albert are buried in nearby Pulcher Spring cemetery.

Although the ranch is off-limits today, the Watts family welcomed both the Conklings and the Centennial Committee.[346] Margaret Conkling wrote that Mose Watts was "most cordial and interested in the old Butterfield Road. We drove through his barnyard and found ourselves riding over the very ruts themselves."[347] In 1930, the ruin of the Pulcher log house still stood on the old road. About a half mile north of the site are Pulcher Spring and the Pulcher Spring cemetery.

Before they resolved the locations of Indian Territory's Butterfield stations, the Conklings thought the Pulcher place was the site of Pusley's Station.[348] To further complicate matters, a mile beyond the Pulcher home site was Buffalo Creek station, established in 1867 on a later mail route at the home of Wade N. Hampton.[349] Illustrating the difficulty in establishing station locations, the Conklings found an Oklahoma Historical Society marker at the Buffalo Creek site indicating it had been a Butterfield station. They contacted the Society to correct the error. This marker had been placed on August 7, 1930, on the trip conducted by John Young Bryce and Muriel Wright to search for historical sites and place markers. Bryce also wrote in the *Chronicles of Oklahoma* that Buffalo Station was a stage stand on the Overland Mail Route.[350]

Margaret Conkling commended the work of the Historical Society in marking and preserving historical sites and wrote in her diary:

We saw several of their markers and noted some slight mistakes in some details. We believe that the designation of the Wade Hampton place rather than the Pulcher place is a mistake. After investigating locally and studying all references available, the Pulcher place seems to us undoubtedly the Butterfield station. The work and study with an investigation of this kind take a great deal of time and it is to be hoped that historical societies all along the way will continue their investigations and place permanent markers at all of these points of interest."[351]

The Conklings would, of course, later learn that their own conclusion about the Pulcher place had also been mistaken. By 1958, the Centennial Committee could see nothing of Buffalo Station, fire having destroyed the structures, but they recommended placement of another historical marker there.[352] There is no indication this ever occurred.

Blackburn's Station

Leaving the Watts Ranch, the stagecoach trail continued through Ti Valley and along Elm Creek, traveling through the later settlements of Ti and Pine Top to Blackburn's Station. The route today crosses the north-south road leading from Hartshorne to Counts, now known as Savage Highway. The westbound county road approximates the original route much of the way, skirting Ti Valley Ranch before reaching the Indian Nation Turnpike. Just east of the bridge passing over the turnpike is the former site of Pine Top School, and about a half-mile south is the location of the Butterfield station operated by Casper B. Blackburn, an intermarried Choctaw originally from Missouri. The actual site of the station is between the turnpike and the county road.[353] The station was at Blackburn's home within a small settlement known as Brushy, sometimes spelled Brushey, probably named for the nearby creek, "whose banks are tangled almost impassably, with briars and brambles," [354]

A few miles east of Blackburn's, Ormsby experienced some excitement. After taking a "splendid" team of horses at Pusley's, the wagon rolled rapidly over the hills, the driver urging on the team, when they came to a patch of woods through which the trail was rocky and twisting. Urgency overcame caution and the driver went "bounding over the stones at a fearful rate." The moon was shining brightly, but the dense tree canopy obscured its light, leaving the driver to find his way in darkness based on his knowledge of the road.[355]

"To see the heavy mail wagon whizzing and whirling over the jagged rocks, through such a labyrinth, in comparative darkness, and to feel oneself bouncing now on the hard seat, now against the roof and now against the side of the wagon, was no joke, I assure you, though I can truthfully say that I rather liked the excitement of the thing," wrote Ormsby.[356] But soon, with two heavy thumps and a jolt that threw everyone from their seats, the wagon made a crashing sound. Stopping to look, they saw only a broken seat in the darkness, but once they reached the station discovered the tongue of the wagon was badly split, requiring a repair. The wagon, as it turned out, was carrying a heavy load of ammunition, which may have contributed to the problem.[357] From Blackburn's, they traveled the next eighteen miles in two hours and a quarter, however, suggesting that the incident did not diminish the driver's haste.

Picking up Ti Valley Road off Savage Highway late one fall afternoon, I am reminded that Ormsby's stage crashed along this very stretch of trail. Heading west, I top a hill and gain a view toward the lowering sun, the descending road offering views of mountains and pine trees in the distance. It is easy to see how the driver gained speed here on the western slope. Over the years any significant rockiness or twistiness has been removed, but for isolation this is another segment that excels. If I squint, I can imagine riding on a stage wagon as evening sets, traveling a little too briskly for comfort. A dip in the road on a curve conjures a likely place for an accident and I catch my breath as a deer runs across the road in front of me. I pass the turn for Pine Top cemetery, where a section of the old mail road once remained on the south and has since been obscured by development. More deer appear. I am in a dark tunnel of road, with tall trees and overcast skies. And then more deer. It is time for me to get out of these woods, I think, wondering whether the stage wagons ever ran into deer.

Deer along the trail between Pusley's and Ti

It turns out the overpopulation of whitetail deer is a modern phenomenon. As early as the 1840s, Benson stated that game had been overhunted in the Fort Coffee area. By 1900, the whitetail deer was nearly wiped out in Oklahoma from hunting, and in 1917 the state's deer population was estimated at only five hundred. By 1922 all deer hunting in Oklahoma was banned. Eleven years later, regulated deer hunting began, and in 1943 deer restoration efforts began. By 2004 the statewide deer population was estimated at nearly half a million. Thus, road hazards at dusk.[358]

Pine Top School was a landmark noted by the Centennial Committee. To its south, the section line road crossed a well-defined trace of the trail near Blackburn's Station. The school is now gone, except for foundation stones and the boys' bathroom, a two-holer outhouse built of stone on a hillside next to the Indian Nation Turnpike, an 80-mile per hour toll road which represents the single biggest change in the area since 1958. Rushing highway traffic below jars the senses after hours of traveling quiet country roads.

Ranchers Larry and Penny James live along Pine Top Road, just east of the turnpike. When Bill and I visit, they show us two deep swales in the earth--distinct and undisturbed segments of the old mail road. The ruins of Pine Top school are also on their property. Larry went to school at Pine Top, a two-room school with about twenty students when he attended. Once achieving the third grade, Larry rode his horse to school, continuing there through the sixth grade, in 1955. Pine Top School closed in 1956, and Larry's family bought this property the same year. They were living there when the Centennial Committee came by in 1958.

In 1930, the Conklings located the mail road near Blackburn's and identified as the remains of the station a pile of chimney stones in a small clearing on the north side of the old road and south of a tributary of Elm Creek. In 1958, the Centennial Committee designated a spot for the marker on the west side of the county road south of Pine Top School, where the road intersected the trail.[359] Today, the damaged concrete base of the station marker still sits along the roadside, hidden in the brush, immediately west of a small tract of land the James' own and where Larry reports seeing remnants of the station in years past. In anticipation of our visit in 2023, Penny cut back the brambles around the marker, showing a respect for history in stark contrast to the vandal who stole the marker's bronze plaque, which is probably now gathering dust in the attic of someone whose ancestor forgot why they stole it.

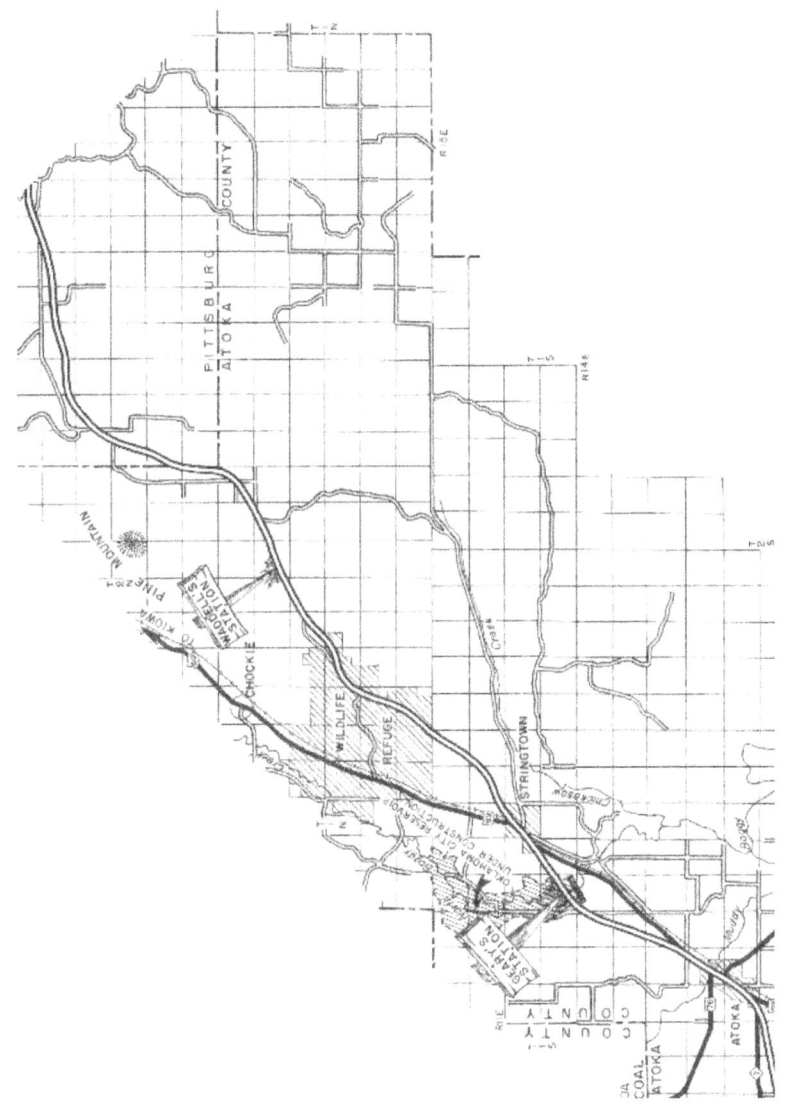

Butterfield Trail - Eastern Atoka County, including Waddell's and Geary's Stations. Adapted from original map courtesy of Oklahoma Historical Society. See Eastern LeFlore County map, page 40, for map legend.

Waddell's Station

Sixteen miles down the road, I step out of a utility vehicle into a thicket and immediately regret it. The berry vines and greenbriers and black locust saplings and their thorns large and small looked from a distance only moderately challenging and the spot looked, again from a distance, a likely place for a cemetery. Now, in the midst of it, I see my mistake on both counts but misplaced bravado prevents me from calling a halt. I trudge out into the prickly mess in my ankle-high boots and blue jeans, stepping as high as possible with my short legs to get over the vines, and stomping them when I can. I fervently wish I had worn tall boots as I look for stones which might indicate the presence of a grave plot near Waddell's Station. I give it a good effort since I got us into this pickle. Doug Van Gundy, my host and driver, does the same. We circle the thicket and finally end up back at the side-by-side. I'm startled to see blood all over his gloves and the sleeves of his camouflage hunting jacket, and his white moustache stained a bright red. He ran into a thorn and his nose has been bleeding profusely. I have nothing to offer, no first aid kit, not even a hankie. Thankfully, the flow has stopped and he is ready to look elsewhere for the cemetery. What a sport. "Let's check out the treeline over there," I say, pointing east as I begin to extract tiny stickers from my pants and socks. We escape the thicket in our scrappy conveyance and approach the trees. I see daffodil foliage, a sure sign of human intervention, and as we close in, notice large stones. We stop and get out. Sure enough, it is the cemetery we are looking for. The Centennial Committee described it as overgrown and abandoned, about one hundred yards east of Waddell's and just south of the road. It contained about fifteen graves, they wrote, each well-defined and with a stone border, but without any inscription. Legend has it that shortly after the Civil War seven outlaws were hanged at Waddell's and that the seven plots in a row were the graves of these individuals. The committee expressed skepticism, however, that such care would have been taken to provide individual graves, each bordered with selected stone, "for such characters!" Van Gundy and I see seven stones in a row which may mark the plots of the outlaws, if the legend is true. Other graves also appear to have fragmented borders of stone. The growth of trees has disrupted the graveyard's order but the presence of the stones is distinctive. This may be the Beal, or Beale, Cemetery, documented in this location by a WPA writer in the 1930s.[360]

Well Founded Fears

Outlaws such as those whose legend lives on at Waddell's did not present much of a problem along the Butterfield route, since the carrying of valuables was prohibited on the stages. But passenger concerns about the potential for threats from Indians were not unreasonable; and Butterfield stations in Texas and beyond did experience such troubles. Raphael Pumpelly commented in 1860 that the fatigue of traveling day and night in a crowded coach in a constantly uncomfortable position was compounded by the anxiety "caused by the danger from Comanches." He wrote, "Every jolt of the stage, indeed any occurrence which started a passenger out of the state of drowsiness was instantly magnified into an attack, and the nearest fellow passenger was as likely to be taken for an Indian as for a friend."[361]

Waterman Ormsby exhibited the same anxiety. "I had read of bands of roving Indians, rambling through the forest but to kill and steal, all rushed to my mind, and transformed each decayed tree or stunted bush into a lurking foe."[362] Between Blackburn's and Waddell's, though tempted to stay up and enjoy a beautiful, clear night, the reporter succumbed to the fatigue of hard travel. Soon, with a jolt, the wagon stopped and Ormsby awoke in a panic. He had been dreaming of Comanche Indians and, half-awake, heard only silence.

Ormsby thought at first the driver and mail agent had been murdered and he had escaped because he was hidden among the blankets. He remembered he had a pistol but thought it best to be still for fear the Indians would find him. Soon, however, he heard the driver's familiar voice saying, "Git up there, old hoss." To Ormsby's relief, the driver was only hitching up a new team at Waddell's. His dream was just that, but real danger was in fact brewing to the northwest where turmoil between settlers and natives in Texas was spilling over into Indian Territory, in particular on the western edges of the Chickasaw Nation.[363]

In 1835 and 1837, the federal government had made treaties with the Comanches, Wichitas and Kiowas to smooth the passage of the migrating eastern Indians during the Removal. The treaties guaranteed peaceful passage through the country north of the Red River for whites and immigrating Indians. These guarantees did not, however, extend to Texans, towards whom these tribes maintained an "implacable hostility."[364] The increased traffic of the 1849 Gold Rush and the killing of bison by whites exacerbated the tensions, and raids of white settlements were frequent. Some peaceful Indians in these tribes stopped raiding but so-called "wilder members" of the Plains tribes continued, returning from raids with scalps, captives and stolen horses to strongholds near the Wichita Mountains, in western Indian Territory. Raiding continued through the 1850s, and in August, 1858, just before the Overland Mail's inaugural outing, the military heard that large bands of Comanches, Apaches, Cheyenne and other tribes were gathered for hostile purposes on the Canadian River near the Antelope Hills, in the far western reaches of Indian Territory. The Indians' purported plans to steal horses for "an incursion against the frontier of Texas" prompted a punitive military expedition.[365] Major Earl Van Dorn brought a command of the Second Cavalry to Indian Territory, arriving on September 26, 1858.

As Overland Mail stages passed back and forth to the southeast in late September, Van Dorn and four hundred cavalrymen made a forced march to a Wichita village near present Rush Springs, Oklahoma, about one hundred thirty miles from the mail road. There, Comanche chief Buffalo Hump's band, on a peaceful mission to return stolen horses to Fort Arbuckle, was in council with the Wichitas. On October 1, 1858, just before daylight, the troops fell upon the Indians, killing four Wichitas and nearly sixty Comanches. Van Dorn was unaware that the Comanches were on a peace mission, a fact known to the command at nearby Fort Arbuckle but not communicated to Van Dorn. Wichita chief Toseqosh was present during the attack and said the worst part of the whole affair was that the Comanches blamed his people and took their horses in revenge, warning: "You lying Wichitas, see what you have done, got all my people killed and it won't be long we will wipe you all out."[366]

This event further inflamed the Comanches[367] and in his 1858 report to the Commissioner of Indian Affairs, Elias Rector, Superintendent of Indian Affairs for the Southern Superintendency, expressed concern for a long and bloody border war and the "entire interruption of the overland mail to California" because of the "apprehended vengeance of the Comanches" if they were not convinced that the slaughter of their people was "the consequence of an unfortunate mistake."[368] The Army ordered two companies of cavalry from Fort Leavenworth, Kansas, to Fort Washita. They arrived on December 29, 1858 and remained at the post until May 1, 1861, when Fort Washita was abandoned for the final time by the U.S. Army.[369] In Rector's 1859 report, the unrest with the Comanches was still uppermost in his mind. Arguing for treating with the Comanches and bringing them in to settle on a reservation rather than "waging a war of extermination," he wrote, "If (the) impression (of treachery) is removed, as it can be by the proper explanations, and satisfaction is made, by presents, for the blood thus shed, the whole of the (tribe) can be colonized." After a long and bloody struggle, most of the Comanches were indeed confined to a reservation by 1875.[370]

The threat of Indian attacks was a serious matter for the Overland Mail. At isolated stations in Texas, New Mexico, and Arizona, Indians routinely ran off the company's horses until they were replaced with mules.[371] In March, 1859, near Mountain Pass about thirty miles east of Fort Chadbourne, Texas, a Comanche was killed just an hour before the stagecoach came through, having been among a band waiting to run off some livestock.[372] Also at Mountain Pass in May 1860, Indians killed a blacksmith in the employ of the Overland Mail and three men living near the station.[373] Another Overland Mail employee died in an attack at Arizona's Apache Pass in February of 1861. This last incident was the result of a series of misunderstandings which disrupted the normally friendly relationship between the Overland Mail Company and the Chiricahua Apaches and their leader Cochise. The Chiricahuas allowed Butterfield to build a station at this pass in the Chiricahua Mountains and traded wood to the station employees in exchange for supplies. A rancher falsely accused Cochise of stealing his cattle and abducting a boy from his ranch and sought help from the military. A young and overzealous Army officer, given orders to retrieve the cattle and the boy, bungled the interaction with Cochise, precipitating the violence in which the hostler at the station was killed and the station keeper wounded.[374] But, in the end, no Butterfield stagecoach passenger was ever killed by Indians, in spite of the fears.

Brushy Creek

Back on the mail road in Indian Territory, discomfort and lack of sleep were the only real misfortunes befalling Ormsby. The sixteen-mile segment where Ormsby napped is even today entirely unpaved and sparsely populated, following a course almost due west from Blackburn's for about a mile to a crossing on Brushy Creek. Just east of the crossing, in woods southwest of the Blackburn's station site, the Centennial Committee found a number of old graves, some enclosed by sandstone walls, and concluded it was Brushey Cemetery. The cemetery's "all-but-obliterated remains" contained a partly legible gravestone of Mora Bell, who died April 12, 1888.[375] Information from other sources and firsthand observation lead to the conclusion that it is probably Colbert Cemetery.[376] The Conklings observed on the east side of Brushy Creek "an old Indian cemetery. We were told the relatives of Holmes Colbert were buried there."[377] A trace of the stagecoach trail is still visible passing north of the well-hidden grave yard.

Although by the 1930s the trail from Blackburn's to the crossing on Brushy Creek had been abandoned for wheeled vehicles, it was still in use at the time by locals traveling on foot or horseback.[378] There at about the same spot, the county road now fords Brushy Creek on a low-water crossing. The site of James Colbert's stage station, established in 1843, is about a half-mile west. Colbert was known as "Brushy Jim" to distinguish him from other Colberts in the Chickasaw Nation. Around 1838, during the Chickasaw migration, Jim's father, Isaac Colbert, moved here where, a few years later, the federal government established one of the first blacksmith shops for the Chickasaws. Today the site of what may be the ruin of Brushy Jim's is marked by a stone well covered by the grill, hood and fenders of an old automobile; part of a flagstone walk or foundation; and partial remains of a chimney.[379]

From Brushy Jim's the stage road followed the north bank of Brushy Creek through a valley between Pine Mountain and a range of hills to the south, curving southwest then almost due south, and passing from Jacks Fork, now Pittsburg, County into Atoka County. The present county road runs in the same general direction as the old road but is located farther north.[380] At the northern entrance to Wesley, the road crosses Nolitubbe Creek then passes through the community's sparse remains. In 1972, an abandoned post office and store building still stood, but now only a cemetery indicates Wesley's existence.[381] Beyond Wesley the county road weaves back and forth across the path of the old trail for about three miles to what was later called the old Beale place, believed to be the location of Waddell's Station. The Beale log house was still standing on the north side of the mail road when the Conklings visited, a very old and well-preserved one-story dogtrot with two chimneys built of limestone slabs. Its location corresponded to the distance of sixteen miles from Blackburn's. "If the old Beale house is not the original station home, it certainly stands on or very near the original site," they concluded, finding the spot conducive to a station location, situated as it was in the "protecting shadow of timber-clad Pine mountain, in the southern extremity of Ti valley, a fertile and productive region which is abundantly watered by McGee creek and its tributaries."[382]

The origin of the name "Waddell" perplexed the Conklings, the name not being of Choctaw origin nor apparently that of someone who married into a Choctaw family. It may have been named for an Overland Mail employee who was temporarily in charge.[383] In 1933, Muriel Wright expounded upon this possibility: one of the organizers of the Pony Express was named William Waddell. He was, she wrote, a man with Cherokee connections and had visited the Cherokee Nation west of the Mississippi. A cousin, Walter Waddell of New York State, joined William in 1856 or 1857 in business in the West before the organization of the Pony Express. Wright hypothesized that one of these Waddells was directly associated with Waddell's Station in Indian Territory, possibly qualifying to run the station by going into partnership with a Choctaw citizen.[384] After the Civil War, when this section of the route was under a local mail contractor, the station became known as Wells' Stage Stand, Wells being a conductor on the Butterfield route who was killed in a quarrel shortly after establishing the station. In the early 1870s, the station was operated by John P.

Rogers, a Cherokee who had married the daughter of Choctaw Chief Samuel Garland.[385] In 1874, Rogers Station was designated a post office, with Burton Doyle as postmaster. The post office closed in 1878.[386]

By 1958 the log house was gone, replaced by a modern home which still occupies a site about forty feet south of the original structure. The Centennial Committee saw an old well, a clear trace of the trail, large cut stones being used for a walk, and a huge bois d'arc tree growing at the end of the house, all suggesting the station location. They placed the historical marker on the north side of the county road and east of the house, near the stump of an old bois d'arc tree being used as a corner post for a fence. Now, however, the explorer searching along the roadside at Waddell's for the marker near a large tree stump will encounter frustration; it has been moved some distance to the north near a modern barn but is visible from the road with some effort.

The drive from Blackburn's to Waddell's is pleasant, splashing through the Brushy Creek crossing and driving through tree-canopied tunnels of well-graded dirt and gravel roads. It was a picturesque trip "full of delight" for the Centennial Committee as they traveled through the Brushy Creek valley in the shadow of Pine Mountain. Ever conscious of the spring flowers during their May excursion, they reported that blue spiderwort and pink mallow "added charm and color to the grass covered hills."[387]

The Brushy Creek crossing

Chapter Seven: The Grandest View

Butterfield Road sign in the Atoka Wildlife Management Area

Bread Town Stage Stand

I glimpse a small yellow sign as we pass a southbound turn off the gravel road traversing the Atoka Wildlife Management Area (WMA). "I think that sign said Butterfield," I tell Bill, and we put on the brakes, turn around, and go back. We have driven only about three and a half miles from Waddell's on a county road that closely follows the Overland Mail route. Sure enough, it's a yellow metal sign with "Butterfield" cut into it. But, lulled into complacency by similar road signs in the refuge announcing Horse Camp Road and Breadtown Road and Chili Bend Road, I fail to grasp the significance, thinking, obtusely, that the sign honors the Butterfield's presence in the region, not that it may be pointing us in the direction of an actual

Overland Mail trace. Which it is. We drive on. Pondering this later, I decide to call the Wildlife Management Area and inquire about the sign. Yes, the sign really does indicate a trace of the Butterfield Road and to top that, there are ruins of a stage stand present. Soon I am back at the refuge, meeting Eric Suttles, WMA biologist, at that yellow sign. We follow Butterfield Road a short distance south and park, then walk into the woods on an old road trace. No more than one hundred feet from our parking spot, the ruins of Bread Town Stage Stand appear. In 1855, Hattie Frazier established the stand along a stream now known as Bread Town Creek. It was not on the Butterfield itinerary but operated during the life of the Overland Mail and after the Civil War. The bread Hattie baked and sold there gave the stand its name. She was known for selling good, reasonably priced food and owned and operated a small farm in connection with her restaurant.[388] Although she is described only as "an Indian woman" in a WPA report, she may have been Hetty Hamalula Tubby Frazier, a Chickasaw who was married to Jackson Frazier, an elected chief of the Chickasaw District of the Choctaw Nation, sometime before 1849 and until his death in 1856. In 1863, she married Cyrus Harris, first governor of the Chickasaw Nation.[389]

In the 1930s, when WPA field worker Joe Southern examined the site, a spring and some foundation and chimney stones remained. Today it is much the same, a stone enclosure protecting the spring and a crumbling rock wall on the creek side harboring a coiled-up cottonmouth on one of my visits. Exploring another day, I walk a visible trace of the trail both north and south of the stand, imagining how the smell of fresh bread once attracted travelers to this spot. Like so many others, the Bread Town site was abandoned with the coming of the railroad. Prompted by the form he was filling out to consider the site's suitability for a state park, Southern wrote that the surrounding area was mountainous and covered with native timber, abundant with deer and other wild game, and its nearby streams were filled with fish. [390] It had apparently changed little since November 1870, when Texas Road traveler Joseph Edmonds reported in the same region panthers and thousands of wolves, deer and wild cats amid mountains covered with evergreens.[391] A perfect place for a future wildlife management area, it seems.

The Overland Mail road continues on its winding course through the refuge. The distance from Waddell's to Geary's Station is only thirteen miles, but required three hours for Ormsby's rig owing to the difficulty of the road, which crossed the hills to avoid going far out of the way to the north. South of the refuge and northeast of Stringtown, the stage road runs through a private ranch, and just south of the ranch the county road closely follows the path of the old road for a short distance. The mail road entered Stringtown through Grants Gap, now occupied by a rock crushing plant.[392] Stringtown's organization dates to 1872 with the coming of the railroad, and the story goes that Stringtown was to have been called "Springtown" because of the "never failing springs of pure water" nearby. Both railroad and postal officials have been blamed for erroneously replacing the "p" with a "t", changing Springtown to Stringtown. Edmonds' 1870 account, however, mentions the community using the "Stringtown" spelling, predating the railroad by one or two years and the post office by four, making these legends suspect.[393] Another tale of the town's naming has an early-day traveler passing through on the stage, noting the village's few buildings strung out along the foot of the hills, and dubbing the place "Stringtown" accordingly.[394] This version is supported by the son of E.H. Culbertson, who came to the area in 1868. "We located at the old Sulphur Springs where Stringtown is now. My father being a blacksmith and carpenter he selected this place to put up a shop, it being about one-half mile below the forks of the Ft. Smith and Texas and the Kansas and Texas road." The road later became the main street of the little town which they named Stringtown, he said, "because it was strung up and down the road." Whatever the origin of its name,

Stringtown was a stage stand on post-war mail routes, reported as twenty-eight miles from Brushy Jim Colbert's. The Conklings were told of a log station building which was demolished in 1884.[395] This may have been E.H Culbertson's stage stop, established in 1869 at his home near a large spring. He maintained a barn there for horses, providing a change of teams for the stages, and his blacksmith shop conducted business with the post-war stage line and travelers along the road.[396]

Nearby, as the Culbertson scion mentioned, the Overland Mail intersected the Texas Road, which Grant Foreman considered the most important of Oklahoma's early thoroughfares. Beginning as a trail leading from St. Louis to trading posts among the Osage, it served as a trade route as early as 1802 and by the 1820s was the primary north-south pathway for settlers through Indian Territory, helping to populate Texas. Emigrants, traders and military expeditions used it heavily until the coming of the railroad. From the northeastern corner of Indian Territory, the Texas Road ran south through the Grand River valley, then crossed the Choctaw Nation on a southwesterly angle to the Red River. Along it in 1820, the United Foreign Mission Society established Union Mission, the earliest Protestant mission in Indian Territory, on the Grand River near present-day Mazie. There the first school in Indian Territory opened in 1821 and the territory's first book was printed in 1835. Near the present town of Salina, influential trader Auguste Pierre Chouteau conducted business and, around 1822, built his large residence, La Grand Saline. In 1824, the U.S. Army established Fort Gibson near the Texas Road. Along its course farther south at Honey Springs occurred the largest military engagement of the Civil War in the Indian Territory. With the battle's outcome favoring the federals, the Confederates lost control of Indian Territory north of the Arkansas River, and a route to Fort Smith was opened to the northern army.[397] At the junction of the Canadian River (the "South Canadian") with its North Fork (the "North Canadian") and the intersection of the Texas Road with the California Road, the important settlement of North Fork Town arose, where gold seekers bound for California rendezvoused and bought supplies. Around 1840, thirty miles farther south, James Perry established the trading post of Perryville then, near Geary's Station, the Texas Road converged with the Fort Smith-Boggy Depot Road, probably on the southwestern outskirts of present-day Stringtown, where the railroad was built. The first railroad built through the Indian Territory, the Missouri, Kansas and Texas ("Katy Railroad"), followed the route of the Texas Road and gradually absorbed the traffic previously traveled over the thoroughfare. Now the same route is followed by U.S. Highway 69.

Geary's Station

For the two and a half miles from Stringtown to Geary's Station the road ran directly southwest. The Overland Mail station was located on the east side of North Boggy Creek at the home of A.W. Geary, to whom the Choctaw government granted the privilege of erecting a bridge and establishing a toll gate near the crossing of North Boggy on October 21, 1858.[398] Before the establishment of the Overland Mail, Geary, an intermarried Choctaw, was already operating a toll bridge and stage station on the North Boggy.[399] Because the road at this point carried traffic from both the Texas Road and the Fort Smith-Boggy Depot Road, Geary's was a busy crossing.

The Celerity wagon carrying Ormsby arrived at Geary's Station on September 20, 1858, at about 2:30 in the morning. The reporter was still awake after the abrupt disturbance of his sleep at Waddell's, and noted Geary's cultivation of an abundance of land in corn, perhaps a secondhand observation given the hour, but visibility may have been good on that bright, clear night for a good look at the Geary cornfields.

During the Civil War, Geary sold his property and left the area. Shortly after, Alexander McKinney established a station on the west side of North Boggy, about a half-mile southwest of Geary's. McKinney's station went out of business, like so many things, about 1872.[400]

We get some idea of the scenery around this time from Texas Road traveler Joseph Edmonds, who found "a beautiful camping place on a clear running creek by name of North Boggy" opposite a mountain three hundred feet high. This was to Edmonds the loveliest scenery he had ever seen. "Beautiful evergreen trees and trees of green, yellow and brown surround open glades that look like fields of grain surrounded with Osage orange fence. We saw . . . mountains . . . covered with green trees, some ranges of hills and some higher that reach to the calling of mountains, all beautifully arranged.[401]

A short distance south of Stringtown on the west side of U.S. 69, the Conklings found a portion of the original trail in the form of a narrow, rough country road with high centers and steep grades leading west from the highway and past the Geary station site, then across North Boggy to the Alexander McKinney place. Part of this trace can still be explored on foot off Lakeshore Drive, which turns west from U.S. 69 about three-fourths of a mile south of Stringtown. A spot to park off the road provides access to nearly a mile of footpath which follows the stagecoach route to the eastern shore of the Atoka Reservoir. Walking this way through the woods one day, I find myself on a beach less than a quarter-mile from the original location of Geary's, now under the waters of the lake.

The Conklings wrote of the North Boggy crossing, "Here the creek has a fine gravel bed and on the south side, deep ruts in three different places give evidence of the early crossing, and show that the drivers were obliged to shift their course from time to time. And, too, here the road is plainly discernable along the west slope of a range of hills." From the North Boggy crossing to the Alexander McKinney place, the Conklings could still trace the road for about a half-mile. It was a deep, single-track depression grown up with grass leading southwest through the McKinney barnyard and into the forest, which they described as second-growth timber.

In 1958, the Geary's site was the only one not visited by the Centennial Committee. Since it had been cleared and was about to be inundated in connection with the construction of the Atoka Reservoir as a water source for Oklahoma City, the committee saw no purpose in finding its exact location.[402] They recommended the Geary's Station marker be located on a high point overlooking the future body of water, with the added words on the plaque "site inundated." More than sixty years later, the reservoir is a long-standing presence, supplying water through a pipeline to Oklahoma City's Lake Stanley Draper more than one hundred miles to the northwest. A plaque on the Atoka Reservoir's dam commemorates Geary's Station and provides a dramatic view of the lake looking north, toward the inundated site of the Butterfield station.

Old Growth

A short distance north of the Atoka Reservoir dam one late November morning, I board a motorboat on the eastern shore of the lake. It is an odd time of year for a boat ride but the weather is sunny and calm, the ride will be short, and I am both warmly dressed and highly motivated. Less than a mile south of the inundated site of Geary's stage stand, I cast off with Bob Jackman, Andy Price, and Art Peters. As the boat speeds up, I hang on and try to stay out of the cold spray. Andy the boatman navigates expertly across the lake, around an island, and into a narrow cove on the western shore.

This would be the first of several expeditions to the Atoka Reservoir, instigated by Bob Jackman, whom I met in the early years of my Butterfield research. Petroleum geology is Jackman's profession, but activism is his passion. In 2001, he successfully led an effort to

"Save Lake Atoka," working to prevent the city of Oklahoma City from logging the west side of the reservoir, where a fragment of the Ancient Cross Timbers survives, a tract of pristine, old-growth, shortleaf pine and post oak forest. What also survives there are remnants of both the Texas Road and the Butterfield Overland Mail Road.

When we arrive on the lake's western shore, a jon boat is already pulled up on the beach, but no one is in sight. A hunter, I think, surprised. It is the opening day of the 2018 rifle season but we did not realize hunting is allowed on the Oklahoma City-owned property. And perhaps it is not. None of us had the foresight to wear blaze orange to avoid being mistaken for a deer, but we proceed with abandon, evidence that our enthusiasm far outweighs our collective wisdom. Armed with a topographical map bearing a dotted line we think might be the old road, we disembark on a rock-strewn beach and fan out. When Jackman explored this side of the lake on foot nearly fifteen years before, he found distinct road traces which he argued were remnants of the Texas and Butterfield roads. He did not have complete success convincing the Oklahoma Historical Society of the historical value of the road fragments, but he has not given up on proving these swales were left by the wagons of families traveling to Texas and Celerity wagons carrying mail to San Francisco.

Disembarking, Bob and Andy go off in one direction. Art and I go in another and quickly find a road depression. We follow it as far as we can, away from the shore. But it is a dead end, perhaps a spur trail to a homestead, long gone. Soon we hear gunshots and then see a fellow in a blaze orange hat and vest walking our way, empty handed, other than his rifle. He speaks as he passes, graciously refraining from pointing out the foolhardiness of our drab attire. Or perhaps he is simply trying to avoid calling too much attention to himself. Eventually we hear Jackman calling that he has found the road and we gather at a southbound path, a well-defined two-track running from the rocky shore of the lake into a meadow. Rocks are occasionally arranged to border the path, including one standing on its edge, and unnatural wear on stones that could have been created by wagon wheels signals to Jackman we have found the trail. We walk a short distance south in the tracks but the hour is getting late, and soon we have to turn around to return to the boat. Comparing our path with the paper map, we believe we have found a trace of the stagecoach road.

A few years later, Jackman gives me documents from his previous work at Lake Atoka, including photographs of the traces he found in the early 2000s. The images look nothing like what we saw in 2018. Instead of a two-track in the prairie, they show a deep swale, more akin to the deep, single-track depression reported by the Conklings. I also acquire a new tool: a map layer in the GaiaGPS smartphone application which allows concurrent GPS navigation against a historical map circa 1900. Comparing our 2018 path with the old road on the historical map, doubt begins to niggle at me about what we found at the Atoka Reservoir. In March 2022 I return for another look. This time, I walk in alone from the south end of the lake, a hard slog of a couple of miles through thick shoreline underbrush. Eventually I find an easy trail that takes me right to the two-track we came across in 2018. But it is a thousand feet east of the old road's location, according to the map. Walking west toward the stagecoach trail, I climb nearly two hundred feet up a ridge. Near the top, I find what looks a road, but it is not quite on the path shown on the map, which appears to be higher still. By that time, the lateness of the hour and a substantial return hike force me to postpone more exploration.

It is nine months before I get back to the Atoka Reservoir, this time with my friends Mary and Kurt McDaniel, vigorous hikers with a high tolerance for uncertainty, essential characteristics for an outing like this. We retrace my earlier path to the point on the ridge where I found what looked like an old road, then tromp northeast over rocky, steep terrain toward the location on the lake shore where we should find the abandoned road entering the woods from the McKinney place. Sticking close to the line on the map, we struggle to maintain any feeling whatsoever that we are on a trail. We are tackling steep, boulder-strewn ascents and negotiating equally steep and rocky descents, a route unfit for a stage wagon. Rarely do we see anything that looks like a road trace until, nearing the lake, we spy a deep rut that is unmistakably a road, coming out of the water. At its deepest point it is perhaps eighteen inches to two feet, eroded by years of wear, converging with the lake about one-half mile west of the McKinney Cemetery, according to a pre-inundation USGS topo map.

After a short break on the lake shore, we turn around for the return hike, this time following the rut visually. It is now so distinct that we stay in it continuously as we walk southwest through large, twisted post oaks and tall pines, parallel to our outbound route, which sits a short distance above us on the ridge. Our road trace is clearly delineated, sometimes with large rocks piled along the roadside. The terrain ascends gradually, a logical path for a wagon versus the difficult route we took on the way out. After walking about a mile to the southwest, we converge with our starting point, and I am convinced we are literally on the historic track of the Overland Mail. There at an elevation some one hundred fifty feet above the lake, I look back toward the east and share Joseph Edmonds' awe at the view, looking out over the rugged terrain and the water below. Near his camp on the west side of North Boggy, Edmonds wrote:

(Went to the) top of the mountain and well it paid us to go: the grandest view I have ever seen. It is impossible to picture it with pen and ink. Mountain scenery, woodland valley and prairie glade all in one view. It is glorious to behold. I don't know what it would be in the sunshine, trees of every hue, size and color. The beautiful clear stream far below glides sweetly past with a gentle murmur. These are some of the glories of our God. These are some of His designs and handiwork.[403]

Looking east from the stagecoach road on the west side of the Atoka Reservoir

This may be one of the only places in Oklahoma where traces of the old trail run through a landscape that looks much as it did in 1858. I contact David Stahle, the dendrochronologist from the University of Arkansas who established the Ancient Cross Timbers Consortium and whom Bob Jackman consulted for help in making his case to prevent logging at the Atoka Reservoir. Stahle's team studied a section of the forest on the west side of the lake and found it one hundred per cent old-growth mixed post oak and shortleaf pine. From that sample, he was able to determine that the old growth is extensive on the west side of Lake Atoka. The steep, rocky slopes were probably never farmed, said Stahle, "Level ground could be cleared and farmed but steep ground not so much. . . . if any old growth is going to survive it's going to be on steep, rocky slopes." The pines and post oaks standing today are two hundred fifty to three hundred years old and, remarkably, were standing when the Overland Mail stage wagons came rushing by.[404]

In 1930, the mail road was already abandoned from Geary's to Boggy Depot, although segments could still be traced through a few sections of fenced land.[405] From the North Boggy crossing, the road ran southwest then turned slightly southeast to a log bridge over the Muddy (Middle) Boggy at Atoka. The bridge was operated by a distant relative of Bob Jackman's, James D. Davis, who, in October, 1858, was granted a charter by the Choctaw General Council to build and operate a toll bridge there.[406] Davis was an intermarried Choctaw, "who took an active interest in the affairs in the Nation during his life time."[407] Just north of that crossing, a short segment of the stagecoach road is preserved at the Atoka County Museum and Civil War Cemetery. A tall granite marker in the middle of the trace memorializes the Butterfield, which runs alongside a cemetery first established by travelers who camped at a spring just north of the river. During the Civil War, Confederate forces occupied the site from time to time and used it as an outpost later in the conflict to guard the route to Boggy Depot, which was by then the main supply depot for Confederate troops in Indian Territory. In the winter of 1862, a measles outbreak killed a number of soldiers with the 19th Arkansas Infantry who were en route to Fort McCulloch to help build earthworks, and they are buried here.

Side Trip: Mrs. Flack's

After crossing the Muddy (Middle) Boggy, the stage wagons traversed the present site of Atoka, passing a well-known traveler's stop, Mrs. Flack's, "on the west side of the old stage line as it passed the present site of Atoka."[408] Eliza Ann Flack was born in 1819 or 1820 into the Juzan family in Mississippi, her father a Frenchman and her mother a Choctaw. About 1838, she married Hugh C. Flack and the couple moved west and settled in the Choctaw Nation. About 1853 or 1854 the Flacks (or Mrs. Flack, it is not clear when her husband died) moved to a site on the south side of the Middle Boggy and there established a stage stand. Mrs. Flack and James D. Davis were described as the oldest citizens of Atoka and owned most of the land in the area.[409] In 1872, the Missouri, Kansas and Texas Railroad purchased one of her cornfields for their Atoka station.[410] Her stand on the Butterfield route was "celebrated far and wide for its clean, nice tables and good eating." She was described as a strong and forceful character and a person of great generosity and large influence.[411] Mrs. Flack died July 25, 1890 and is buried in Atoka's Westview Cemetery. The location of her stage stand was in the vicinity of present-day A Street between Pennsylvania and Ohio Avenues in Atoka.[412]

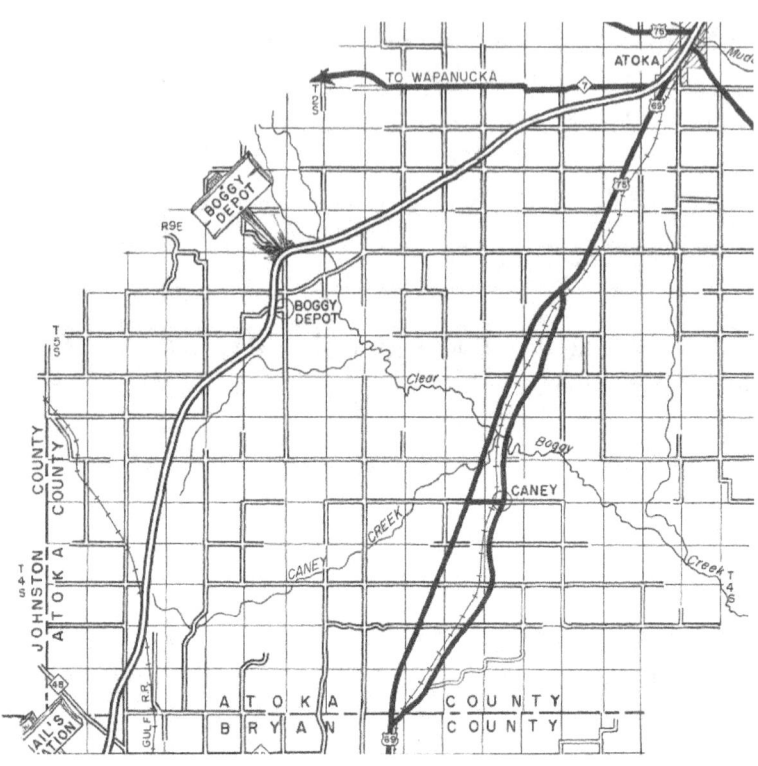

Butterfield Trail - Western Atoka County, including Boggy Depot. Adapted from original map courtesy of Oklahoma Historical Society. See Eastern LeFlore County map, page 40, for map legend.

The Skullyville Constitution

Beyond Atoka, westbound stagecoach passengers were probably relieved to leave the rough mountain roads behind and enjoy flatter terrain as they approached Boggy Depot.[413] Ormsby's transport made short work of the seventeen-mile trip from Geary's, arriving in only two and a half hours. In Boggy Depot, Ormsby learned that "an Indian" had been shot in a quarrel over the Skullyville Constitution a few days before. "The nation is divided on the question of forming a State government," he wrote. "The two parties wax strong on their respective sides, and frequent collisions are the consequence. I do not wish to be unfair on the subject, but I am given to understand that the half-breeds and whites and more intelligent full-bloods are in favor of the State government."[414] This situation resulted from radical changes to the Choctaw constitution following the 1855 separation from the Choctaws. When the Choctaws first moved to the Indian Territory, they re-established the same three autonomous political districts they had in the old country, each with its own elected chief. The new constitution, adopted in Skullyville in 1857, abolished the traditional office of district chief and consolidated the executive role into the office of Governor. This centralization of power was an unwelcome shift for those who adhered to traditional ways, as was the fact that the governing document's structure seemed to be laying the groundwork for statehood. The constitution also authorized the Choctaw General Council to permit slaveowners to emancipate slaves and to limit the introduction of slaves into the nation, actions interpreted by opponents as abolitionist.[415] The legality of the document's adoption was also questioned since it was not submitted to a vote of the people and, not surprisingly, the jurisdiction of Tandy Walker, serving as Governor under the new constitution, was considered illegitimate by many. Opponents of the Skullyville Constitution met at Doaksville in May of 1858, wrote a new constitution and elected their own set of officers. The Choctaw Nation verged on civil war over this dispute and Ormsby passed through when the crisis had reached its highest intensity, precipitating violence and bringing the nation's government to a halt. Ultimately the federal government intervened, sending its agents Elias Rector and Albert Pike to meet with representatives of both Choctaw factions. Under threats of military force if no resolution could be reached, the Choctaw council acted within days to restore the offices of the district chiefs, although the bulk of the power remained with an elected governor. Ten days later the council agreed to submit the question of a new constitutional convention to a popular vote. In January 1860 at a convention in Doaksville, delegates framed a new constitution retaining the traditional district organization with its chiefs and courts, but also providing for a national government with a principal chief, bicameral general council, and supreme court. With few changes, this constitution remained in effect throughout the remainder of the nineteenth century. One legacy of the Skullyville constitution is its official seal which, with bow, crossed arrows and combined pipe and hatchet, now forms part of the Great Seal of Oklahoma.[416]

Boggy Depot

Ormsby's description of Boggy Depot as "several painted houses and a few stores"[417] sounds inconsequential, but the settlement was the largest on the Indian Territory segment of the Butterfield route. It was the temporary capital of the Choctaw Nation under the Skullyville Constitution when Ormsby stopped there before dawn on September 20, 1858. He would have seen little of the town but may have eaten an early breakfast at Guy's Hotel, where the station was located, on the public square. Besides the hotel, a number of homes, a church and school, several stores and warehouses, a livery, blacksmith shop, grist mill and brick kiln comprised the community.[418] Thomas J. Bond, a physician in Boggy Depot, wrote to Peter Pitchlynn in September 1858 that the Overland Mail coaches were enlivening the community as they passed by each day, reminding them of the "March of Civilization." The road between Fort Smith and Boggy Depot was, he reported, "very much improved and the streams were then being bridged."[419]

Boggy Depot's origin coincides with the 1838 migration of the Chickasaws to the western part of the Choctaw Nation. A road had to be opened for their journey from Fort Coffee, and the effort to get the Chickasaws to their new homes met with many challenges, including a smallpox epidemic in which 500 to 600 died. A poor corn crop caused by drought required that corn be shipped up the Red River, then hauled overland, and beef had to be driven on the hoof from Arkansas. In 1838, government agent William Armstrong reported most of the migrating Chickasaws settled near the Blue and Clear Boggy Rivers, where a supply depot was established, thus the depot on the Boggy became "Boggy Depot." In these early days establishing blacksmith shops was a high priority in order to provide tools and other essential works of metal. In 1838 Armstrong reported a blacksmith up and running on the Boggy, a stream which also boasted sufficient water for grist and saw mills. Armstrong pledged to get construction of the grist and saw mills underway, writing he would endeavor to have a good mill as soon as possible where only a year or two before "the wild Indians roamed."[420]

William R. Guy, whose hotel hosted Overland Mail passengers, came west with the Chickasaws in 1837 as a commissary and assistant conductor, settling in Boggy Depot and marrying Jane McGee, a Chickasaw. During the early 1840s he established a mill on Clear Boggy and became the town's first postmaster in 1849 when a post office was established for weekly mail service between Fort Smith, Boggy Depot, and Fort Washita.[421] By 1858, Guy had died and the Choctaw government granted his heirs permission to build a bridge across Clear Boggy and a tollgate near their mill about a mile east of Boggy Depot on the stagecoach road.

Confederate troops occupied the town during the Civil War, and after the conflict Boggy Depot soon went into decline in the familiar story . . . the coming of the railroad sounded its death knell. In 1870, the stage road still passed through, and Edmonds described it as an old government station and a "tolerable village for the Nation."[422] But in 1871 the stage road took a new route south of Boggy Depot and the town gradually moved south. The new community was called New Boggy Depot.[423] Eight miles to the east, the railroad laid its tracks through what is now Tushka and, predictably, trade diminished. Gradually the population shifted to towns near the railroad until by the early 1880s Boggy Depot was almost deserted.[424] By 1927, "Old" Boggy Depot, so-called to distinguish it from New Boggy Depot, had disappeared except for the ruins of a few houses. One of these was Allen Wright's, built in 1860 and by that time one of the last antebellum homes in Oklahoma. Wright was arguably Boggy Depot's most famous resident and made what has been the most enduring of Boggy Depot's contributions to Oklahoma, the state's name. Born in Mississippi in 1826, Wright moved with his family in a self-emigrating party in 1833 to Indian Territory. By 1856 he was an ordained Presbyterian minister and elected to the Choctaw General Council. In 1866 he became principal chief and was re-elected in 1868. At the onset of the Civil War, Wright signed the Choctaw treaty of alliance with the Confederacy, and he served in the Confederate Army. He represented the Choctaws at the Fort Smith Council and signed the Reconstruction Treaty of 1866. When U.S. commissioners proposed the consolidation of Indian Territory's tribes under an intertribal council, Wright suggested the region be designated the "Territory of Oklahoma," "Oklahoma" being a Choctaw phrase meaning "Red People." After that, the name was in common usage, given officially to Oklahoma Territory in 1890 and to the state in 1907. Allen Wright died at Boggy Depot on December 2, 1885, and was buried in the Boggy Depot cemetery.[425] Another of Wright's lasting legacies was his granddaughter, historian Muriel Wright. She died in 1975 and was buried at Rose Hill Burial Park in Oklahoma City, but a large granite memorial in her honor stands in Boggy Depot cemetery.

The Allen Wright home was still owned by the family in 1927, its chimneys of brick made by Englishman Charles Sparrow, remaining at the time "as perfect as when they were first erected." Clumps of chinaberry trees then marked empty home sites and a trace of the stage road remained.[426] By 1932, the other houses were "crumbling ruins of . . . foundations, half-hidden among china berry trees and brambles" and only Allen Wright's house still stood.[427] It was destroyed by fire on March 28, 1952.

In 1958, the State of Oklahoma made Boggy Depot a memorial state park in conjunction with Oklahoma's 1957 Semi-Centennial. When the Centennial Committee came through that year they could see the "well defined outlines" of the stagecoach trail between the crossing on Clear Boggy and the park as they entered Boggy Depot from the east. In the center of the trace, at the extreme eastern limit of the park, they placed the historical marker.[428]

Today Boggy Depot is a peaceful and attractive recreation area, far from the beaten path. It is managed by the Chickasaw Nation and offers space for camping and picnicking. Signage marks the sites of Allen Wright's home and other landmarks, and a map at the entrance offers a key to the layout of the old town. The historical marker placed in 1958 sits intact at the east entrance to the park, in the trace mentioned by the committee. On the south side is a notable depression where the old road exits.

Memorial to Muriel Wright in the Boggy Depot Cemetery

On one of our journeys, Bill and I camp in this hallowed spot, the only people to do so that night. The tree-shaded grounds make for lovely camping and we enjoy a roaring fire and the howls of nearby coyotes. Just before sunrise the next morning I walk a quiet nature trail to a large pond, "Little Cedar Lake," on the western edge of the park. During these same pre-dawn moments Ormsby's wagon rolled away from this place--once a bustling community and now only a distant memory--for more adventure farther west.

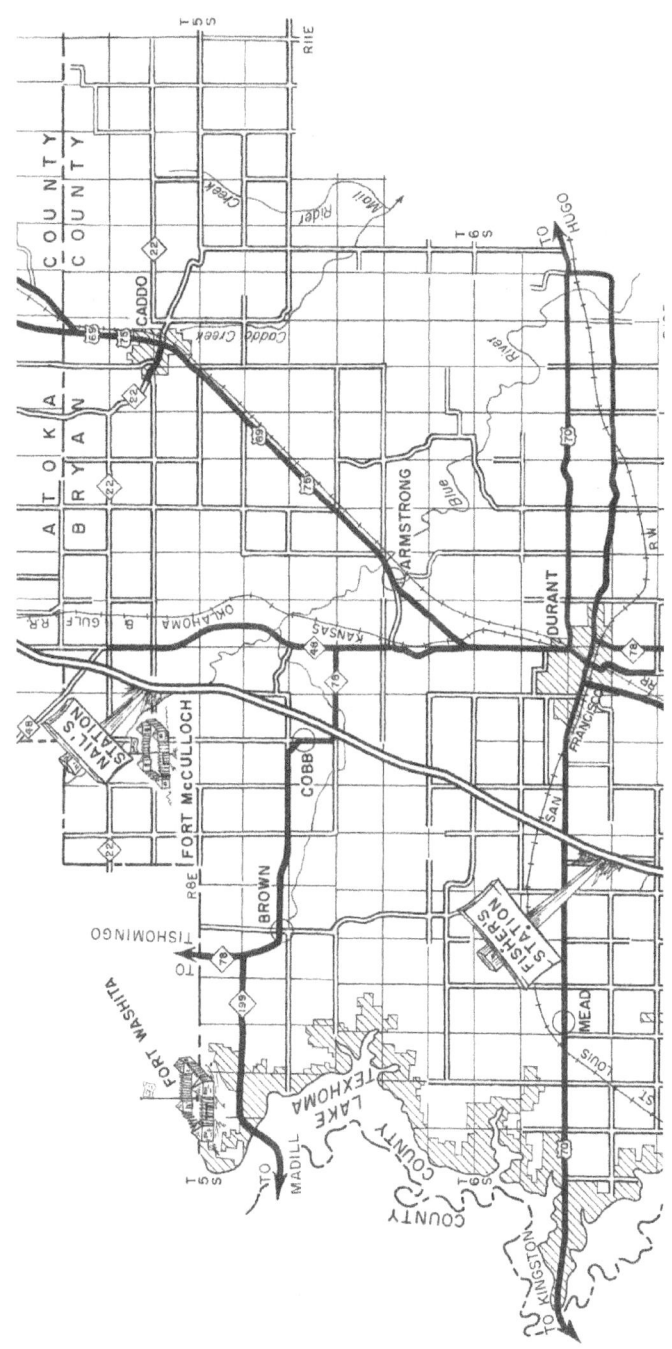

Previous Page: Butterfield Trail - Northern Bryan County, including Nail's and Fisher's Stations. Adapted from original map courtesy of Oklahoma Historical Society. See Eastern LeFlore County map, page 40, for map legend.

Chapter Eight: A Limpid Stream and the New York Herald

Shawn Rowland at the Nail's Crossing marker

Nail's Crossing

"Do y'all need some help?" The sun has fallen below the horizon and Bill and I have given up our search. We walk across the field, heading back to the truck. That afternoon we had driven to the end of Nails Crossing Road near the community of Kenefic and set off on foot to find the remnants of the Butterfield station and the Nail family cemetery. We located the grave plot easily enough but now are stymied in our attempt on the monument marking the site of the Nail station.

The imminent darkness hastens our steps, but the figure calling out stops us in our tracks.

"We sure do," I tell the young man approaching us. Shawn Rowland and his family are neighbors and run cattle on this property. His father informed him we were here looking around and, since it was getting dark, he came to check on us.

Thankful for his kindness, I tell him we're looking for the station marker.

"Okay, I think I can take you there," says Rowland. And he does. We walk briskly through tall grass among copses of cedars, past the cemetery and off to the northwest. Finally in near darkness we find it between two piles of rubble, the 1958 Oklahoma Historical Society marker for Nail's Station, its concrete base and bronze plaque in perfect condition. Except for Waddell's, it is the only marker in the series not located on a public road, accounting for its well-preserved state. We look around for a few minutes but it is getting too dark to find the stagecoach road and river crossing, so we discuss a return trip as we walk back to the truck with Rowland. "You should talk to Russell Washington. He's lived here for a long time and knows a lot about the trail," he says. We agree to do that on our next visit and call it a day, thankful for Rowland's intervention and highly satisfied at getting to see this historical treasure.

Ormsby's arrival at Nail's was on the other end of daylight from ours, at nearly seven o'clock in the morning on Monday, September 20, 1858. He had traveled seventeen miles from Boggy Depot, crossing several streams in the first few miles, then rolling over prairies. By the time the Conklings came through, this stretch of road was abandoned, though they could plainly see traces in fenced fields and stream crossings. They also noticed deep ruts across a large outcropping of limestone a short distance north of Nail's. Today a rock quarry sits about a mile north of Nail's, likely the remnant of that outcropping.[429] Flourishing in the bottomlands, the "peculiar bois d'arc," or Osage

Orange tree, was a point of interest for the Conklings. Sixty years before, Edmonds also commented on the bois d'arcs, spotting specimens two to four feet thick.[430] Large bois d'arcs continue to thrive in the Blue River bottom, as Bill and I can attest after hours wandering around looking for the marker.

At Nail's, Ormsby found a copy of his own newspaper, the *New York Herald*, surprisingly far from New York City. Station keeper Jonathan H. Nail belonged to a prominent mixed-blood Choctaw family, among the dominant political faction before removal and remaining so in the west.[431] Born in 1825 in Mississippi, Nail settled on Blue River in the 1840s, establishing a mill on the stream, which appeared deep blue as it ran over a bed of blue limestone and clay.[432] Sometimes the river was called by its French name, "L'eau Bleu," spelled "Low Blue" or "Loe Blue" in English.[433] As farmer, rancher and slaveholder,[434] Nail had reason to be interested in the important events of the United States and reading the *Herald* was one mechanism for staying informed. He was not unique in this: Red Oak post office customers in 1868 subscribed to such periodicals as *Harper's Monthly* and *Frank Leslie's Monthly* along with regional newspapers.[435] Jonathan Nail's land holdings extended to the east eight miles from Blue River to the present town of Caddo and touched the Twelve-Mile Prairie on the south and southwest. Built around 1850, Nail's large house on high ground just east of the river was originally a one-and-a-half story double log structure, forty-two feet long by twenty feet wide. The red brick in the tall outside chimneys came from Charles Sparrow, English brick mason of Boggy Depot whose product was also used in Allen Wright's chimney. Jonathan Nail's son Joel inherited the property and lived on the place until the late 1870s. In 1930 it was still in the family, and by that time the house's log exterior was clapboarded. The original chimneys were still in place, each of its six rooms having a fireplace.[436] Modern structures had replaced log outbuildings and barns, but foundation ruins were visible as were remains of a wooden fence with tall oak posts and ornamental tops which once enclosed the station.[437] A high stone stile marked the entrance to the front yard from the mail road. Surmising that in its heyday it must have presented an "air of distinction and comfort," the Conklings also noted that the Nail home, along with Walker's, was among the last four remaining log house stations along the entire Butterfield route. By the time the Centennial Committee arrived in 1958, only piles of brick and stone marked the location of the house. They selected a site for the marker between the heaps of rubble, which is where we found it.

During Ormsby's visit, a heavy bridge was under construction across the Blue River for the use of the Overland Mail. Whether this bridge survived the Civil War is unknown, although with Confederate troops encamped on the west bank of the Blue at Fort McCulloch, a bridge over the stream may have been maintained. There is reference to Confederate General Albert Pike's presence at "Nail's Bridge" during the war.[438] In 1866, the Choctaw General Council granted Jonathan Nail a five-year charter for a toll bridge across Blue River at his premises on "the Boggy and Sherman Road," referring to the endpoint of Sherman, Texas, across the Red River. The next year, Nail died at the age of 42. His widow, Catherine Nail, married David A. Folsom, of another powerful mixed-blood family. Before the end of 1867, Folsom obtained a renewed charter in his name.[439] Over the years, various bridges spanned the Blue River at this spot. A photograph from a September 1910 issue of the *Caddo Herald* pictures a wagon bridge. W.B. Morrison wrote in 1926 that remains of a dam were still to be seen, and bits of the cable for the ferry boat, "used in times of high water or for those who preferred not to risk the ford, or the crude bridge, for at times a wooden bridge spanned the stream at this point."[440]

The Conklings were able to identify "some of the decayed timbers of the old bridge . . . submerged along the east bank of the stream at the crossing." In later years, according to Jonathan Nail's grandson,

Claude Nail, the water at the crossing was about knee deep and rocks were placed across the river so it could be forded without getting wet. Even when bridges were present the embankments on each side would sometimes wash out, so that the stage and other horse-drawn buggies still had to ford the river.[441]

Margaret Conkling extolled the beauty of late fall at Blue River, "flowing gently between elm, oak, and sycamore-lined banks, all russet and scarlet with glimpses of grassy slopes extending down to the water's edge." The Conklings called Nail's Crossing "an ideal resort location"[442] and the Centennial Committee described it as "one of the most beautiful spots on the entire Oklahoma route."[443] Indeed, its recreational opportunities were enjoyed by the surrounding community and the *Caddo Herald* kept folks abreast of the many outings occurring at "Nail Crossing."[444] In August 1912 the Thursday Music Club entertained with a moonlight picnic at Nail Crossing, having "a most delightful time."[445] In May 1911 an auto party from Caddo drove to Nail Crossing, taking their kodaks along.[446] Picnicking, baptism, and overnight camping took place there. In September 1915 Durant Boy Scout Troop No. 1 spent a week at Nail's "fishing, swimming, and in fact, everything that goes to make up a healthful body and an alert, sound mind."[447] In 1895 R.P. Dickey, Physician and Surgeon, advertised his services at the Jackson & Co. store on Blue, near Nail Crossing and the community that grew up around the crossing also had its own Odd Fellows Lodge, instituted in 1924.[448]

Visible evidence of this once-thriving community is noticeably absent today. Other than the historical marker amid the rubble, there are a cistern, a set of stone steps descending into a nearly buried cellar, a road trace leading north, vestiges of a bridge, and the Nail family cemetery.

The Nail family cemetery

The grave plot, southeast of the station site, is surrounded by a wrought iron fence and dominated by a tall monument. Upon Catherine Nail Folsom's death in 1917, the *Caddo Herald* reported she was interred "in the depths of that silent forest inclosed (sic) by an iron fence, in the midst of the square a stately cedar and beneath its drooping branches a family monument with four sides."[449] The monument, purchased by Mrs. Folsom before her death, bears the name of her first husband, Jonathan Nail, her second husband, David

Folsom, and her brother, J.H. Foster. The fourth side, intended for an inscription honoring Mrs. Folsom, is blank, but a marker placed in 2011 at its base indicates she is buried there. In 1958, the cemetery was unkempt, "a jungle of trees, wild vines, climbing roses and iris, all in bloom." The Centennial Committee hoped that the Historical Society would acquire the plot and maintain it as a memorial. It did not. The cemetery was just as untidy in 2019. The tall central marker still stood erect, though with a list suggesting support would soon be needed to prevent its collapse. Soon after, the brush and trees in the cemetery were cleared by the Choctaw Nation, improving things somewhat.

In February 2021 we visit the site again, following up on Shawn Rowland's recommendation to connect with neighbor Russell Washington, who, we learn, played a role in another significant event in Oklahoma history. In 1978, escaped murderers Claude Dennis and Michael Lancaster were driving a truck they stole from Washington when their thirty-three-day, multi-state killing spree finally ended at nearby Caddo. The pair had escaped from the Oklahoma State Penitentiary in McAlester and gone on a rampage that left eight people dead, including three Oklahoma Highway Patrolmen, triggering manhunts in eleven states. The killers came to Washington's home and held him captive but, miraculously in his opinion, left him unharmed when they took his truck and drove into a roadblock near Kenefic, where the pair were finally killed.[450] A marker at the Indian Territory Museum in Caddo memorializes the lost troopers, and visitors can learn more about the incident from a newspaper collection. The museum also houses quirky collections illuminating the history of Caddo including a jail cell and replicas of a blacksmith shop, photographer's darkroom, dentist's office, lawyer's office, and post office. The photo-lined walls include an image of the Nail house.

We walk with Washington to the river on the trace of the mail road, winding through thorny black locust trees covered with lichen and moss. The embankment is steep on the east side of the river, but the crossing spot itself is shallow, with a wide rock ledge. "Blue river here is a limpid flowing stream that has cut a channel for itself through thin and almost horizontal beds of limestone," the Conklings wrote. One of Margaret Conkling's photos shows Roscoe wading across the stream,[451] where they saw "a profuse distribution of fossil marine animal and plant life exposed in the limestone beds, evidently of Cretaceous age," including cephalopods and other mollusks. A short distance north of the Nail house they found a coiled mollusk twenty-six inches in diameter lying in the eroded track of the old mail road. In 1958 the Centennial Committee also commented on the "fossiliferous" nature of the limestone bed of Blue River, where they saw clear traces of the ford and imagined great excitement at Nail's Crossing for both the stage drivers and passengers of the Overland Mail: "With four fresh horses, eager to go, and a fairly steep river bank to descend, the driver must really have had to ride the brake and pull leather to avoid a catastrophy (sic)."[452]

Side Trip: Fort McCulloch

On the opposite bank of Blue River, west of Nail's, Bill and I find ourselves squeezing through a barbed wire fence with only the most minimal of instructions. "You'll feel the road," Jack Risner assures us, sending us into the river bottom on foot.

After crossing Blue River, the stagecoach road came to a crossroads. A westbound spur led to Fort Washita, about ten miles away. The mail road turned south and continued about fourteen miles over rolling prairies to Fisher's Station. During the Civil War, Fort McCulloch, the main Confederate fortification in southern Indian Territory, occupied this site on the west bank of the Blue. In the spring of 1862, after the battle of Pea Ridge, General Albert Pike withdrew to this point deep in the Choctaw Nation and established the outpost, naming it for General Benjamin McCulloch, who died at Pea Ridge.

Extensive earth works were the only permanent structures; the troops lived in tents and other temporary dwellings. The strategic location of Fort McCulloch at the crossroads allowed Confederate control of the roads leading north to Missouri, east to Fort Smith, west to Fort Washita, and south to Sherman, Texas.[453] The Conklings stopped here on their explorations, describing the fort's ruins as "a large earthwork forming a sort of redoubt in the shape of a great four or five pointed star." It was overgrown with weeds, grass and young trees and the couple saw resemblance between the manmade emplacement and the work of native Mound Builders. "Some enterprising investigator," they wrote, "evidently possessed of this view, has cut a cross-section through one part of the earthwork. Near the earthwork are a number of ruins which appear to have been dug-outs or rude shelters of some sort." These may have been remains of the arsenal pits, where ammunition was stored.[454]

Only the earthworks now remain at Fort McCulloch, where we meet property owner Risner and his potbellied pig, Ophelia. Her benign nature contrasts sharply with the noise coming from the house of loudly barking, vicious-sounding dogs. Thankfully, they are locked up securely, or so we hope. We examine the tall manmade mounds with our host, then, with his vague directions, begin our trudge through the river bottom to look for traces of the stagecoach trail. The road is barely discernible and we track it only briefly before it disappears.

Artifacts from Fort McCulloch

Soon we are bushwhacking through dense undergrowth and postholing in soft, deep mud as we turn north along the river bank looking for the crossing. Eventually we find a cut in the bank, steep for a wagon crossing but many years of erosion could have changed the spot considerably. Our visit here precedes our access to the east bank, so we lack that point of reference, and Risner says there are several crossings in the area. We have, at least, located what appears to be one of them.

As we return to the Risner place, an opening in the trees starts to feel very much like a road, and we realize we are on track. Or at least on some track. Risner said large flat stones stood up on edge are an indicator of the trail and we see these along the clear, level path. We emerge on a westbound trace, which we conclude is the road to Fort Washita.

Ruins at Fort Washita Historic Site

Side Trip: Fort Washita

In 1834, when the Chickasaws negotiated a treaty with the U.S. government, they agreed to migrate west if provided protection from the Plains tribes controlling the adjoining lands. They were assigned a tract in the western section of the Choctaw Nation, but at first stayed close to existing Choctaw settlements. By 1838 the government had not fulfilled its promise of protection and the Chickasaws refused to settle on their assigned lands, insisting a fort be built near the mouth of the Washita River. "During this time, tensions continued to grow between the Chickasaw and Choctaw, who initially occupied the same area of the Indian Territory," wrote retired Chickasaw historian and archaeologist Towana Spivey. "The Chickasaw wanted to regain their political independence and secure lands of their own. The fear of being completely absorbed under the political control of their old adversaries, the Choctaw, weighed heavily on tribal leaders."[455] In 1842 the fort was finally established and the Chickasaws began to settle in their designated territory. Construction of permanent buildings on the high, forested land about one and one-half miles east of the Washita River began in 1843 and the post's structures, built of limestone quarried in the region, some of them two stories high, eventually included a hospital and barracks. The fort even boasted such luxuries as a bar, library, newspaper and bowling alley. The Conklings wrote, "No other army post on the western frontier could boast of a more healthful and picturesque location than Fort Washita. Epidemics of illness, often so fatal at many other posts, were never recorded here."

Fort Washita served as supply depot and military stronghold during the Mexican War, 1846 to 1848, and after the war was a launching point for military explorers headed into the newly acquired territory to the southwest. In the 1850s, it served as a stop for gold seekers bound for California, where they could refresh and regroup. With the establishment of the Overland Mail, the Butterfield line supplied the post's mail via the Boggy Depot post office. On May 1, 1861, federal troops abandoned Fort Washita; one day later a company of Texas Rangers took possession. Confederate forces occupied the fort during the Civil War, using it as a supply depot and hospital. Later, Fort Washita became the property of the Chickasaw Nation. Eventually the grounds were allotted to tribal members, the Colbert family.[456]

The Conklings noted that Fort Washita was one of three early military posts which were abandoned but still stood along the old mail road, remote and isolated but "well enough preserved in their old setting to permit one to peer back over the years and picture them as they were in that old time." The other two are Fort Phantom Hill near Abilene, Texas, and Fort Chadbourne near Bronte, Texas, and both are still maintained as historic sites. When the Conklings saw Fort Washita, many of the barracks and officers' quarters were still standing along grass-grown streets. Some of the buildings had been converted into homes. In 1962 the State of Oklahoma purchased the land and transferred it to the Oklahoma Historical Society, which began restoration. One of the barracks was reconstructed but later burned. Fort Washita Historic Site is now owned by the Chickasaw Nation; it is a beautiful spot where visitors can tour tree-shaded grounds, admiring both restored structures and those in ruins, some retaining a haunting grandeur.[457]

Chapter Nine: The End of the Line

Fisher's Station

Back on the Overland Mail road, Waterman Ormsby had nothing to say about Fisher's Station, the last stand in the Choctaw Nation. The stagecoach road enters the Chickasaw Nation about three hundred yards west of Fisher's, known after the Civil War as Carriage Point. There the road forked, one branch running southeast toward Colbert's Ferry and Sherman, Texas; the other going southwest, entering Texas at Preston Bend.[458]

Fisher is another station keeper about whom we know little. Correspondence between Roscoe Conkling and Muriel Wright in 1935 indicates she believed the station was connected to Fisher Durant, the father of Dixon Durant, a Choctaw whose family migrated from Mississippi around 1846 and for whom the town of Durant was named. In trying to determine the identity of the station keeper, Wright had first researched the Choctaw Fisher family – Silas Fisher, Osborn Fisher, et al. But she concluded that since Silas Fisher had remained in the lower Red River country after the removal and Osborn Fisher ranched and operated a store near Daisy in northeast Atoka County and then settled in Tishomingo, this would be unlikely. Instead, she noted that the earliest location of the site of the city of Durant was actually made by Fisher Durant, and it was known in early days as "Fisher's Place." She promoted the idea that the Butterfield road had actually come through Durant, and Fisher's Place had been Fisher's Station. Conkling doubted this conclusion, first pointing out that the Fisher Durant location did not fit into the Butterfield table of distances and the route would have required "a rather rank bend to the east and then southwest again," a deviation that the road builders would have avoided. "I have investigated the route from Nail's to Carriage Point and from there to Colbert's in the field with some of the oldest men in the region and if there was any other road between these points followed by the Overland Mail, these men had never heard of it," wrote Conkling.

But, Conkling conceded, this did not mean that the station could not have been named for Fisher Durant. He could have been employed by the Overland Mail Company as a station keeper and the station named for him even if his home was near the present location of Durant, but it would seem that some reference to this would have been handed down to his descendants. More likely, wrote Conkling, Fisher was among the more than two hundred Butterfield employees from New York brought west to work on the Overland Mail and placed in charge of stations during the first year of operations. "I was told by the then oldest living employee of the old Wells-Fargo Company, who died some years ago in Utica, that Mr. Butterfield transported more than two hundred of his old employees in New York to the western field to work on the Overland. Many of these were placed in charge of stations during the first year of operations," Conkling wrote. Few of these remained long, but long enough to have their names identified with the stations along the route, and "for that reason no record can be found to prove their identity," he added. Conkling included Holloway and Waddell among these.

Wright stuck to her guns, however, asserting it would be too much of a coincidence if Fisher Durant, "the most prominent Choctaw citizen in his locality" had nothing to do with Fisher's Stand, in spite of the fact that his known dwelling was in Durant, four miles east of the stage stand. "He could have owned an extra ranch cabin or erected one specially for a stand on the stage line road west of his home place," she explained. Wright concluded, "And now I feel almost certain, it must have been that of Fisher Durant."[459] It appears the two agreed to disagree. Ultimately the Conklings wrote, "Because the station ceased to be known as Fisher's after the Company abandoned the route in

1861, and the old name of Carriage Point restored, it has been suggested that Fisher may have been in the Company employ and temporarily installed there." Wright later wrote in an appendix to her 1957 article, "The Butterfield Overland Mail One Hundred Years Ago," that Fisher was a member of a well known Choctaw family.[460] And in the 1958 Committee Report, she simply quotes Conkling's conclusion.

Although Conkling believed the name, "Carriage Point," preceded the Overland Mail, others suggest it came about after the beginning of the Civil War. One account has it so named because an old carriage broke down nearby during the Civil War and was left to the ravages of time.[461] In 1869, Calvin Colbert bought the stage stand and it became an overnight stop for stagecoach travelers.[462]

Miss Frances

"Am I scaring you with my driving?"

I realize that, like at Fort McCulloch, I am feeling the road again but in a different way as I careen across a field at Fisher's Station in a side-by-side with a grinning Frances Sexton. "Miss Frances," as she's called, is very hard of hearing and needs a walker to get around on foot but, behind the wheel of this motorized buggy, her eyes sparkle and she's agile and confident. I will not say she's a speed demon, but suspect such a description may have fit in her younger days.

"A little," I think in response, but keep my thoughts to myself and hang on for dear life while assuring her I'm perfectly comfortable with her driving. Miss Frances is eighty-six and clearly enjoys entertaining guests this way. She is giving me a tour of Fisher's Station on a hot July day in 2022. I called to make the appointment just a few weeks before and spoke with her caregiver, Jaquita. When I suggested visiting the following winter when the weather cooled down, Jaquita said I had better not wait.

Miss Frances' parents, Odes and Agnes Cross, bought this property in 1950 and were living here in 1958. It was Odes and Agnes the Centennial Committee were talking about when, after selecting a spot for the marker in the front lawn of the site, they wrote that Mr. and Mrs. Cross "expressed interest, and offered to mow around the marker and keep it tidy."[463] To this day the grass around the marker is kept neatly trimmed on the east side of the county road.

Bumping along through the pasture east of the double-wide mobile home which replaced her parents' house, Miss Frances points out where the old station building sat, though nothing remains to indicate its presence. The Conklings saw "a caved-in well, some decaying hand-hewn timbers, and scattered foundation stones." The Centennial Committee also saw rubble and scattered stones, concluding it was ample evidence of the station buildings' locations.[464]

"Now I didn't guarantee you this wouldn't be a rough ride," she chuckles as we roll north to the caved-in stone well and, nearby, the burial place of Thomas Rider. The grave stone, enclosed by an iron fence, is about four feet high and indicates he died August 17, 1863, at age 19. Miss Frances says that some of Rider's family came in the past and asked if they could put up the iron fence. In 1958, other grave stones were evident, indicating the presence of a small cemetery. A larger cemetery, the Carriage Point burial ground, is located about one-half mile southeast of Fisher's Station, but is not on our itinerary today.

We head east toward a tributary of Mineral Bayou, parking close to a well which she says indicates the site of Carriage Point about one thousand feet away. I get out to explore. "I'd give anything if I could get out and walk with you," she says. I wish she could too. The earth is badly eroded on the north side of the structure but the rock-lined well is otherwise intact. Back in her hot rod, we follow the creek south to a crossing, where the stream rises from a spring. "Since 1950 this creek has never gone dry." There she points out a tree she loves. "I want to show you a tree down here, I'll bet you'll want to take a picture of it." It is an old post oak whose exposed roots are naked from erosion and have grown bark. She smiles as she reminisces about sunbathing nearby many years ago "after making sure the gates were closed." On the way back to the house, she shows me where the Overland Mail Road ran across the property on its southbound journey and comments on the ancient trees where her mother once picked up pecans.

The author (left) with "Miss Frances" Sexton

My visit with Miss Frances ends with cake fresh from the oven and iced tea and a hug. I am sad to leave, feeling I have had a rare privilege in meeting this woman who has allowed me to travel back in time with her. I promise to come back and visit but I never do, and one day shy of four months after our day of adventure, on November 5, 2022, Frances Sexton died at the age of eighty-seven, a stark reminder not to wait.

Side Trip: Isaac Alberson House

In 1958, Muriel Wright wrote that the Edwards Store was "the only original building located along the Overland Mail in Oklahoma that is standing today."[465] But she had stated in 1957, "The Alberson house built in 1844 is still standing about a mile from present Colbert,"[466] referring to the home of Chickasaw leader Isaac Alberson, which remains today along the Overland Mail route southeast of Colbert. It is unclear why Wright omitted the Alberson house in her later reference to original buildings along the mail route. Originally the house was one and one-half story with a stone chimney, two rooms each measuring eighteen by twenty feet comprising the main part of the original house. It has since been expanded and clapboarded and is vastly changed on the exterior. But inside, vestiges of the log cabin are visible through openings in the modern walls, and the original stone chimney still stands along the south elevation.[467] The Alberson House is privately owned, and while not publicly accessible it is easily admired from the road, a rambling two-story structure with a porch running its length.[468]

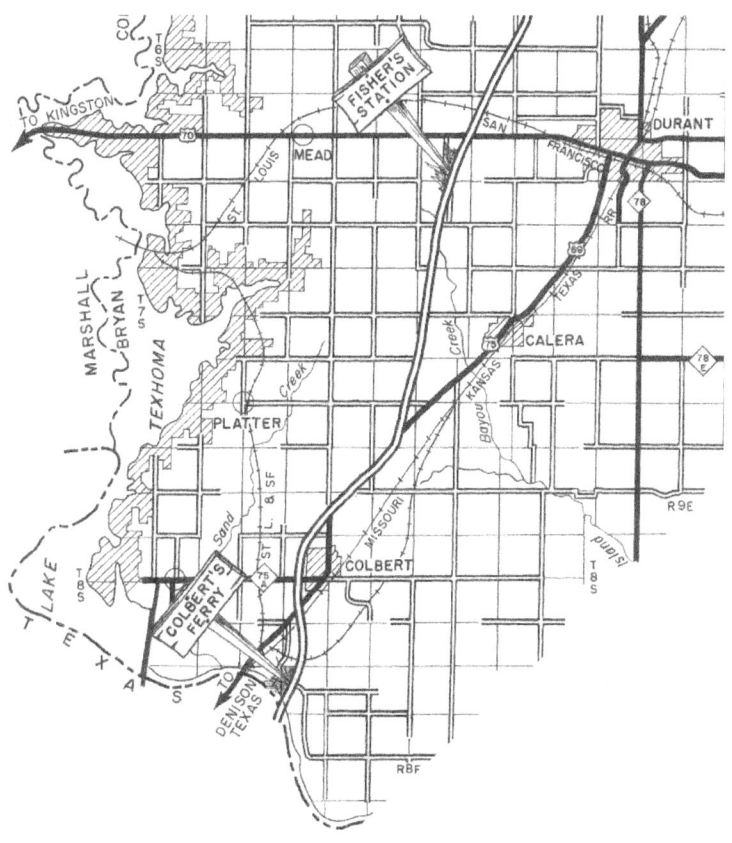

Butterfield Trail - Southern Bryan County, including Colbert's Ferry. Adapted from original map courtesy of Oklahoma Historical Society. See Eastern LeFlore County map, page 40, for map legend.

Colbert's Ferry

The rain refuses to stop and our determination to wait it out erodes as the day wears on.

Bill and I are at Colbert's Ferry in the home of Brandon and Kim Poteet along with author Rusty Williams, who wrote *The Red River Bridge War: A Texas-Oklahoma Border Battle*. We bide our time examining artifacts the Poteets have found and historic photographs that Rusty has brought. But the downpour becomes more insistent and finally we decide to brave the weather as the afternoon wanes. It's an opportunity not to be wasted, rain or shine. For Rusty, it's a chance to see, up close, the remnants of the bridge central to the border conflict he wrote about, and for me and Bill to tread the spot where the Overland Mail stage wagons boarded a flat boat and crossed the "wide, shallow and muddy" Red River into Texas. We don raingear and face the showers and the mud. What we find makes the damp worthwhile.

The first westbound Butterfield stage arrived at Colbert's Ferry on September 20, 1858 at 9:50 in the morning, thirty-four hours ahead of schedule, making its last stop in the Indian Territory. Colbert's, the only Overland Mail station in the Chickasaw Nation, lay thirteen miles slightly west of south of Fisher's Station, at the home and ferry of B.F. Colbert on the north bank of the Red River. The stage was so far ahead of schedule that no team awaited, so Ormsby had time for a good meal and a visit with Colbert, a mixed-blood Chickasaw born in Mississippi in 1828 to Martin and Sallie Colbert. Ormsby applauded Colbert's "great sagacity and business tact," and described him as jovial and pleasant.[469] Originally, the Preston crossing about seven miles above Colbert's was designated for the Overland Mail route. But Colbert and a contingent from Sherman, Texas, convinced the authorities to move the crossing to his ferry, which he had operated since 1852, when he bought the farm and ferry of Joseph G. Mitchell, on the north bank of the Red River in Panola County, Indian Territory.[470] Colbert advertised in the April 7, 1852 edition of the *Chickasaw Intelligencer*, published at Fort Washita, that he had two new ferry flats manned by experienced ferrymen and pledged to keep the approaches in good condition. His advertisement urged persons from Illinois, Indiana, Iowa, Wisconsin, western Kentucky, Missouri, and northwestern Arkansas to use his ferry on their way to north and west Texas. Rates ranged from two dollars for a wagon with six horses or oxen to twenty-five cents for a man and horse to five cents per head for hogs or sheep.[471] By ferrying the Overland Mail stages free of charge and keeping adjoining roads in good condition, Colbert assured his enterprise would benefit from the increased travel. The fare for a four-horse team not associated with the Overland Mail was a dollar and a quarter, netting Colbert about one thousand dollars   per year. It was a month after the inaugural run of the Butterfield when the Chickasaw government granted Colbert an official charter for the ferry, protecting his operation from infringement.[472]

Colbert enslaved about twenty-five people and told Ormsby he considered them "about the best stock there is, as his increase is about four per year." It was these slaves who worked the river banks, cutting away sand to make the slope less steep, and pushing the ferry across the river with poles.[473] And it was this same Colbert, "Master Frank," who was "loved" by former slave Kiziah Love. Yet Colbert considered her one of his livestock, if his comment to Ormsby is taken seriously.

At the time of his conversation with the reporter, Colbert was considering installing a cable-and-horsepower mechanism so that one man could manage the boat. Ormsby suggested that Colbert obtain a piece of the Atlantic cable, intending to be humorous, given that difficulties being experienced with the operation of the Atlantic telegraph cable were being lampooned in the press at the time. Ormsby never said whether Colbert appreciated his sarcasm, but the ferry's means of propulsion had not changed by July 1860, when Tallack traveled through. By 1871, however, the ferry was, perhaps by necessity, no longer operated solely by manual labor but rather being run by cable. John Malcolm found two black men operating it when he took the job of ferryman at Colbert's that year. Malcolm was associated with Colbert from 1871 to about 1887 and said Colbert was one of the best men he ever worked for. "He was strictly honest and a perfect gentleman in every sense of the word, and expected everyone else to be the same."[474]

When B.F. Colbert died of pneumonia December 18, 1893, his death notice was published in papers all over the United States, calling him the most illustrious and wealthiest of the Chickasaw tribe of Indians. *Our Brother in Red (Muskogee, Indian Territory)* wrote cryptically that he was a man of "many excellent dispositions, though his own worst enemy."[475]

By the time of the coming of the Katy Railroad in 1872, Colbert's Ferry drew heavy traffic, requiring the addition of a second boat. Each boat could carry six to seven two-horse wagons, often heavily laden with freight. But the construction of a railroad bridge over the Red River created a slump in the ferry business. [476] The enterprising Colbert built the first wagon bridge across the Red River, a heavy wooden structure five hundred seventy-seven feet long and sixteen feet wide, and opened it to traffic in 1875. Flood waters washed the bridge away the same year it opened, so Colbert put the ferry back into operation and in 1890, having organized the Red River Bridge Company with associates in Denison, Texas, built a new toll bridge at the same location. After Colbert's death, the Red River Bridge Company continued the operation. Another flood in 1908 destroyed the new bridge, and ferry service resumed, this time using a powered boat until another bridge was built in 1915. This was still in use as a toll bridge when the Conklings were there in 1930, though they wrote it was doomed to be replaced by a free bridge which had been erected nearby.[477]

That free bridge would trigger the Red River Bridge War of July, 1931. Though never an actual shooting war, the conflict erupted between the governors of Texas and Oklahoma after construction of the free bridge at Colbert and two others across the Red River on U.S. Highways 77 and 81. The owners of private toll bridges already in use in those locations objected to the opening of the free bridges before they had recovered their costs from the toll bridges. To block the opening of the free bridge at Colbert, the owners of the toll bridge obtained a federal injunction. The Texas governor then ordered Texas Rangers to barricade the southern end of the bridge to comply with the injunction. In response, the colorful William H. "Alfalfa Bill" Murray, governor of Oklahoma, declared martial law and sent the Oklahoma National Guard to seize the bridge and remove the barricades to let traffic flow undisturbed. He then plowed up the highway approaching the Oklahoma end of the toll bridge and had the paving removed, stationing armed troopers on both sides of the river to keep the free bridge open. Toting a gun, Murray made a personal visit to the site, remaining two days and spending the night in the temporary headquarters of the Oklahoma National Guard, an abandoned brick building at the north end of the toll bridge. A federal court dissolved the injunction in August and the free bridge finally opened on Labor Day, 1931.[478] Today a side trip to the Colbert City Park on the north end of Colbert reveals a span of that first free bridge across the Red River. The span was moved to the park after the bridge was replaced in 1996.

The foundations of the brick building used for the National Guard headquarters during this drama were recently rediscovered by Colbert resident Anthony Irwin when clearing land on West Toll Bridge Road. The substantial structure where Alfalfa Bill apparently slept on a cot amid the guardsmen was used before that time by the Southern Surety Company, but the identity of its original owner is uncertain.

Below it are the abutments of the toll bridge. In 1958, the old span was deteriorated, its timbers rotting, but still used occasionally by pedestrians. The Centennial Committee wrote that it would "soon fade into the limbo of history side by side with the ferry that it, in its turn, had superseded." They walked onto the bridge, noting the tranquility of the scene from their vantage point as they looked down Red River to the site of Colbert's Ferry. Time and erosion had lowered the slope of the north bank and the spot was deeply shaded with tall cottonwoods and elms. The committee tried to imagine "the shouting, confusion and excitement that must have prevailed as the whip for the Overland Mail brought his Celerity wagon, pulled by a four-in-hand, down that steep bank to the waiting ferry to be pulled across the Red River, . . . , into Texas and towards the unknown West."[479]

In 1972 Kent Ruth, the historian who wrote the application for the National Register of Historic Places listing for Colbert's Ferry, visited the site. The toll house which served the bridge, rotting but not totally in ruins, still stood on the east side of the sunken dirt road. Beyond it an eroded path dropped down to the ferry site at the water level. Ruth stood beside the old toll house with the property owner who recalled three cottonwood trees on the Texas side of the river to which the ferry cable was anchored and the big single cottonwood on the Oklahoma side. "All are gone now," wrote Ruth, "but he pointed out their location, indicated the course of the road down to the ferry, and expressed the wish that perhaps someday a reconstructed ferry could once again carry the nostalgically-inclined traveler across the river as it had over a century ago." No reconstructed ferry has appeared to date.

Toll bridge piers at Colbert's Ferry

The downpour has subsided into a steady drizzle by the time we reach the site of Riverside, the large home B.F. Colbert built upon the hill above the ferry around 1881.[480] It was as "finely appointed as any house in the Indian Territory."[481] Like most structures of that vintage it is long gone. In November, 1898, large timber and prairie fires in the Colbert area destroyed everything in their path, and the Colbert estate at Riverside was amid the conflagration.[482] Brandon Poteet points out where it sat on the summit of the hill, "high up on a wooded bluff of the Red river, on a level plat of fine farm land," according to the Conklings. They also reported that the old road leading to the ferry landing, west of the station site, was eroded and overgrown.[483] Today the path is still visible, a deep recess winding through the earth. In 1870, Joseph Edmonds traveled "down the long winding hill into the ferry boat, which is a flat boat run with ropes and pulley, and a few strokes and pulls and we land safely on the Texas shore." On Farwell's eastbound journey he found the Red River's muddy waters much lower than usual, and was ferried across by slaves, "from one deep red earthy bluff of bank to another similar one on the eastern side, up which we scrambled."[484]

The family cemetery with its large granite marker in memory of B.F. Colbert is located east of the knoll where the house stood. The nearly buried remains of a cistern identify the location of the station house, both captured in a photo by the Conklings in the 1930s.[485] Nearer the river, broken gravestones protrude from the earth amid the fallen and leaning trunks of a copse of soapberry trees in their death throes. One is that of Henry Colbert, brother to B.F., born 1832, his date of death hidden beneath the surrounding earth.

The two piers of the toll bridge still stand in the Red River, visible looking east from the modern highway bridge on U.S. Highway 69/75. A gas pipeline fire destroyed the bridge's main span and the remainder was demolished in 1961.[486] We scramble down the muddy embankment to explore the site of the ferry landing and the bridge pilings. I look up to the north bank at the first abutment, wishing I could go back and walk across that bridge like the Centennial Committee did in 1958. From ground level, the tall concrete piers are imposing, but even more remarkable is the wreckage from the old bridge. In pools of water on the river bank and in the stream, girders and cables and wooden planks from the bridge decking, machinery and hardware create a feeling of utter destruction, especially in the cold rain.

It never occurred to me that the remnants of the bridge would still be there, but of course thousands of pounds of steel do not simply float off down the Red River to the Mississippi and into the Gulf of Mexico. The river—dark gray rather than red on this gloomy day-- looks narrow at this point, with Texas only a stone's throw away.

Cephalopod fossil on the shore of the Red River at Colbert's Ferry

Walking along the shore, we see fossils embedded in the stone. Like the ones at Blue River, these ocean-dwelling cephalopods which died out eons ago remind us of the longer view of history, that sixty years, or a hundred and sixty, is infinitesimal in the grand scheme of things.

The Oklahoma Historical Society's marker sits intact on the south side of the county road near the Colbert burial plot, the final marker in Indian Territory, a lonely symbol on a quiet road memorializing a tiny link in the long chain of the Butterfield Overland Mail stage line, a system using a technology so outmoded today as to render it almost fantastical. Its two hundred miles across Oklahoma can be driven in a matter of hours, even considering the circuitous back-roads route. But why hurry? It's something to absorb, slowly, to gaze to the west across the Poteau, drink from the spring at Skullyville and walk through historic cemeteries under majestic oaks. Have a picnic at the Edwards Store and consider the significance of the accident at Mountain Station.

Go for a hike at the Atoka Reservoir and adventure through an ancient forest, camp a night at Boggy Depot and imagine the thriving town it once was. Then, ending up here, look across another river into Texas and ponder the daunting journey that lay ahead for passengers on that Butterfield stage. For them, Indian Territory was only the beginning.

Chapter Ten: Epilogue

Waiting for a team of horses at the Red River, Ormsby looked back on the journey he had just completed. His first five hundred miles in the stagecoach and wagon were just the warm-up for a long and arduous trip. After four days of travel through southern Missouri, northwest Arkansas and the southeastern corner of Indian Territory Ormsby found the inconveniences a worthwhile exchange for the variety of scenery and terrain, the "curious characters" he met and the novelty of "roughing it overland." Writing twelve days later from Tucson, Arizona, he remembered the Indian Territory even more fondly in contrast to what he experienced in between:

> Though the country through which we had passed was but sparsely peopled, it seemed like leaving home to bid farewell even to these settlements to proceed through the wilds of Texas, along its lonely plains and barren hills and dangerous frontier to the Rio Grande. The very log huts of the friendly Choctaws were like home in comparison to the almost uninhabited wilds which we were to traverse, where all the evidence of the presence of man was the faint trail of the teamsters.[487]

Two thousand miles and not quite twenty days from the Red River, Ormsby's stagecoach rolled into San Francisco at 7:30 a.m. on Sunday, October 10. Other than delays caused by wild mules, which several times had to be lassoed and settled down before they could be harnessed to the wagon while the stage waited, the trip had been expeditious and reasonably smooth. The mail reached its destination one day and one-half hour quicker than the contracted time of twenty-five days. Ormsby declared the overland mail route "permanently established and its success placed beyond the possibility of a doubt."

In reality the Butterfield Overland Mail's Southern Route was transitional, both in its path and its mode of transportation, a fleeting step in the determined advance toward the transcontinental railroad. It was, however, in its time, "the most popular institution of the Far West," bringing welcome news from home to the pioneers of California and by 1860 carrying more letters than the ocean steamers.[488] But the spring of 1861 brought new circumstances. Seven states had seceded and the southern Confederacy formed. Interference with the Butterfield line's mail service through Texas by Confederate sympathizers was becoming a problem. On March 2, 1861, Congress transferred the Butterfield line to the Central Route via Salt Lake City.

In Indian Territory, regular postal service and stage lines came to a halt during the Civil War but the road's use continued after the war. Toll gate and toll bridge privileges were renewed or granted to new operators in 1866 and 1867: to Charles LeFlore for a toll bridge across Clear Boggy a mile east of Boggy Depot; James D. Davis, a toll bridge across Muddy (Middle) Boggy; Jonathan Nail, toll bridge across Blue River; George Riddle (son of Butterfield station keeper John Riddle), toll bridge across the Fourche Maline; and Wade Hampton, a toll gate at Buffalo Station on the west of Buffalo Creek Crossing near Pulcher. To Olasechubi, a full-blood Choctaw and perhaps the only full-blood to be granted a toll gate or toll bridge privilege during this period, a toll gate at Mountain Station; John Wilkin, a toll bridge over Bayouzil (Brazil Creek) in the vicinity of the McDaniel and James' bridge; Jack McCurtain, a toll gate at The Narrows; John James, a toll bridge on James Creek, a branch of Blue River a few miles south of Nail's Crossing; and David Folsom, a toll bridge at Nail's Mill on Blue River (placing the privilege under Folsom's name after the death of Jonathan Nail, Folsom having married his widow).[489]

A new line of stations came into being along the Overland Mail route in 1868 with the establishment of regular stages from Fort Smith. Included at different times were Skullyville, Brazil Station, Council

House, Edwards, McCurtain's, Riddle's Station, Mountain Station, Buffalo Station, Jim Colbert's on Brushy, Wells' Station, Rogers' Station, McKinney's, Mrs. Flack's, Boggy Depot, Nail's Crossing, Carriage Point and Colbert's Ferry.[490]

The road from Fort Smith to Boggy Depot and on to Texas had been essential to the settlement of the Chickasaws, a main highway for the Choctaws, a critical military artery and a thoroughfare by which travelers and migrants journeyed north and south for decades. From 1858 to 1861 the Butterfield Overland Mail increased outside traffic and put the Indian Territory on a national stage. During the three years of its existence the Choctaws and Chickasaws were settled and re-established but also faced continued threats to their national existence, drought, internal conflict over the structure of their government, and growing pressures associated with the onset of the Civil War. Beginning in the 1870s with the coming of the railroad and the development of the coal mining industry, populations dwindled along the old mail road and post offices closed. New towns sprang up along the railroad and many of the old communities ceased to exist.[491] The important towns of the Choctaw Nation--Boggy Depot, Skullyville, and Doaksville—passed away as communities, and in many places the southwestern trajectory of the road was eventually replaced with streets laid out on a one-mile east-west-north-south section-line grid. Today the towns of any size along the route—Spiro, Wilburton, Atoka, Durant--have their origins in the railroad or coal mining. In a historical preservation sense this is a blessing; road fragments and ruins still exist along the Butterfield which may have been obliterated had the Katy Railroad chosen that route instead of the Texas Road.

One Hundred Years Later

In the early 1950s, organizations in states across the length of the Southern Route started planning a centennial celebration for the Overland Mail. A non-profit organization, the American Association for State and Local History, created a national committee led by Texas historian H. Bailey Carroll, who appointed subcommittees in each of the states involved. Vernon H. Brown chaired the Oklahoma committee, which first met in November, 1953 and laid out plans for Oklahoma's celebration, which would coincide with the state's semi-centennial in 1957 and continue into 1958.[492]

From the outset, the Oklahoma group's plans included marking the Overland Mail route through the state,[493] which they accomplished in May of 1958, hoping to be the first state to mark all its Butterfield stations.[494] Whether they were successful with the goal to be first is unclear, but to date not all states along the route have marked their stations. A Concord coach restored by committee member John D. Frizzell would be the centerpiece of the celebration. The coach had belonged to Pawnee Bill and was found disintegrating in a field when Frizzell rescued it.[495] This was the first of many stage coaches restored by Frizzell, who later established Frizzell Coach and Wheel Works, an international business which his son John, Jr. carried on after the elder Frizzell's death in 1981.[496]

Oklahoma's centennial celebration began in June 1957 with a commemorative cancellation on mail, "Centennial Butterfield Overland Mail 1857-58." This occurred at four post offices: Spiro, Wilburton, Atoka and Durant.[497]

That summer at the Semi-Centennial Exposition of Oklahoma's statehood, the Butterfield's one hundred years were recognized with a replica of Fisher's Station, a log cabin housing an exhibit of historical relics from a century before. Outside the cabin on either end stood Frizzell's stagecoach and a modern post office bus used in collecting mail from post offices without a railroad. This display stood at the fairgrounds in Oklahoma City from June 14 to July 7, 1957.[498]

After the exposition, the log cabin was moved to the courthouse grounds in Durant for a continuation of the celebration September 13-15. That weekend the mail was carried by stagecoach from Atoka to Boggy Depot, then to Durant and on to Colbert's Ferry. About three thousand people greeted the coach in Atoka and more lined the streets of Durant to see the departure and arrival of the stagecoach, which carried 3,870 pieces of mail weighing 44 lb. 3 oz.[499] At Boggy Depot an estimated one thousand people attended special festivities surrounding the dedication of the property as a state park and conveyance of the deed to the State of Oklahoma by J. Brookes Wright of McAlester, son of Chief Allen Wright and uncle of Muriel Wright.

The process of creating Boggy Depot State Park was fraught with difficulty and delay. As told by J. Brookes Wright, the idea came to him in the fall and winter of 1952-53 to establish a memorial park at Boggy Depot, primarily to preserve the historic cemetery. The state soon passed legislation and an appropriation for establishment of the park and Wright's sister, Anna Wright Ludlow, agreed to donate the land.

But the process became drawn out and soon Mrs. Ludlow became ill and was unable to execute the deed. After her death, two years passed before the estate was settled and in the meantime the state funding was cancelled. Finally, with a new state appropriation, J. Brookes Wright purchased the land so that he could deed it to the state.

Preparing the future park for the September, 1957 celebration presented another challenge, however. "I began in the winter of 1957 to make Old Boggy presentable for the Semi-centennial and the Butterfield Centennial celebrations," wrote Wright. "Mr. Ernest Fabray, a former President of the Old Boggy Depot Cemetery Association, and I began working on the cemetery and by the time spring came we had it in good condition. Then the rains came and it was early summer before we got to work anymore. In the meantime the bushes, the weeds and the grass grew prodigiously in the cemetery and on the Old Boggy townsite until they appeared a wilderness. Then the real job began." Eventually, the Oklahoma governor allowed prison inmates to help with the cleanup and the property was in "fine condition" for the celebration on September 13.[500]

The nationwide celebration the following year brought even more fanfare. Its climax was a re-enactment of the westbound journey of the first Butterfield stagecoach. A caravan traveled from Tipton, Missouri to San Francisco along the Overland Mail route from September 16 to October 10, mirroring the timing of that inaugural journey. Frizzell's Concord stagecoach and U.S. Highway Post Office No. 1, a bus which picked up mail at two hundred post offices along the route, led the convoy, presenting "dramatically the progress of one hundred years in mail transportation and postal service."[501] Also comprising the procession were a "highway chapel"; an Anvil Unit; a "California state unit," carrying a collection of Overland Mail books; and Hugh Park, editor of Press-Argus, Van Buren, Arkansas, with an early American handpress, which would print a daily caravan paper, the "Stagehorn."[502]

The "Highway Post Office" was first used in 1941 to deliver mail to communities not served by the railroad and its success led to more highway postal routes. The Post Office brought back the first coach for the event.

"A group of bewhiskered, red-shirted descendants of the '49ers," comprised the Anvil Unit. These individuals represented California's Platrix Chapter of E. Clampus Vitus, a fraternal organization dedicated to the preservation of the heritage of the American West. Their prairie schooner carried the remnants of a Butterfield blacksmith shop and at each stop the members of the "Centennial Anvil Chorus" fired an anvil into the air with gunpowder in memory of the Butterfield.[503]

Even a song writing duo, Pat and Marge Patrick of Springdale, Arkansas, accompanied the caravan in a car with loud speakers, playing their musical tale of the Overland Mail.[504] As planned, the convoy left Tipton on September 16, 1958 and arrived in San Francisco on October 10.[505] Festivities greeted the entourage in communities along the way. The stagecoach was actually carried between towns by truck and semi-trailer and unloaded and hitched to the four-horse team for local parades.

In Oklahoma, Governor Raymond Gary proclaimed "Overland Mail Days" on September 19 and 20, the two days the first Butterfield stage spent in Indian Territory. The procession entered Oklahoma September 19[506] and made it to Durant on September 20, although its arrival there was delayed more than two hours thanks to mud and heavy traffic. The horses were exhausted and the coach had to be brought in on the trailer.

By this time, the Highway Post Office was carrying nearly 90,000 pieces of mail.[507] Each post office along the route could deposit mail on the coach for transportation to San Francisco where a special "back stamp" showing the date of arrival in San Francisco was placed on the letter before its dispatch to the addressee. Postmasters also applied special markings or "cachets" to outgoing mail placed on the caravan, and numerous post offices in Oklahoma created their own designs. Red Oak's was a side view of a stage coach, with four horses galloping toward the left of the envelope. The magenta marking included the words: "Red Oak, Oklahoma (Indian Territory) Stage Station." (Red Oak was not an official Butterfield station but such liberties were frequently taken during the centennial.) Colbert's large cachet, also in magenta, displayed a stage coach on a flat bottom ferry being poled across the river, with the wording, "1858 Colbert's Ferry, I.T. The Overland Mail Crosses Red River Colbert, Oklahoma 1958."[508] Oklahoma towns on the route were Spiro, Panama, Shady Point, Poteau, Wister, Fanshawe, Red Oak, Panola, Wilburton, Gowen, Hartshorne, Haileyville, Dow, Bache, Alderson, Krebs, McAlester, Savanna, Kiowa, Stringtown, Atoka, Tushka, Caney, Caddo, Durant, Calera and Colbert. A number of these were near, but not actually on, the original Overland Mail route.

On October 10, the U.S. Post Office issued an Overland Mail Centennial Commemorative stamp through the San Francisco post office, making it available at other post offices the following day. One hundred twenty million of the four-cent stamps comprised the initial printing. The stamp depicts an Overland Mail coach under attack, overlaid on a map of the southwestern United States, with the route shown between Tipton and San Francisco.[509]

The Writing on the Wall

In the fall of 1858, as the first Butterfield Overland Mail stage wagons rolled through Indian Territory, the tenuous possession of this land by the Five Tribes was already slipping through their fingers. Overland Mail passengers traversing Indian Territory were impressed not only with the vast, fertile tract of land but that in their observation so little of it was cultivated. The opinion that this abundance was wasted upon the Indians was a common thread. "The land is well watered, and with little cultivation could be made to yield abundantly; but they prefer to let their stock grow and increase without their care, and draw their small pensions from the government," wrote Ormsby.[510] Tallack was even more direct, stating,

> As we traversed the sunny forest glades and fertile undulations of open land, our American passengers expressed, in no gentle terms, their disapprobation of the forbearance of the Federal Government in reserving such an ample and splendid region for a population so scanty and so evidently unable to avail themselves of even a small portion of the vast and easily attainable advantages set before them."[511]

The inevitability of statehood, right or wrong, was on the mind of Elias Rector, writing October 26, 1858, to Charles E. Mix, Commissioner of Indian Affairs:

> The country possessed by (the Cherokees, Creeks, Seminoles, Choctaws and Chickasaws), picturesque and fertile, must at some day become a State of the American Union. It is useless for white man or Indian to shut his eyes to that fact; . . . . Necessity is the supreme law of nations. All along the Indian border the country is now populous, and the railroad will soon reach their frontier.

Necessity will soon *compel* the incorporation of their country into the Union, and before its stern requisitions every other consideration will give way, and even wrong find, as it ever does, in necessity its apology."[512]

Even as early as 1832, before the Choctaws' westward migration was complete, Commissioner of Indian Affairs Elbert Herring noted that the twenty-one million acres allotted to the Choctaws at more than 1,200 acres per individual was a "vast extent of territory . . . beyond any possible requirement for their use."[513]

The Five Tribes' alliance with the Confederacy during the Civil War gave the United States government a golden opportunity. As historian Angie Debo put it, the tribes were

> . . . Left completely at the mercy of the Federal Government, for they had violated the most fundamental principle of their "foreign" policy when they had taken up arms against the United States. The people of Kansas were clamoring for the removal of the Indian tribes who owned land in that state, and millions of liberated Negroes were trustfully expecting "forty acres and a mule" from the authorities at Washington. The homes of the "rebel Indians" might be confiscated as a cheap and convenient solution of these two problems.[514]

It would be another forty years before that confiscation would be fully consummated, but the trajectory was set. With the Reconstruction Treaty of 1866 the Choctaws and Chickasaws surrendered the Leased District and granted right of way for the railroad. The railroads brought more whites, as did coal mining. Pressure to open up Indian lands for non-Indian settlement intensified. In 1889, the federal government finally gave in and opened up to settlers the Unassigned Lands, purchased from the

Creek and Seminole Nations. The Land Run of 1889 led to the opening of other Indian lands and pressure grew for allotment, the process of dividing communally held land into individually owned private property, paving the way for statehood. A territorial government was created in 1890 and Oklahoma Territory was born.

Federal legislation authorized allotment negotiations and a commission chaired by U.S. Senator Henry Dawes went to work with the Five Tribes in 1893, finally completing the allotment process in 1906. Under the Atoka Agreement of 1897, the lands of the Choctaws and Chickasaws were divided equally among their members. Freedmen and their descendants received smaller land allotments. The agreement also provided for the termination of the two tribal governments on March 4, 1906, although the Choctaw government lived on in a diminished form to deal with matters related to communally owned coal and mineral lands. After this time, principal chiefs or governors were appointed by the President of the United States, not elected by their members. With the joining of Indian Territory to Oklahoma Territory in statehood in 1907, the Choctaw and Chickasaw Nations seemed to pass out of existence as separate political entities. But this was not the end of the story.

From the 1930s to the 1970s, legislation restored to the Indian nations the management of their assets, including land and mineral rights; reversed the goal of cultural assimilation of Native Americans into American society; and promoted tribal self-determination. The Indian nations regained the ability to elect their own leaders, re-establish their governments, and decide how their funds should be spent. In the 1980s, the federal Indian Gaming Regulatory Act was passed into law, permitting tribal governments to operate specific kinds of gambling, with profits to be used to benefit tribes and their members. In 2004, Oklahoma voters approved casino gaming operated by tribal governments, which led to the proliferation of casinos throughout the state and gaming revenues going into the coffers of the tribes. Today the Choctaw and Chickasaw Nations run diverse businesses to generate income and provide their citizens with a wide range of services. The Choctaw Nation is the third largest Indian nation in the U.S., with more than 200,000 tribal members, and the Choctaw Nation of Oklahoma is the largest of the three federally recognized bands of Choctaws.

Finding the Butterfield

When I was in the tenth grade at Okmulgee High School, in the capital of the Muscogee (Creek) Nation, Oklahoma history seemed to begin in 1907, or so I gleaned from my textbook. But somehow that did not ring true, for the Creek Council House, built in 1878, was sitting right there in downtown Okmulgee and still is. Many of my friends were Creek Indians, but I had no idea of their history. Much later in life I discovered a great deal happened here before 1907, and I was intrigued. I wanted to dig, farther and farther into the past. Before statehood, before the Land Run, before the Civil War, before Removal, shedding light on what is obscure to so many, to those who have not been exposed to the rich and distinct early history of Oklahoma.

In finding the Butterfield I found antebellum Oklahoma. Not just the physical remnants but a real sense of connection with the people and events of the past. Bumping along in the stagecoach with Ormsby, riding with the Conklings in their 1930 Buick, and tagging along with the Centennial Committee from the Oklahoma Historical Society as their entourage sought out the old stations on back roads brought me in touch with that time long ago. Like Ormsby I enjoyed the variety in scenery and terrain, the curious characters I met and the many hours spent on isolated rural roads. I saw new beauty in a land that over my lifetime had grown too familiar. The flowery language of other travelers reminded me that southeastern Oklahoma is a lush, green, beautiful place. Mountains where I would have seen only hills. A clear, running creek now hidden beneath the depths of a large reservoir. An old growth forest in a place previously unknown. Flowing springs with an infinite history. Grave yards, telling so much of the story. I did not find every inch that remains of the old road. There is much more to explore. But a book must be finished at some point.

While Grant Foreman saw the Texas Road as the most important of Oklahoma's early trails, I see the Butterfield, the Fort Smith-Boggy Depot Road, at least as important to Oklahoma's early history. The fact that it passed from the scene so long ago has preserved much of it. As of this writing, development of the Butterfield National Historic Trail by the National Park Service is in its early stages. It will bring about new awareness and new ways to access the trail in Oklahoma and the six other states it crosses. I hope this volume contributes to a greater understanding of the trail and its significance, and inspires others to go out and find the Butterfield, and early Oklahoma, for themselves.

Appendix

Locations of station markers and other sites noted in this volume are listed below in geographical order from east to west.

Fort Smith National Historic Site: 301 Parker Avenue, Fort Smith, Arkansas, 35.38857, -94.43127

New Hope Cemetery: New Hope Road and Orchard Lane east of Spiro, Oklahoma, at 35.24966, -94.58312

Spiro Mounds Archeological Center: North of Spiro at 18154 First Street, 35.31173, -94.56843

Walker's Station: About one and one-half miles northeast of Spiro at 18570 Spring Road, at 35.25206, -94.59097

Skullyville Cemetery: West of Walker's Station off Spring Road at 35.25128, -94.59434

Skullyville County Jail: About three miles west of U.S. Highway 59 near Panama, Oklahoma, at 35.17351, -94.71793

Brazil Cemetery: About seven miles west of Shady Point, Oklahoma just off County Road N4640 at 35.13499, -94.76732

Trahern's Station: About nine miles west of Shady Point on County Road E1300 at 35.12351, -94.80336

Dog Creek School: About fourteen miles southwest of Shady Point on County Road D1340 at 35.08107, -94.86539

Norris Cemetery: About nine miles northeast of Red Oak on Norris Road at 35.00862, -94.95217

Edwards Store: About eight miles northeast of Red Oak on Norris Road at 34.99750, -94.97420

Holloway's Station: About three miles northeast of Red Oak on Norris Road at 34.97586, -95.05120

Riddle's Station: One and one-half miles east of Wilburton on Lutie Road at 34.92015, -95.25645

Mountain Station Cemetery: About eleven miles southwest of Wilburton at 34.83669, -95.42445

Pusley's Station: About three miles southwest of Higgins at 34.79684, -95.46578

Blackburn's Station: About seven and one-half miles south of Blanco on County Road N4090 at 34.669567, -95.742133

Waddell's Station: About three miles southwest of Wesley at 34.593483, -95.886033

Bread Town Stage Stand: About three-quarters of a mile south of Wesley Road on Butterfield Road in the Atoka Wildlife Management Area, at 34.52545, -96.99224

Trail at Atoka Reservoir (eastern shore): About one-half mile west of U.S. Highway 69 on Lakeshore Drive at 34.46058, -96.07044

Geary's Station: About one and one-half miles southwest of Stringtown at 34.454675, -96.083900 (inundated)

Atoka County Museum and Civil War Cemetery: About one mile north of Atoka, on U.S. Highway 69 at 34.40011, -96.11710

Boggy Depot: Ten miles south and west of Atoka, and about four miles south of the bridge across Clear Boggy River at 34.319939, -96.308308

Nail's Crossing: On the east bank of Blue River, about two miles southwest of Kenefic at 34.13108, -96.39078

Fort Washita: Fifteen miles northwest of Durant on Highway 199 at 34.10264, -96.54700

Fisher's Station: About four miles west of Durant at 33.98527, -96.45444

Colbert's Ferry: About three miles south of Colbert at 33.818369, -96.516139

For a comprehensive set of resources for the Butterfield Trail in Indian Territory see https://susandragoo.com/butterfield-oklahoma/

Acknowledgments

To my husband Bill, who was my travel partner for most of this project and has been my partner in life for twenty amazing years. Thank you for your love and support; without you none of this would be possible.

To all the family and friends who have supported me in this, thank you. Your patience in having to listen to the latest update on "The Butterfield" will hopefully be well rewarded.

I have made many new friends along this journey, historians and fellow researchers who have guided and encouraged me. Many thanks to these, including Bob Jackman, Gerald Ahnert, Dr. Carroll Messer, Dr. John Fahey, Dr. Bill Corbett, Dr. Joe Schiller, June Chubbuck, Ken Rainbolt, Earl Shero, Joseph Wolf, Dr. Kim Hinson, and Kristina Wyckoff.

And to all the land owners who so graciously shared access, their time, and their stories, I am deeply grateful.

About the Author

Susan Dragoo is a native Oklahoman, born and raised in Okmulgee and now a resident of Norman. She holds a Bachelor of Arts degree in Telecommunications from the University of Tulsa; and Master's degrees in Management from Southern Nazarene University; and Biostatistics from the University of Oklahoma.

Her journalism career began in 1977 at the *Okmulgee Daily Times* and, after a long hiatus for a career in healthcare, she has been busy writing about adventure travel and history for regional and national magazines, including *Overland Journal, Oklahoma Today, OutdoorX4* and the *Chronicles of Oklahoma*.

Susan and her husband Bill find joy in their children, grandchildren and ongoing pursuits of adventure in the outdoors.

For more information and access to publications see www.susandragoo.com.

"But seek first the kingdom of God and his righteousness."
Matthew 6:33

Contact Susan at susan.dragoo@gmail.com.

Index

Congress, 9, 10, 16, 28, 31, 32, 34, 88, 198

Conkling, Margaret, 23, 71, 104, 129, 130, 174

Conkling, Roscoe, 174, 181, 183

Conkling, Roscoe and Margaret, 17, 19, 20, 21, 27, 57, 59, 68, 71, 72, 78, 79, 90, 101, 104, 105, 121, 123, 129, 130, 131, 134, 141, 142, 148, 150, 151, 153, 168, 169, 170, 171, 174, 175, 178, 182, 184, 190, 193, 194, 208

Connecticut, 101

Corbin, T.R., 26

Council House, 73, 74, 75, 76, 79, 199

Counts, Oklahoma, 131

Courthouse Gap, 107

Creek Council House, 208

Creek Nation, 69, 208

Creeks, 14, 53, 55, 83, 88, 90, 91, 92, 205

Crocker, Hugh, 13, 26

Cross Timbers, 115, 152, 156

Cross, Odes and Agnes, 184

Culbertson, E.H., 147

Cummings, Alexander, 32

Daily Alta, 38, 85

Daily Oklahoman, 98

Daisy, Oklahoma, 181

Darnell, Jim, 84

Davis, James D., 45, 156

Dawes, Henry, 207

Debo, Angie, 15, 206

Denison, Texas, 190

Dennis, Claude, 173

Dent, Frederick T., 35

Dickey, R.P., 171

Doaksville, 15, 48, 54, 74, 159

Dog Creek, 81, 82, 83, 84, 211

Dole, William P., 93

Doña Ana, 35

Dow, Oklahoma, 204

Doyle, Burton, 143

Dragoo, Bill, 62, 114, 127, 134, 145, 164, 167, 169, 174, 188

Dukes, Joseph, 87

Durant, Dixon, 181

Durant, Fisher, 181

Durant, Oklahoma, 22, 182, 199, 200, 203, 204, 213

E. Clampus Vitus, 203

Eagletown, 87

Eastern Oklahoma Historical Society, 97

Edmonds, Joseph, 147, 150, 154, 162, 169, 193

Edwards Store, 90, 94, 95, 96, 100, 102, 105, 186, 195, 212

Edwards Trading Post, 69

Edwards, Martha J.. *See* Chapen, Martha Riddle

Edwards, Thomas, 91, 92, 93, 98

El Paso, Texas, 13, 19, 35

Elm Creek, 131, 134

Emachaya, 76

Emancipation Proclamation, 82

Notes

[1] Waterman L. Ormsby. *The Butterfield Overland Mail.* Edited by Lyle H. Wright and Josephine M. Bynum. San Marino, Calif.: Huntington Library, 1942, 121. Although the government contract set a 25-day deadline, the Overland Mail Company was striving for 24 days.

[2] Walter B. Lang. *The First Overland Mail: Butterfield Trail, St. Louis to San Francisco1858-1861.* Washington, D.C.: privately printed, 1940, 32.

[3] LeRoy R. Hafen. *The Overland Mail, 1848-1869: Promoter of Settlement, Precursor of Railroads.* Cleveland, Ohio: Arthur H. Clark, 1926. 48-49.

[4] "The Transcontinental Railroad," History of Railroads and Maps. Library of Congress. https://www.loc.gov/collections/railroad-maps-1828-to-1900/articles-and-essays/history-of-railroads-and-maps/the-transcontinental-railroad/

[5] Memorial of Asa Whitney . . . Praying a Grant of Land, to Enable Him to Construct a Railroad from Lake Michigan to the Pacific Ocean (28th Congress2nd sess., Senate Doc. 69, Serial 451, Jan. 28, 1845). http://www.cprr.org/Museum/Eastward.html

[6] Roscoe P. and Margaret B. Conkling, *The Butterfield Overland Mail, 1857–1869: Its Organization and Operation over the Southern Route to 1861; Subsequently over the Central Route to 1866; and Under Wells, Fargo and Company in 1869.* 3 vols. Glendale, Calif.: Arthur H. Clark, 1947. Vol. 1 of 3, 154.

[7] John Butterfield, Report to the Directors of the Overland Mail Company, August 2, 1858, quoted by Bob Crossman in *Butterfield National Historical Trail Passenger Diaries & Stories.* Ingram Spark Press, 2024. 61-66.

[8] Conkling, *The Butterfield Overland Mail*, 166. *Daily Republican,* St. Louis. February 6, 1861, 4.

[9] Lang, *The First Overland Mail,* 110.

[10] *Daily National Democrat* (Marysville, Calif.) October 23, 1859, 2.

[11] Conkling, *The Butterfield Overland Mail*, 137.

[12] Ormsby, *The Butterfield Overland Mail*, 90.

[13] Lang, *The First Overland Mail,* 110.

[14] Ormsby, *The Butterfield Overland Mail,* 64.

[15] Lang, *The First Overland Mail,* 131.

[16] Conkling, *The Butterfield Overland Mail*, 140.

[17] Lang, *The First Overland Mail,* 131.

[18] Conkling, *The Butterfield Overland Mail*, 126.

[19] Michael F. Doran. "Negro Slaves of the Five Civilized Tribes." *Annals of the Association of American Geographers* 68, no. 3 (September 1978): 346.

[20] Angie Debo, *The Rise and Fall of the Choctaw Republic.* Norman: University of Oklahoma Press, 1934. 56-70.

[21] Blue Clark. "Chickasaw Colonization in Oklahoma," in Gibson, Arrell M. (ed.), *America's Exiles: Indian Colonization in Oklahoma.* Oklahoma City. Oklahoma Historical Society, 1976. 44-59.

[22] Debo, *The Rise and Fall,* 78.

[23] Debo, *The Rise and Fall,* 37.

[24] Report of the Acting Superintendent of the Western Territory. Annual Report of the Commissioner of Indian Affairs . . . for the Year 1837. 20-21.

[25] Debo, *The Rise and Fall,* 71, 78-79.

[26] Clara Sue Kidwell. *The Choctaws in Oklahoma, From Tribe to Nation, 1855-1970.* Norman, Okla.: University of Oklahoma Press, 2007. 4-7, 10.

[27] "The Choctaws to their White Brethren in Ireland," *Arkansas Intelligencer,* April 3, 1847, 2.

[28] John Butterfield to the Directors of the Overland Mail Company, August 2, 1858. Quoted in Crossman, *Butterfield National Historic Trail,* 62.

[29] Lang, *The First Overland Mail,* 13-14.

[30] Hafen, *The Overland Mail,* 214.

[31] Significance Statement, Final Butterfield Overland Trail Special Resource Study, parkplanning.nps.gov, 42-44.

[32] Personal interview with John Fahey, January 15, 2022, regarding search for Harbin's Station in southern Missouri.

[33] Transmittal Letter, Final Butterfield Overland Trail Special Resource Study, 3-4.

[34] Muriel H. Wright. "Historic Places on the Old Stage Line from Fort Smith to Red River," *Chronicles of Oklahoma* 11, no. 2 (June 1933): 798.

[35] Wright, "Historic Places," 801.

[36] Grant Foreman. *Down the Texas Road: Historic Places Along Highway 69 Through Oklahoma.* Norman, Okla.: University of Oklahoma Press, 1936. 6-9.

[37] Significance Statement, Final Butterfield Overland Trail SRS, 43. Books and articles retracing the trail in other states have subsequently been published, including Glen Sample Ely's comprehensive *The Texas Frontier and the Butterfield Overland Mail, 1858-1861.* Norman: University of Oklahoma Press, 2016.

[38] Wright, "Historic Places," 800.

[39] John Young Bryce (1863-1937), Hartshorne, a Methodist minister, moved to Indian Territory with his parents in 1868, served as Secretary of the Oklahoma Historical Society 1925-1930, edited the *Chronicles of Oklahoma,* and surveyed historical spots of Oklahoma. See "John Young Bryce (Necrology)," *Chronicles of Oklahoma* 15, no. 3 (September 1937): 362-363.

[40] "History Tablets," *Chronicles of Oklahoma* 11, no. 2 (June 1933): 754.

[41] Muriel Wright to Judge R.L. Williams, November 26, 1930. Muriel Wright Collection. Box 7, Folder 22. Oklahoma Historical Society, Oklahoma City.

[42] Leroy H. Fischer, "Muriel H. Wright, Historian of Oklahoma," *Chronicles of Oklahoma* 52, no. 1 (Spring 1974): 17.

[43] Muriel H. Wright. "The Butterfield Overland Mail One Hundred Years Ago." *Chronicles of Oklahoma* 35, no. 1 (Spring 1957): 56, Note 2.

[44] Wright, "The Butterfield Overland Mail," 68.

[45] Muriel H. Wright; Vernon H. Brown, John D. Frizzell, Mildred Frizzell, James D. Morrison, Lucyl A. Shirk, and George H. Shirk. "Committee Report Butterfield Overland Mail." *Chronicles of Oklahoma* 36, no. 4 (Winter 1958): 446.

[46] Roscoe Conkling Papers. Seaver Center for Western History Research, Los Angeles, Calif. Box 9 Stage Photos Folder 46 Oklahoma Research - Manuscript Material. Diary Pages, M.B.C., Fall, 1930.

[47] Wright, "Historic Places," 798.

[48] Ormsby, *The Butterfield Overland Mail,* 24.

[49] Ormsby, *The Butterfield Overland Mail,* 17-18.

[50] Gerald T. Ahnert. "Identifying Butterfield's Overland Mail Company Stages on the Southern Trail, 1858–1861," *Overland Journal* 32, no. 4 (Winter 2014–15), 143. Also Gerald T. Ahnert, "The Maker of Butterfield's Overland Mail Company Stage Wagons," *The Carriage Journal* 58, no. 1 (January 2020), 31-35.

[51] Ormsby, *The Butterfield Overland Mail,* 22.

[52] "Boston Mountains," Encyclopedia of Arkansas. https://encyclopediaofarkansas.net/entries/boston-mountains-2389/

[53] Conkling, *The Butterfield Overland Mail,* 210.

[54] Ormsby, *The Butterfield Overland Mail*, 22-24. Conkling, *The Butterfield Overland Mail,* 215.

[55] Edwin C. Bearss and Arrell M. Gibson. *Fort Smith: Little Gibraltar on the Arkansas.* Norman, Okla.: University of Oklahoma Press, 1979. 5-13.

[56] Bearss and Gibson, *Fort Smith,* 66.

[57] Ben Collins Pickett. "William L. McClellan, Choctaw Agent, West." *Chronicles of Oklahoma* 39, no. 1 (Spring 1961): 42.

[58] William McClellan to Peter B. Porter, September 28, 1828. National Archives. War Department, Office of Indian Affairs, 1824-1849. Records of the Bureau of Indian Affairs. Letters Received. Choctaw Agency, 1824-1876: Choctaw Agency, West, 1825-1838. NAID: 163824570 Container ID: Reel 184. 42-43.

[59] John W. Frank, Roland S. Moore, and Genevieve M. Ames. "Historical and Cultural Roots of Drinking Problems Among American Indians." *American Journal of Public Health* 90 no. 3 (March 2000): 344-351.

[60] Pickett, "William L. McClellan," 47.

[61] John Stuart to the Adjutant General. September 19, 1833. *The Territorial Papers of the United States*, Volume 21, 794.

[62] "The Civil War and Malaria, *Scientific American,* July 14, 2011. https://www.scientificamerican.com/article/quinine-the-civil-war-and-malaria/.
[63] Bearss and Gibson, *Fort Smith,* 105.
[64] William P. Corbett. "Rifles and Ruts: Army Road Builders in Indian Territory," *Chronicles of Oklahoma* 60, no. 3 (Fall 1982): 294-309.
[65] Patrick B. McGuigan. "Bulwark of the American Frontier: A History of Fort Towson," in Odie B. Faulk, Kenny A. Franks and Paul F. Lambert. *Early Military Forts and Posts in Oklahoma.* Oklahoma City: Oklahoma Historical Society. 1978. 10-11.
[66] Carolyn Thomas Foreman. "Report of Captain John Stuart on the Construction of the Road from Fort Smith to Horse Prairie on Red River." *Chronicles of Oklahoma* 5, no. 3 (September 1927): 333-347.
[67] Grant Foreman. *Indian Removal: The Emigration of the Five Civilized Tribes of Indians.* Norman: University of Oklahoma Press. 1932. 220-221.
[68] Muriel H. Wright. "Old Boggy Depot," *Chronicles of Oklahoma* 5, no. 1 (March 1927): 4.
[69] Bearss and Gibson, *Fort Smith.*
[70] Wright, "The Butterfield Overland Mail," 69.
[71] Bearss and Gibson, *Fort Smith,* 198.
[72] Grant Foreman. *Marcy and the Gold Seekers: The Journal of Captain R. B. Marcy with an Account of the Gold Rush over the Southern Route.* Norman, Okla.: University of Oklahoma Press, 1939.
[73] "Overland Mail Exploring Party." *Arkansas Intelligencer* (Van Buren, Ark.) April 23, 1858, 2.
[74] "California Overland Mail." *Arkansas Intelligencer* (Van Buren, Ark.) April 16, 1858, 2.
[75] "The Overland Mail." *Arkansas Intelligencer* (Van Buren, Ark.) August 13, 1858, 2.
[76] McClellan-Kerr Arkansas River Navigation System, U.S. Army Corps of Engineers Tulsa District Website. https://www.swt.usace.army.mil/Missions/Navigation/
[77] According to the Conklings, the first westbound Butterfield stagecoach departed for Indian Territory via Second Street at a river crossing a short distance south of the fort at the foot of South E Street. This is inconsistent with the geography of the location. Second Street, as it turned southwest toward the river, would have had to run into and through the walls of the military installation to be consistent with their map. And the foot of South E Street is too far away, another half-mile to the south. The street shown running down to the river is most likely present-day Third Street. The federal government confirms this, see http://npshistory.com/publications/foundation-documents/fosm-fd-2017.pdf
[78] Lang, *The First Overland Mail,* 126.

[79] Albert D. Richardson, *Beyond the Mississippi: From the Great River to the Great Ocean*. Hartford, Conn.: American Publishing Co., 1867. 219.

[80] Carroll J. Messer, "Beale Wagon Road to the Pacific Coast. Western Camel Road and Eastern Iron Bridge Road." Texas A&M University, College Station. October 26, 2021. 23-45. Muriel H. Wright. "Lieutenant Averell's Ride at the Outbreak of the Civil War." *Chronicles of Oklahoma* 39, no. 1 (Spring 1961): 2-14. "Arrival of Volunteers for the Capture of Fort Smith. Midnight Abandonment of the Post by Federal Troops." *Arkansas True Democrat* (Little Rock, Ark.) May 2, 1861, 2. Quoted from the *Fort Smith Times and Herald*, April 21, 1861.

[81] Thomas Nuttall. *A Journal of Travels into the Arkansas Territory During the Year 1819*. Edited by Savoie Lottinville. Norman, Okla.: University of Oklahoma Press, 1980. 159.

[82] Lang, *The First Overland Mail*, 41-42.

[83] Raphael Pumpelly. *My Reminiscences.* New York: Henry Holt and Company, 1918. 183.

[84] Foreman. "Report of Captain John Stuart," 339.

[85] Henry C. Benson. *Life Among the Choctaw Indians, and Sketches of the South-West.* Cincinnati, Ohio: L. Swormstedt & A. Poe, 1860. 99.

[86]H. B. Möllhausen. *Diary of a Journey from the Mississippi to the Coasts of the Pacific with a United States Government Expedition.* London: Longman, Brown, Green, Longmans, & Roberts, 1858. 27-28.

[87] W.B. Parker. *Through Unexplored Texas.* Philadelphia: Hayes and Zell, 1856. 12.

[88] Ormsby, *The Butterfield Overland Mail*, 26.

[89] John Ring Plantation. July 22, 1937. Indian-Pioneer Papers, Western History Collections, University of Oklahoma Libraries.

[90] Frank Haddox. January 8, 1938. Indian-Pioneer Papers.

[91] Benson, *Life Among the Choctaw Indians,* 108-109. Oak Lodge Cemetery History and Inscriptions. June 28, 1937. Indian-Pioneer Papers.

[92] Grant Foreman (editor). *A Pathfinder in the Southwest: The Itinerary of Lieutenant A.W. Whipple During His Explorations for a Railway Route From Fort Smith to Los Angeles in the Years 1853-1854.* Norman: University of Oklahoma Press. 1941. 27-29.

[93] The influence of these intermarried whites, along with that of Christianity, changed gender roles in the traditionally matrilineal society of the Choctaws, where the position of women was one of honor. Debo wrote that white observers perceived traditional gender roles among the Choctaws as unequal division of labor: it seemed women performed the drudgery and the men hunted and fished. Such a generalization, however, failed to account for "the importance and difficulty of the chase," in Debo's opinion. She wrote, "The women performed a large part of the labor of the fields, made the clothing, prepared and stored the food, and carried the burdens; the men provided the game, built the houses,

manufactured the wooden and stone implements, carried on the governmental activities, and protected the tribe in war." Debo, *The Rise and Fall*, 18.

[94] Ormsby, *The Butterfield Overland Mail*, 27.

[95] Conkling, *The Butterfield Overland Mail*, 235.

[96] John Young Bryce, "Perryville At One time Regular Military Post," Chronicles of Oklahoma 4, no. 2 (June 1926): 187.

[97] Debo, *The Rise and Fall*, 114-116.

[98] Wright, "Historic Places," 806.

[99] *Acts and Resolutions of the General Council of the Choctaw Nation at the Called Sessions thereof Held in April and June, 1858, and the Regular Session Held in October, 1858.* Fort Smith, Arkansas: Josephus Dotson, Printer for the Nation. 1859. 49-50.

[100] *Acts and Resolutions for the General Council of the Choctaw Nation*, 1859. 38.

[101] *Fort Smith Times,* July 7, 1858.

[102] David McClellan to John H. Eaton. March 25, 1830. National Archives. War Department, Office of Indian Affairs, 1824-1849. Records of the Bureau of Indian Affairs. Letters Received. Choctaw Agency, 1824-1876: Choctaw Agency, West, 1825-1838. NAID: 163824570 Container ID: Reel 184. 78-79.

[103] Conkling, *The Butterfield Overland Mail,* 235. Wright, "Historic Places," 810. Pickett, "William L. McClellan," 46.

[104] Francis Armstrong to Elbert Herring, September 25, 1834. National Archives. War Department, Office of Indian Affairs, 1824-1849. Records of the Bureau of Indian Affairs. Letters Received. Choctaw Agency, 1824-1876: Choctaw Agency, West, 1825-1838. NAID: 163824570 Container ID: Reel 184. 448.

[105] Pickett, "William L. McClellan," 46, Note 14.

[106] Foreman, "Report of Captain John Stuart," 339.

[107] "1000 Spinning Wheels 400 Looms." *Arkansas Gazette*, Arkansas Post, Ark., July 17, 1833, 4.

[108] Marcy, Randolph B., *The Prairie Traveler*, New York: Harper & Brothers, 1859. 257.

[109] Grant Foreman, "Early Post Offices of Oklahoma," Chronicles of Oklahoma 6, no. 1 (March 1928): 5.

[110] Cameron Blevins, *Paper Trails: The US Post and the Making of the American West.* Oxford University Press, 2021. 27-29.

[111] Debo, *The Rise and Fall,* 35.

[112] Muriel H. Wright and George H. Shirk. "Artist Möllhausen in Oklahoma – 1853." *Chronicles of Oklahoma* 31, no. 4 (Winter 1953-54): 404-405.

[113] Benson, *Life Among the Choctaw Indians,* 186.

[114] Debo, *The Rise and Fall*, 41-61.

[115] Report of the Commissioner of Indian Affairs . . . for the Year 1860. 129, 135.

[116] Debo, *The Rise and Fall*, 41.

[117] "Deaths," *Army and Navy Chronicle* 7, no. 10 (September 6, 1838): 240.

[118] Peter James Hudson. "A Story of Choctaw Chiefs, Part 1." *Chronicles of Oklahoma* 17, no. 1 (March 1939): 7-16.

[119] W. B. Morrison. "The Saga of Skullyville." *Chronicles of Oklahoma* 16, no. 2 (June 1938): 236. Foreman, *Indian Removal,* 50-51. Debo, *The Rise and Fall,* 64-65.

[120] Carolyn Thomas Foreman. "The Armstrongs of Indian Territory," *Chronicles of Oklahoma* 30, no. 3 (Autumn 1952): 295, 306.

[121] Richardson, *Beyond the Mississippi,* 219.

[122] I.C. Gunning. *The Butterfield Overland Mail Through Eastern Oklahoma.* Eastern Oklahoma Historical Society. 22.

[123] Barbara Krauthamer. *Black Slaves, Indian Masters: Slavery, Emancipation, and Citizenship in the Native American South.* Chapel Hill, NC: University of North Carolina Press, 2013. 18-23. Doran, "Negro Slaves," 337.

[124] Benson, *Life Among the Choctaw Indians,* 348, 359.

[125] Doran, "Negro Slaves," 340-349.

[126] Fay A. Yarbrough. *Choctaw Confederates: The American Civil War in Indian Country.* Chapel Hill: The North Carolina Press, 2021. 47-49. Keith Tolman. "Tea Kettle on a Raft: A History of Navigation on the Upper Red River." *Chronicles of Oklahoma* 81, no. 4 (Winter 2003): 400. Krauthamer, *Black Slaves,* 80. Doran, "Negro Slaves," 340, 346.

[127] Ormsby, *The Butterfield Overland Mail,* 26.

[128] Lang, *The First Overland Mail,* 161.

[129] Wright and Shirk, "Artist Möllhausen," 400.

[130] Ethan Allen Hitchcock. *A Traveler in Indian Territory.* Edited by Grant Foreman. Norman, Oklahoma: University of Oklahoma Press, 1930. 187.

[131] Parker, *Through Unexplored Texas,* 38.

[132] Doran, "Negro Slaves," 345.

[133] Kidwell, *The Choctaws in Oklahoma*, 32-33.

[134] Donald L Parman. "Reverend William Graham's Stay at Fort Coffee and New Hope 1845-1847," *Chronicles of Oklahoma* 76, no. 3 (Fall 1998): 273.

[135] N. Sayre Harris. "Journal of a Tour in the Indian Territory." Edited by Carolyn Thomas Foreman. *Chronicles of Oklahoma* 10, no. 2 (June 1932): 231.

[136] Benson, *Life Among the Choctaw Indians*, 115-117.

[137] Library of Congress, Digital Collections, Born in Slavery: Slave Narratives from the Federal Writers' Project, 1936-1938.

[138] Interview with Polly Colbert, Library of Congress, Federal Writers' Project: Slave Narrative Project, Vol. 13, Oklahoma, Adams-Young. 1936. Manuscript/Mixed Material, 33.

[139] Interview with Kiziah Love, Slave Narrative Project, 192.

[140] Mary Grayson, Slave Narrative Project, 117-121.

[141] Matilda Poe, Slave Narrative Project, 242-244.

[142] Krauthamer, *Black Slaves*, 58-59, 164 (notes 31, 32).

[143] Lang, *The First Overland Mail*, 156.

[144] Henry I. and Ida L. Falconer, July 15, 1937. Indian-Pioneer Papers. Doran, "Negro Slaves," 341.

[145] Debo, *The Rise and Fall*, 59-60.

[146] Ormsby, *The Butterfield Overland Mail*, 26-30.

[147] Report of the Acting Superintendent of the Western Territory. Annual Report of the Commissioner of Indian Affairs . . . for the Year 1837. 20.

[148] Annie Heloise Abel. *Manuscript of the Slaveholding Indians, Vol. 3 The American Indian Under Reconstruction.* Cleveland: The Arthur H. Clark Company, 1915.

[149] Ormsby, *The Butterfield Overland Mail*, 26-27.

[150] Parker, *Through Unexplored Texas,* 60.

[151] Elias Rector to Charles Mix, October 26, 1858. *Report of the Commissioner of Indian Affairs . . . for the Year 1858.* 126.

[152] Kevin Sweeney. "Twixt Scylla and Charybdis: Environmental Pressure on the Choctaw to Ally with the Confederacy." *Chronicles of Oklahoma* 85, no. 1 (Spring 2007): 72-93.

[153] Wright and Shirk, "Artist Möllhausen," 399.

[154] Conkling, *The Butterfield Overland Mail,* 234.

[155] Thomson McKenney and W.L. McAlister to Col. D. Cooper, August 29, 1853. Office of Indian Affairs. *Annual Report of the Commissioner of Indian Affairs for the Year 1853.* 184.

[156] Personal interview with Dale Stout, Spiro, Oklahoma, March 4, 2023.

[157] *The Tecumseh Herald*, Tecumseh, Oklahoma, January 30, 1897, 2.

[158] Personal interview, Dale Stout.

[159] Conkling, *The Butterfield Overland Mail,* 236.

[160] Mrs. Jessie Moore. June 23, 1937. Indian-Pioneer Papers.

[161] Wright and Shirk, "Artist Möllhausen," 405.

[162] Jessie Moore, July 23, 1937, Indian-Pioneer Papers.

[163] Wright, et al., "Committee Report," 447.

[164] Oak Lodge Cemetery, Indian-Pioneer Papers.

[165] Wright, et al., "Committee Report," 448.

[166] John Frizzell Collection. 1957-1994. Box 4, Folder 12. Butterfield Oklahoma Trip/George Shirk Oklahoma Historical Society, Oklahoma City.

[167] Wright, et al., "Committee Report," 448.

[168] Peterson retired in 2022.

[169] Dennis A. Peterson, "Spiro Mounds," The Encyclopedia of Oklahoma History and Culture, https://www.okhistory.org/publications/enc/entry.php?entry=SP012.

[170] Nuttall, *A Journal of Travels*, 185.

[171] Benson, *Life Among the Choctaw Indians*, 65.

[172] Parman, "Reverend William Graham's Stay," 267.

[173] Möllhausen, *Diary of a Journey,* 31.
[174] Personal interview with Dennis Peterson, February 25, 2022.
[175] Grant Foreman (ed.). "Journal of the Proceedings of Our First Treaty with the Wild Indians." *Chronicles of Oklahoma* 14, no. 4 (December, 1936): 396, via Foreman, "The Armstrongs," 306.
[176] Lula Neighbors. January 13, 1938. Indian-Pioneer Papers.
[177] Wright, "Historic Places," 802, n.5.
[178] Debo, *The Rise and Fall,* 176-177
[179] Dianne Everman. U.S. Department of Interior. National Park Service. National Register of Historic Places Inventory., Skullyville County Jail, Choctaw Nation, 80004286. April 21, 1980, 2-3.
[180] Izora James. May 27, 1937. Indian-Pioneer Papers.
[181] As of February, 2022, this picturesque bridge had been replaced.
[182] Roscoe Conkling Papers. Box 9 Stage Photos, Folder 46 Oklahoma Research - Manuscript Material. Diary Pages, M.B.C., Fall, 1930.
[183] Robert Anderson Welch. June 18, 1937. Indian-Pioneer Papers.
[184] Bob Srout. "Letter from Brazil." *The Indian Champion,* Atoka, I.T. March 7, 1885, 4.
[185] "Women Postmasters," AboutUSPS.com. 3.
[186] George H. Shirk. "First Post Offices Within the Boundaries of Oklahoma." *Chronicles of Oklahoma* 26, no. 2 (Summer 1948): 190.
[187] Wright, "Historic Places," 807.
[188] "Brazil Creek Bridge," bridgehunter.com.
[189] There are several variants in the spelling of this name. The one used here is consistent with the Oklahoma Historical Society's Encyclopedia of Oklahoma History and Culture. See James P. Pate, "Moshulatubbe," The Encyclopedia of Oklahoma History and Culture, https://www.okhistory.org/publications/enc/entry?entry=MO025.
[190] Wright, Muriel H. "Oklahoma Historic Sites Survey." *Chronicles of Oklahoma* 36, no. 3 (Autumn 1958): 291.
[191] "Proposal for Building Council and Chiefs' Houses." *Arkansas Gazette,* Arkansas Post, Ark., June 21, 1836, 3.
[192] William Armstrong to Elbert Herring, July 21, 1836; Armstrong to C.A. Harris, October 14, 1836, September 3, 1837. National Archives, Choctaw Agency, 1824-1876: 1832-1838. War Department, Office of Indian Affairs, 1824-1849. Records of the Bureau of Indian Affairs: Letters Received.
[193] Muriel H. Wright. "Historic Spots in the Vicinity of Tuskahoma." *Chronicles of Oklahoma* 9, no. 1 (March 1931): 32.
[194] Parker, *Through Unexplored Texas,* 30-31.
[195] James C. Milligan and L. David Norris. "The Last Choctaw Execution: A Case of Law and Disorder." *Chronicles of Oklahoma* 73, no. 4 (Winter 1995): 391.

[196] The Conklings placed the Council House approximately two hundred feet northeast of the Latham store. Muriel Wright's 1933 report placed the Council House about fifty yards north of Trahern's grave. The Committee located the Council House about one hundred feet from the spring, but did not comment in print on its orientation. A map hand-drawn by one of the Committee members and a draft of their manuscript situated it northeast of the spring. An Oklahoma Historic Sites Survey published in 1958 placed the Council House about four hundred yards southeast of the spring. The 1972 NRHP application stated the spring was "a bit farther to the north" of the presumed site of the Council House. These reports are difficult to reconcile. A potentially useful observation comes from the Committee's interview with Everett Bledsoe, who died a week after the 1958 visit. Bledsoe had come to the Latham community in 1908 and said that, when he was a boy, "The older settlers would align their sight upon the grave of Moshulatubbe by sighting a certain way through the windows and doors of the Council House."

[197] W.A. Welch. August 26, 1937. Indian-Pioneer Papers. Conkling, *The Butterfield Overland Mail,* 239-240. Wright, "Historic Places," 819.

[198] Conkling, *The Butterfield Overland Mail,* 239.

[199] Wright, et al., "Committee Report," 451.

[200] Personal visit to Council House with Amanda Regnier of the Oklahoma Archeological Survey; Kristina Wyckoff and Michael Mayes from the Oklahoma State Historic Preservation Office, and representatives of the Choctaw Nation, 11/29/2023.

[201] Mary Ann Blochowiak, "Oklahoma Historians Hall of Fame: Robert L. Williams. Notes and Documents." *Chronicles of Oklahoma* 82 no. 2 (Summer 2004): 240-241.

[202] Wright to Williams, November 26, 1930.

[203] Debo, *The Rise and Fall,* 5.

[204] John R. Swanton. *Source Material for the Social and Ceremonial Life of the Choctaw Indians.* Washington, D.C.: Smithsonian Institution, U.S. Bureau of American Ethnology, United States Government Printing Office, 1931, 170-194.

[205] Benson, *Life Among the Choctaw Indians,* 294-295.

[206] Wright, "Historic Places," 810-811.

[207] Wright, "Historic Places," 810-11, 819. Conkling, *The Butterfield Overland Mail,* 239-40. Roscoe Conkling Papers, Box 9 Folder 49, August 21, 1932 and Box 7 Folder 7. Wright, et al, "Committee Report," 451.

[208] Kent Ruth. "Trahern's Station." National Register Historic Properties Inventory – Nomination Form, 72001073. April 25, 1972. 4. U.S. Department of Interior. National Park Service.

[209] Parker, *Through Unexplored Texas,* 32.

[210] Walt Wilson. "Freedmen in Indian Territory During Reconstruction." *Chronicles of Oklahoma* 49, no. 2 (Summer 1971): 230.

[211] Debo, *The Rise and Fall,* 99.

[212] Krauthamer, *Black Slaves*, 101-119.

[213] Yarbrough, *Choctaw Confederates*, 179.

[214] Angela Y. Walton-Raji. "Freedmen Neighborhood School Roster, Choctaw Nation." *The African-Native American Genealogy Blog.* https://african-nativeamerican.blogspot.com/

[215] Susan Lewis. June 19, 1938. Indian-Pioneer Papers.

[216] W. David Baird. *Works Progress Administration (W.P.A.) Public Buildings, Recreational Facilities and Cemetery Improvements in Southeastern Oklahoma, 1935-1943* (Thematic Resources). 88001399. June 15, 1985: 23. State Historic Preservation Office, Oklahoma Historical Society.

[217] Frizzell Collection. Box 4, Folder 12.

[218] Ormsby, *The Butterfield Overland Mail*, 29.

[219] Lang, *The First Overland Mail*, 132, 157.

[220] John Edwards. "The Choctaw Indians in the Middle of the Nineteenth Century," Edited by John R. Swanton. *Chronicles of Oklahoma* 10, no. 3 (September 1932): 406-408.

[221] Sue L. McBeth. "Diary of a Missionary to the Choctaws." Edited by Anna Lewis. *Chronicles of Oklahoma* 17, no. 4 (December 1939): 439-440.

[222] Pitchlynn to Pitchlynn, February 10, 1860. Peter Pitchlynn Collection, Native American Manuscripts. Western History Collections, University of Oklahoma Libraries.

[223] Pitchlynn to Dukes, September 5, 1860. Peter Pitchlynn Collection.

[224] Elias Rector to A.B. Greenwood, September 24, 1860. *Report of the Commissioner of Indian Affairs . . . for the Year 1860*, 117.

[225] Memorial of the Representatives of the Choctaw Nation of Indians in general council assembled, praying the payment amount due the Choctaw under the treaty of June 1855, January 9, 1861. Quoted in Sweeney, "Twixt Scylla and Charybdis."

[226] Hiram Rumsfeld, August 9, 1860, quoted in Crossman, *Butterfield National Historic Trail,* 327.

[227] Annie Heloise Abel. *Manuscript of the Slaveholding Indians, Vol. 1 The American Indian as Slaveholder and Secessionist.* Cleveland: The Arthur H. Clark Company, 1915. 58-61.

[228] Abel, *The American Indian as Slaveholder,* 77-79.

[229] Abel, *The American Indian as Slaveholder,* 77-79.

[230] Yarbrough, *Choctaw Confederates*, 99.

[231] Wright, et al, "Committee Report," 452. Edwards Store should not be confused with Edwards' Trading Post, established about 1835 southeast of present Holdenville, on the right bank of Little River about three miles above its confluence with the Canadian River. Situated about 130 miles west of Fort Smith along the California Road, Edwards's Post was a stop for California-bound travelers after 1849.

[232] Conkling, *The Butterfield Overland Mail*, 246.

[233] The 1860 census lists Thomas Edwards, age 28, born in England, his occupation a day laborer. Four stage drivers are listed in the same dwelling, their places of birth Maryland, New Hampshire, New York, and Arkansas. They are located at the dwelling of A.H. Pulscher (sic), which is that of Albert H. Pulcher, a native of Germany, whose land was located west of Pusley's Station on the present-day Watts Ranch.

[234] I.C. Gunning. *The Edwards Store or Old Red Oak.* Eastern Oklahoma Historical Society. 12-13, 22-23.

[235] John Bartlett Meserve. "Chief Opothleyahola." *Chronicles of Oklahoma* 9, no. 4 (December 1931): 439-453.

[236] Coffin to Dole, September 24, 1864, *Report . . . for the Year 1864.* 303-307.

[237] Isaac Colman to W.G. Coffin, September 1, 1864. *Report of the Commissioner of Indian Affairs for the Year 1864.* 313-315.

[238] Elijah Sells to D.N. Cooley, October 16, 1865. *Report of the Commissioner of Indian Affairs for the Year 1865.* 257.

[239] Gunning, *The Edwards Store,* 29-31.

[240] Abel, *The American Indian Under Reconstruction,* 15-19.

[241] William S. Phillips to W.P. Dole, March 22, 1864. *Report of the Commissioner of Indian Affairs for the Year 1864.* 328.

[242] Phillips to Dole, March 22, 1864, 328.

[243] Kent Ruth. "Edwards Store." National Register Historic Properties Inventory – Nomination Form, 72001069. April 13, 1972. 4. U.S. Department of Interior. National Park Service.

[244] Conkling, *The Butterfield Overland Mail,* 242-244.

[245] Abel, *The American Indian,* 18-21.

[246] Wright to George Shirk, January 21, 1956. Muriel Wright Collection. Box 9, Folder 47. Oklahoma Historical Society, Oklahoma City.

[247] Wright, et al, "Committee Report," 452.

[248] Wright, et al, "Committee Report," 453.

[249] "Edwards Store Restoration Proceeding." *Mistletoe Leaves* 53, no. 1 (January/February 2022): 5.

[250] Gunning, *The Edwards Store,* 56.

[251] Conkling, *The Butterfield Overland Mail,* 246.

[252] Roscoe Conkling Papers, Box 9 Folder 49, August 21, 1932. Wright, "Historic Places," 805, note 9.

[253] Roscoe Conkling Papers, Box 22, Notebooks.

[254] Roscoe Conkling Papers, Box 9 Folder 49, August 21, 1932.

[255] Roscoe Conkling Papers, Box 15, Correspondence H-R.

[256] Roscoe Conkling Papers, Box 14 Folder 50, Correspondence I.C. Gunning 1970.

[257] "Ledger of History Given to University." *Daily Oklahoman,* May 28, 1955, 8.

[258] Conkling, *The Butterfield Overland Mail,* 242-247.

[259] "Accident to the Overland Stage," *The Cincinnati Enquirer,* August 3, 1860, 3. This report was likely first printed in a Fort Smith, Arkansas newspaper and subsequently reprinted in other newspapers, including the *Cincinnati Enquirer.*

[260] Wright, et al. "Committee Report," 452.

[261] Muriel Wright. "Tour Along the Old Butterfield Overland Mail Route in Oklahoma, 1955," Notes and Documents, *Chronicles of Oklahoma* 33 no. 3 (Autumn 1955): 395.

[262] Parker, *Through Unexplored Texas,* 24.

[263] Wright, et al, "Committee Report," 453.

[264] Bryan Bickers. "Brazil (Gap) Stage Stand." July 8, 1936. Works Progress Administration Historic Sites and Federal Writers' Projects Collection. Western History Collections, University of Oklahoma. Box 17 Stage Stops and Newspapers, Folder 4.

[265] *Acts and Resolutions of the General Council of the Choctaw Nation . . . October, 1858.* 49-50. Wright, "Historic Places," 807.

[266] Conkling, *The Butterfield Overland Mail,* 247-249.

[267] Wright to Conkling, November 7, 1935. Muriel Wright Collection.

[268] *Constitution and Laws of the Choctaw Nation Together with the Treaties of 1855, 1865 and 1866.* Chahta Tamaha: Joseph Folsom, 1869, 462.

[269] Parker, *Through Unexplored Texas*, 24-25.

[270] John Bartlett Meserve. "The McCurtains." *Chronicles of Oklahoma* 13, no. 3 (September 1935): 300.

[271] Hudson, Peter James. "A Story of Choctaw Chiefs (continued)." *Chronicles of Oklahoma* 17, no. 2 (June 1939): 204.

[272] Wright, "Historic Places," 817.

[273] Robert Anderson Welch, June 18, 1937; James S. Latimer, June 21, 1937; Bud Cutler, June 15, 1937; William Dellwood Fields, June 16, 1937; James A. Blalack, July 9, 1937. Indian-Pioneer Papers.

[274] Roscoe Conkling Papers. Box 7, Folder 7, Okla. Stage Photos with Written Material. Box 9 Folder 46 Okla Research - Manuscript Material, Diary Pages, M.B.C., Fall, 1930, 71.

[275] Conkling, *The Butterfield Overland Mail,* 250.

[276] Conkling, *The Butterfield Overland Mail,* 250.

[277] Works Progress Administration Historic Sites and Federal Writers' Project Collection. Box 4, Folder 4 (Latimer County).

[278] Debo, *The Rise and Fall,* 177.

[279] Robert Anderson Welch, Indian-Pioneer Papers.

[280] Devon Abbott Mihesuah. "Unfinished Choctaw Justice: The Murder of Charles Wilson and the Execution of Jackson Crow." *Chronicles of Oklahoma,* 86, no. 3 (Fall 2008): 303. Wright, "Oklahoma Historic Sites," 297.

[281] Debo, *The Rise and Fall,* 22, 39-40, 47, 199-200.

[282] This distinction, however, may belong to the execution of William Going at the Sulphur Springs (Alikchi) courthouse in July, 1899. See Coleman, Louis,

"The Execution of William Going." *Chronicles of Oklahoma* 76, no. 1 (Spring 1998) 38-47.

[283] Devon Abbott Mihesuah. *Choctaw Crime and Punishment 1884-1907.* Norman, Okla.: University of Oklahoma Press, 2009, 70.

[284] Benson, *Life Among the Choctaw Indians,* 215.

[285] Debo, *The Rise and Fall,* 174.

[286] The Execution of Silan Lewis. February 9, 1938. Indian-Pioneer Papers.

[287] Ormsby, *The Butterfield Overland Mail,* 29.

[288] Muriel H. Wright. "Some Geographic Names of French Origin in Oklahoma," *Chronicles of Oklahoma,* 7, no. 2 (June 1929): 189.

[289] Wright, "Historic Places," 807.

[290] Conkling, *The Butterfield Overland Mail,* 253.

[291] Wright, et al, "Committee Report," 456. Conkling, *The Butterfield Overland Mail,* 250-251.

[292] Wright, *Historic Places,* 798-822. Also "Choctaw Journeys into the Past," choctawspirit.wordpress.com, web site of Choctaw historian Kathy Leach, and "Story Map, A Land Resplendent with Memories," https://storymaps.com/stories/9e8fe809390640408f62ec29a3bd292f.

[293] Ormsby, *The Butterfield Overland Mail,* 30.

[294] John Stuart. October 1, 1835. Office of Indian Affairs: Schools (Choctaws West). Compiled from original records selected by Grant Foreman 1930. Oklahoma Historical Society Library. E93, U5F7 Volume 3. 213-216. Report of the Acting Superintendent of the Western Territory. Annual Report of the Commissioner of Indian Affairs . . . for the Year 1837. 21. Parker, *Through Unexplored Texas,* 24-2.

[295] Steven L. Sewell, "Coal," The Encyclopedia of Oklahoma History and Culture, https://www.okhistory.org/publications/enc/entry.php?entry=CO001.

[296] Shero, Earl. Personal interview February 2, 2023. Conkling, *The Butterfield Overland Mail,* 251-252.

[297] Wright, et al, "Committee Report," 456.

[298] Foreman, *Down the Texas Road,* 42.

[299] Ormsby, *The Butterfield Overland Mail,* 30.

[300] Parker, *Through Unexplored Texas,* 41.

[301] Greene, A.C. *900 Miles on the Butterfield Trail.* Denton, Tex.: University of North Texas Press, 1994, 36.

[302] William Dellwood Fields, Indian-Pioneer Papers.

[303] James Wilson Baird. July 21, 1937. Indian-Pioneer Papers.

[304] William Dellwood Fields, Indian-Pioneer Papers.

[305] Sampson Collin. June 9, 1937. Indian-Pioneer Papers.

[306] W.B. Morrison Collection, Box 4 Folder 43, Research Notes, Materials, Choctaw Indians. Western History Collections, University of Oklahoma Libraries.

[307] Angie Debo, *The Road to Disappearance, A History of the Creek Indians.* Norman: University of Oklahoma Press, 1979, 18, 301.

[308] Mrs. Irwin A. Watson. "Creek Indian Burial Customs Today." *Chronicles of Oklahoma* 28, no. 1 (Spring 1950): 102.

[309] Wright, et al, "Committee Report," 457.

[310] Fort Smith is actually about 85 miles distant.

[311] "The Muybridge Trial," *San Francisco Chronicle,* February 6, 1875, 3.

[312] George F. Spaulding. *On The Western Tour with Washington Irving; The Journal and Letters of Count de Pourtales.* Norman, Okla.: University of Oklahoma Press, 1968, 78-79.

[313] "The Muybridge Trial," *San Francisco Chronicle,* February 6, 1875, 3.

[314] Arthur P. Shimamura. "Muybridge in Motion: Travels in Art, Psychology and Neurology." *History of Photography* 26, no.4 (2002), 348-349.

[315] "News of the Day," *The New York Times*, July 23, 1860, 4.

[316] "Accident to the Overland Stage," *The Cincinnati Enquirer,* August 3, 1860, 3.

[317] Muybridge, although unnamed, was likely the eighth passenger.

[318] "Accident to the Overland Stage," *The Cincinnati Enquirer.*

[319] Muriel H. Wright. "Notes on the History of Mountain Station," *Chronicles of Oklahoma* 36 no. 4 (Winter 1958-59): 476-477.

[320] Grant Foreman. "Early Post Offices of Oklahoma," *Chronicles of Oklahoma* 6, no. 1 *(*March 1928): 6.

[321] James A. Blalack, Indian-Pioneer Papers.

[322] 1850 United States Federal Census for Andrew McKey, Athens, Gentry County, Missouri. https://www.ancestry.com/imageviewer/collections/8054/images/4200559_00420?pId=3778780

[323] The average speed of the Pony Express was 10 miles per hour, but that speed was achieved because a fresh horse was acquired every 10 to 15 miles. At that brisk rate an express rider could have reached Fort Smith in about 10 hours, although in reality it would likely have taken longer.

[324] Gunning, *The Butterfield Overland Mail,* 26.

[325] Wright, "Historic Places," 816.

[326] Wright, "Notes on the History of Mountain Station," 476.

[327] Parker, *Through Unexplored Texas,* 41.

[328] Built by the WPA in 1937-38 and now abandoned but still intact. See Oklahoma Landmarks Inventory Nomination, Thematic Surveys, WPA Region Reports, Latimer County, State Historic Preservation Office, 10.

[329] Conkling, *The Butterfield Overland Mail,* 255.

[330] https://www.findagrave.com/memorial/40721513/eastman-pusley

[331] Wright, "Historic Places," 809-810.

[332] Wright, et al, "Committee Report," 458.

[333] Ormsby, *The Butterfield Overland Mail,* 30.

[334] Kent Ruth. "Pusley's Station." *National Register of Historic Places Inventory - Nomination Form.* 72001068. (Restricted property.) April 13, 1972, 2.

[335] Wright, et al, "Committee Report," 459.

[336] Ormsby, *The Butterfield Overland Mail,* 30-31.

[337] "Choctaw Stickball." Culture, Traditions. Mississippi Band of Choctaw Indians. https://www.choctawnation.com/about/culture/traditions/stickball/.

[338] Parker, *Through Unexplored Texas,* 21.

[339] Debo, *The Rise and Fall,* 8-9.

[340] Möllhausen, *Diary of a Journey,* 46-49.

[341] Debo, *The Rise and Fall,* 9, 228.

[342] *The McAlester Capital,* Oct 19, 1899, p

[343] *McAlester Daily News,* Aug. 13, 1905, p. 3

[344] "Choctaw Stickball." Mississippi Band of Choctaw Indians.

[345] Conkling, *The Butterfield Overland Mail,* 257.

[346] The Committee recommended, however, that readers detour around the ranch via Hartshorne to Ti.

[347] Roscoe Conkling Papers, Box 9, Folder 46, Oklahoma Research --- Manuscript Material. Diary Pages, M. B.C., Fall, 1930. 79.

[348] Roscoe Conkling Papers, Box 17 Correspondence, Folder 188, Correspondence Watts, Mose, 1931, 1934.

[349] Conkling, *The Butterfield Overland Mail,* 256.

[350] J.Y. Bryce, "Temporary Markers of Historic Points," *Chronicles of Oklahoma* 8, no. 3 (September 1930) 288.

[351] Roscoe Conkling Papers Box 9, Folder 46, Oklahoma Research --- Manuscript Material. Diary Pages, M. B.C., Fall, 1930. 80-81.

[352] Wright, et al, "Committee Report," 460.

[353] Gunning, *The Butterfield Overland Mail,* 28.

[354] Parker, *Through Unexplored Texas,* 51. Wright, "Historic Places," 811. Conkling, *The Butterfield Overland Mail,* 258.

[355] Ormsby, *The Butterfield Overland Mail,* 31.

[356] Ormsby, *The Butterfield Overland Mail,* 31.

[357] Ormsby, *The Butterfield Overland Mail,* 36.

[358] "White-Tailed Deer Timeline." Oklahoma Department of Wildlife Conservation. https://www.wildlifedepartment.com/hunting/resources/deer/timeline. Also, Benson, *Life Among the Choctaw Indians,* 33.

[359] Wright, et al, "Committee Report," 461.

[360] "Beal Cemetery." Recorded by Joe Southern, March 31, 1938. Works Progress Administration Historic Sites and Federal Writers' Project Collection, Western History Collections. Box 11 Cemeteries and Burial Sites, Folder 18 Pittsburg County.

[361] Pumpelly, *My Reminiscences,* 186.

[362] Ormbsy, *The Butterfield Overland Mail,* 16.

[363] Ormsby, *The Butterfield Overland Mail,* 32.

[364] Foreman, Grant. "Historical Background of the Kiowa-Comanche Reservation." *Chronicles of Oklahoma* 19, no. 2 (June 1941): 130.

[365] Foreman, "Historical Background," 131-135.

[366] James C. Milligan and L. David Norris. 1991. "Keeping the Peace; William H. Emory and the Command at Fort Arbuckle." *Chronicles of Oklahoma* 69, no. 3 (Fall 1991): 257-261.

[367] Foreman, "Historical Background," 133.

[368] Elias Rector to Charles E. Mix, October 26, 1858. *Report of the Commissioner of Indian Affairs . . . for the Year 1858,* 126-134.

[369] James A. Howard II. "Fort Washita," in Faulk, et al, *Early Military Forts and Posts in Oklahoma.* 57.

[370] Rector, Elias to Charles E. Mix, September 20, 1859. *Report of the Commissioner of Indian Affairs . . . for the Year 1859,* 166.

[371] Glen Sample Ely. 2016. *The Texas Frontier and the Butterfield Overland Mail 1858-1861.* Norman: University of Oklahoma Press. 2016. 128, 145-156.

[372] "Arrival of the Overland Mail," Daily Missouri Republican, March 10 1859, 2.

[373] Wisconsin State Journal, May 10, 1860, p. 1. "Murder and Robbery." *The Weekly Butte Democrat* (Oroville, Calif.), May 12, 1860, 2.

[374] Gerald T. Ahnert. *The Butterfield Trail and Overland Mail Company in Arizona 1858-1861,* Canastota, New York: Canastota Publishing Co. 2011. 15, 27-30.

[375] Wright, et al, "Committee Report," 461.

[376] "Colbert Cemetery." Recorded by J.H. Moore, April 13, 1938. Works Progress Administration Historic Sites and Federal Writers' Project Collection. Western History Collections. Box 11 Folder 18, Pittsburg County.

[377] Roscoe Conkling Papers, Box 9, Folder 46, Oklahoma Research, Manuscript Material. Diary Pages, M. B.C., Fall, 1930. 85.

[378] Conkling, *The Butterfield Overland Mail,* 260.

[379] Wright, et al, "Committee Report," 461-463. Wright, "Historic Places," 819. "Colbert Stage Crossing on Brushey Creek," "Colbert's Station and the Isaac Colbert Home." Works Progress Administration Historic Sites and Federal Writers' Project Collection. Western History Collections. Box 17 Stage Stops and Newspapers, Folders 8 and 9.

[380] Wright, et al, "Committee Report," 462-463.

[381] Gunning, *The Butterfield Overland Mail,* 29.

[382] Conkling, *The Butterfield Overland Mail,* 262-263.

[383] Conkling, *The Butterfield Overland Mail,* 262. Wright, et al, "Committee Report," 461-463.

[384] Wright, "Historic Places," 811-812.

[385] Wright to Conkling, November 7, 1935. Muriel Wright Collection.

[386] "Wells Station on Fort Smith – Boggy Depot Road," Works Progress Administration Historic Sites and Federal Writers' Project Collection. Western History Collections. Box 17 Stage Stops and Newspapers, Folder 31. *Laws of the Choctaw Nation Passed at the Choctaw Councils of 1876 and 1877,* 51. Foreman, "Early Post Offices," 6.

[387] Wright, et al, "Committee Report," 461-463.

[388] Joe Potts (Second Interview), October 2, 1937. Indian-Pioneer Papers. Meserve, John Bartlett, "Governor Cyrus Harris," *Chronicles of Oklahoma* 15, no. 4 (December 1937): 373-387.

[389] Personal email communication with Kati Cain, Chickasaw Nation Research Specialist and Genealogist, December 13, 2023.

[390] "Bread Town Stage Stand," Works Progress Administration Historic Sites and Federal Writers' Project Collection. Western History Collections. Box 17 Stage Stops and Newspapers, Folder 6.

[391] Joseph A. Edmonds. "Diary of Joseph A. Edmonds." Edited by James W. Moffitt. *Chronicles of Oklahoma* 17, no. 3 (September 1939): 313.

[392] Conkling, *The Butterfield Overland Mail,* 263-264. From a geological viewpoint, Stringtown lies within "a zone of fracturing and faulting of the country rock on a grand scale." "Local displacement of the heavily bedded limestones may be observed at a point where the old road made the descent of the rock quarry hill. Over a greater part of the distance from present-day Red Oak to Stringtown, the road appears to follow in the great trough or depression lying between the Choctaw fault on the north, and the Winding Stair fault on the south."

[393] Edmonds, "Diary," 309-314.

[394] J.Y. Bryce. "Some Notes of Interest Concerning Early Day Operations in Indian Territory by Methodist Church South." *Chronicles of Oklahoma* 4, no. 3 (September 1926): 239. V.V. Masterson. *The Katy Railroad and the Last Frontier.* Norman, Okla.: University of Oklahoma Press, 1952, 190.

[395] Conkling, *The Butterfield Overland Mail,* 264.

[396] Bryce, "Some Notes of Interest," 237-239.

[397] Foreman, *Down the Texas Road,* 5-46.

[398] Wright, "Historic Places," 808.

[399] Conkling, *The Butterfield Overland Mail,* 265. Wright, "Historic Places," 808.

[400] Conkling, *The Butterfield Overland Mail,* 266.

[401] Edmonds, "Diary," 313-314.

[402] Wright, et al, "Committee Report," 464.

[403] Edmonds, "Diary," 313.

[404] Personal interview with David Stahle, February 12, 2022.

[405] Conkling, *The Butterfield Overland Mail,* 266-267. Wright, et al, "Committee Report," 464. By 1958, the route of the trail from the North Boggy crossing to Boggy Depot was then "all but obliterated and . . . obscure in every detail,"

although since they didn't visit the Geary's site it is unclear how the Committee could have drawn this conclusion about the segment from North Boggy to Atoka. Today, after the segment of trail at the Atoka Museum, the trail is lost from Atoka to Boggy Depot.

[406] Wright, "The Butterfield Overland Mail One Hundred Years Ago," 70.

[407] Wright, "Historic Places," 808.

[408] Wright, "Historic Places," 820-821.

[409] Mrs. R.J. Inge, Diary of Reverend Dr. J.B. Murrow, August 22, 1937. Indian-Pioneer Papers. *Atoka Independent,* January 25, 1878, 5.

[410] "Atoka Station Grounds." *Indian Citizen,* August 3, 1899, 2.

[411] "Mrs. E.A. Flack." *The Indian Missionary,* August 1, 1890, 4.

[412] Mrs. Flack's was probably located at NW¼ NW¼ S14 T2S R11E, east of present-day A Street and Mississippi Avenue in Atoka.

[413] Vernon H. Brown. "American Airlines along the Butterfield Mail Route." *Chronicles of Oklahoma* 33, no. 1 (Spring 1955): 11.

[414] Ormsby, *The Butterfield Overland Mail,* 33.

[415] Kidwell, *The Choctaws in Oklahoma,* 51-55.

[416] Debo, *The Rise and Fall,* 74-75.

[417] Ormsby, *The Butterfield Overland Mail,* 33.

[418] Conkling, *The Butterfield Overland Mail,* 268-271.

[419] Bond to Pitchlynn, September 18, 1858, Peter Pitchlynn Collection, Western History Collection.

[420] Report of William Armstrong, *Annual Report of the Commissioner of Indian Affairs for the Year 1838.* 510.

[421] Wright, "Historic Places," 809.

[422] Edmonds, "Diary," 313.

[423] Shirk, "First Post Offices," 189.

[424] Conkling, *The Butterfield Overland Mail,* 270.

[425] John Bartlett Meserve. "Chief Allen Wright." *Chronicles of Oklahoma* 19, no. 4 (December 1941): 314-321.

[426] Muriel H. Wright. "Old Boggy Depot." *Chronicles of Oklahoma* 5, no. 1 (March, 1927): 4.

[427] Conkling, *The Butterfield Overland Mail,* 270.

[428] Wright, et al, "Committee Report," 466.

[429] Wright, et al, "Committee Report," 466.

[430] Edmonds, "Diary," 314.

[431] Kidwell, *The Choctaws in Oklahoma,* 8.

[432] Parker, *Through Unexplored Texas,* 51.

[433] Foreman, *Indian Removal,* 220.

[434] "Fatal Accident." *The South-Western.* Shreveport, Louisiana, August 3, 1859, 2. Quoted from the *Choctaw Herald.* Twelve of the people Nail enslaved were separating some powder and coffee which had gotten mixed and one "young

negro, thinking to frighten the balance, threw a coal of fire into the powder."
Two were killed and nine wounded in the accident.

[435] Conkling, *The Butterfield Overland Mail,* 246-247.

[436] Joe Stanford. "Nail's Crossing" (Interview with Claude Nail). US GenWeb Archives. http://files.usgwarchives.net/ok/bryan/history/towns/nail.txt

[437] Wright, "Historic Places," 812.

[438] W.B. Morrison. "Fort McCulloch Bryan County's War Fortress, History Shows." *Durant Weekly News and Bryan County Democrat,* June 4, 1926, 7.

[439] Wright, "Historic Places," 815.

[440] Morrison, "Fort McCulloch," 7.

[441] Stanford, "Nail's Crossing."

[442] Roscoe Conkling Papers, Box 9, Folder 47, Oklahoma Research – Manuscript Material. Diary Pages, M.B.C., Fall, 1930.

[443] Frizzell Collection, Box 4, Folder 12.

[444] *Caddo Herald,* September 2, 1910, 8.

[445] *Caddo Herald,* August 2, 1912, 7.

[446] *Caddo Herald,* May 12, 1911, 3.

[447] *Durant Weekly News and Bryan County Democrat,* September 17, 1915, 4.

[448] *Caddo Herald,* August 8, 1913, 7. August 23, 1918, 1. August 5, 1910, 8. December 25, 1924, 1. *Caddo Banner,* March 22, 1895, 1.

[449] "Gone Home," *Caddo Herald* (Caddo, Oklahoma) September 14, 1917, 1.

[450] http://www.ohptrooper.com/30thanniversary1.htm
http://www.ohptrooper.com/tulsa_may27a.htm

[451] Roscoe Conkling Papers, Box 7, Folder 7, Oklahoma Stage Photos with Written Material.

[452] Wright, et al, "Committee Report," 467.

[453] William P. Corbett. "Confederate Strongholds in Indian Territory: Forts Davis and McCulloch," in Faulk, et al, *Early Military Forts and Posts in Oklahoma.* 73.

[454] Muriel H. Wright and Leroy H. Fischer. "Oklahoma Civil War Sites." *Chronicles of Oklahoma* 44, no. 2 (Summer 1966): 164-65.

[455] Towana Spivey. *Exploring the Depths of History, A Selection of Nineteenth Century Water Wells in Indian Territory,* 2019. Ada: Chickasaw Press. 26-32.

[456] Howard, "Fort Washita," in Faulk, et al, *Early Military Forts and Posts in Oklahoma.* 63.

[457] Jon D. May, "Fort Washita," The Encyclopedia of Oklahoma History and Culture, https://www.okhistory.org/publications/enc/entry.php?entry=FO046.

[458] Bryce, "Temporary Markers," 283-294.

[459] Muriel Wright to and from R.P. Conkling, October 28, 1935, November 1, 1935, November 7, 1935. Muriel Wright Collection. Box 7, Folder 34.

[460] Wright, "The Butterfield Overland Mail One Hundred Years Ago," 71.

[461] M. Ruth Hatchett. "Necrology: Isabelle Rebecca Colbert Yarborough." *Chronicles of Oklahoma* 37 no 3 (Autumn 1959): 382-384.

[462] "Carriage Point," Works Progress Administration Historic Sites and Federal Writers' Project Collection. Western History Collections. Box 17 Stage Stops and Newspapers, Folder 4.

[463] Wright, et al, "Committee Report," 468-469.

[464] Wright, et al, "Committee Report," 468-469.

[465] Wright, "Committee Report," 452.

[466] Wright, "The Butterfield Overland Mail One Hundred Years Ago," 55.

[467] Isaac Alberson House, Oklahoma Landmarks Inventory, http://oli_shpo.okstate.edu/query_result.aspx?id=46508&pbc=P

[468] Carolyn Thomas Foreman, "Pierce Mason Butler." *Chronicles of Oklahoma* 30, no. 1 (Spring 1952): 20, note 33. Isaac Alberson House, Oklahoma Landmarks Inventory, http://oli_shpo.okstate.edu/query_result.aspx?id=46508&pbc=P

[469] Ormsby, *The Butterfield Overland Mail,* 33-35.

[470] Wright, "The Butterfield Overland Mail One Hundred Years Ago," 66, note 29.

[471] Ruth Ann Overbeck, "Colbert's Ferry." *Chronicles of Oklahoma* 57 no. 2 (Summer 1979): 214-215.

[472] Wright, "Historic Places," 812-813.

[473] Ormsby, *The Butterfield Overland Mail,* 35.

[474] W.B. Morrison. "Colbert Ferry on the Red River, Chickasaw Nation." *Chronicles of Oklahoma* 16 no. 3 (September 1938): 309.

[475] *Our Brother in Red,* Muskogee, Indian Territory, December 21, 1893, 5.

[476] Morrison, "Colbert Ferry," 307-311.

[477] Conkling, *The Butterfield Overland Mail,* 283.

[478] Dianna Everett. "Turnpikes and Toll Bridges," The Encyclopedia of Oklahoma History and Culture, https://www.okhistory.org/publications/enc/entry.php?entry=TU022.

[479] Wright, "Committee Report," 471.

[480] Morrison, "Colbert Ferry," 314.

[481] Conkling, *The Butterfield Overland Mail,* 281.

[482] "Prairie Fire Losses," *Indian Citizen,* Atoka, Indian Territory, November 24, 1898, 4.

[483] Wright, et al, "Committee Report," 469.

[484] Lang, *The First Overland Mail,* 156

[485] Roscoe Conkling Papers. Box 7, Folder 7, Oklahoma Stage Photos with Written Material.

[486] http://bridgehunter.com/ok/bryan/red-river/

[487] Ormsby, *The Butterfield Overland Mail,* 10, 41.

[488] Hafen, *The Overland Mail,* 98-99.

[489] Wright, "Historic Places," 814-817.

[490] Wright, "Historic Places," 817-818.

[491] Conkling, *The Butterfield Overland Mail,* 254-255.

[492] Muriel Wright. "Centennial of the Butterfield Overland Mail Organization." Notes and Documents. *Chronicles of Oklahoma* 35, no. 4 (Winter 1957-58): 474.

[493] "Overland Mail Celebration." Notes and Documents. *Chronicles of Oklahoma* 33, no. 1 (Spring 1955): 12.

[494] Shirk to Clement M. Silvestro, editor of History News, June 20, 1958. George Shirk Collection. Butterfield Overland Mail Centennial Committee Correspondence. Box 9, Folder 3. Oklahoma Historical Society, Oklahoma City.

[495] Excerpt from Overland Mailbag, Volume 1, February 16, 1958. George Shirk Collection. Box 9, Folder 3.

[496] "Move 'Em Out! Wagon Maker Builds Them All: Stages, Buggies, Chariots, Etc." *The Sunday Oklahoman*, April 26, 1981. 93. "John Frizzell: His Heart is On the Next Stage," *Valley News* (West Lebanon, New Hampshire), June 22, 1981. 20.

[497] Wright, "Centennial of the Butterfield," 474.

[498] Muriel Wright. "Notes on the Butterfield Overland Mail Centennial." Notes and Documents. *Chronicles of Oklahoma* 35, no. 2 (Summer 1957): 228.

[499] Shirk to Harry Weiss, Holton, Kansas, September 17, 1957. George Shirk Collection. Box 9, Folder 3.

[500] J. Brookes Wright, "Establishment of Boggy Depot State Park." Notes and Documents. *Chronicles of Oklahoma* 36, no. 2 (Summer 1958): 204-206.

[501] Muriel Wright. "Butterfield Overland Mail, 1958 in Oklahoma." Notes and Documents. *Chronicles of Oklahoma* 36, no. 4 (Winter 1958-59): 478-479.

[502] Butterfield Overland Mailbag, undated. George Shirk Collection. Box 9, Folder 3.

[503] Missouri Historical Review, July 1958. George Shirk Collection. Box 9, Folder 3.

[504] Joseph E. Howell, "Butterfield Stage Caravan Arrives; In Durant Tonight." *The Tulsa Tribune.* September 20, 1958, 1.

[505] "Stagecoach Rerouted by Traffic Rule." *San Francisco Examiner.* October 11, 1958, 1.

[506] "Fort Smith Hails Butterfield Stage." *Daily Oklahoman.* September 20, 1958, 1.

[507] "Caravan Over Two Hours Late But 3,000 Remain to Greet It. Stagecoach Finally Gets Here But Sans Horses; Postal Unit is Loaded." *Durant Daily Democrat.* September 21, 1958, 1.

[508] Wright, "Butterfield Overland Mail, 1958 in Oklahoma," 478-481.

[509] Reprint from Postal Bulletin No. 20105, September 11, 1958. George Shirk Collection. Box 9, Folder 3.

[510] Ormsby, *The Butterfield Overland Mail,* 28-29.

[511] Lang, *The First Overland Mail,* 157-58.

[512] Elias Rector. *Report of the Commissioner of Indian Affairs . . . for the Year 1858.* 126-127.

[513] Elbert Herring. *Report from the Office of Indian Affairs.* November 22, 1832. 161.

[514] Debo, *The Rise and Fall,* 84.